San Juan Hill

To order additional copies, please contact us.
BookSurge, LLC
www.booksurge.com
1-866-308-6235
orders@booksurge.com

HORACE
MUNGIN

SAN JUAN HILL

2006

San Juan Hill

CONTENTS

ACKNOWLEDGEMENTS

Special thanks to Geraldine Mungin, Barbara Lewis, Alicia White and to all those who revealed a moment or awaken a memory.

AUTHORS NOTE

Grady Lee Murrow's story, though, in large part a work of fiction, reminds me of my own history. The events and people in his story so closely resembles those in my own life that reading Grady Lee's story gives me that feeling of dejavu we have at times when we experience the sensation of reliving an event that has past in time. But because Grady Lee Murrow is a fictional character in my novel San Juan Hill, as are the events and people in the yarn, this is a startling development. This being the case, reading San Juan Hill, provokes a kind of dream quality of familiarity in me. This intimacy makes me theorize whether my acquaintance with the protagonist and his tale originates from the fact that I wrote the story or because maybe I lived the story in my writing of it or…maybe, I actually lived the story? The story is set in a real place where I, in fact, once lived, so that might be yet another reason for this blaring of the line between creativity and reality. Whose story is this, Grady Lee's or my own—is it real or fiction?

Metaphysics is a branch of philosophy dealing with the nature of existence. Many people in this field grapple with the questions that explores which state of our mindfulness is real, our dream or our reality—and how do we distinguish between the two? When it comes to the question of whose story this is, I submit that the solution to my dilemma awaits their explanation.

I have told the story that follows this commentary from creativity, and not from memory. But creativity has a recollection of its own and works from its own retrospective. This is how the real gets combined with the imaginary. This is called art. In this case the art of story telling. And for me, the art of story telling is to make the tale seem real and believable to the reader. I also believe that the story should have purpose. It should be about more than itself, it should be the mirror that project and reflect the readers' thoughts about the subject that the tale has invoked. After all, the reader's involvement is the last element in the writing of the story—the reader is also the most important contributor to the story's overall affect. For it is each reader's interpretation, that, in the end, is what the story documents.

This is the story of a unique community and a time of innocence. A racially diverse community coalescing to overcome street gangs, delinquency, apathy and drug abuse to prepare its youth for their future. It is the saga of a community's triumphs and failures—it is the story of how from the wretched arose the worthy.

It is also the memoir of a young boy growing up in a midtown Manhattan public housing project; a coming of age story, if you will, told in his own voice. Grady Lee is a boy who missed a chance at a formal education, but somehow manages to keep himself out of the joint and even obtain a degree of self scholarship and the will to nurture his one gift. Grady Lee Murrow has not forgotten his years growing up in the project, though, if possible, forgetting would have been a much easier route. Even knowing all the pitfalls of trying to recreate the past, Grady Lee has not forgotten, although remembering in many instances, is so much more a chaotic activity.

Horace Mungin

To: Miles and Taylor
Nazareth and Natalie
Fatima and Haru

CHAPTER ONE
The Amsterdam Projects

<u>1</u>

I spent my formative years, the years that solidified my value system, growing up in a housing project in midtown Manhattan, hanging out with Brad Buffert and Ozzie Donaldson. Two factors that contributed greatly to my many failures and my youthful inclination for apathetic expectations, but at the same time, made my survival possible. Now I am wise enough to know that if I hadn't survived there, there would not have been any failures. Also, that to fail just as to succeed is to be alive, and life makes *all things* possible. When I think back, with this in mind, I find myself grateful for the misfortune of my prior circumstances. I know that without the lessons I learned in that milieu, I would not have survived in, as it were, a stacked deck.

"Don't let me ever see you with your nose running and your eyes watering wild," Albee Woods once told me as he nodded away in a heroin stupor. I gave him a bizarre stare, but I knew that he was trying to be helpful.

"Thanks man, I got ya'."

"Gonna be plenty of times in life when you don't get what you want," Bobby Lenin advised me once when my mother didn't have the money to give me to buy a ticket for a neighborhood boat ride to Bear Mountain. I was out in the streets, my eyes tearing up and acting glum about it. "So you better get used to it."

"I sure hope not," was my response to Bobby, really feeling that his prophecy would be abundantly true throughout my life, but I had enough hope to say "I'm gonna make it out of here, you'll see."

"Don't feel sorry for nobody, 'cause they ain't gonna feel sorry for you," Polly Wolly often told me. "Take advantage of the sucker, don't you be the sucker. Never take pity—never show pity."

"Polly, I need a quarter, you got one you can let me have?" I asked, not wanting to delay receiving the benefit of this new insight.

These older guys were looking out for me, they were instructing me on the road ahead from their own experiences. They knew that drug addiction, deprivation and deception were but some of the wickedness I would have to dodge in the coming years. This neighborhood of poor souls, blacks, whites and Puerto Ricans, with their unorthodox, harsh, and often perverted value system, provided the impetus for my endurance in the larger society where genuine venality thrived. Life was severe, but this community also had a humane side. It had the enduring characteristics of yearning and ambition that offered many possibilities.

It was by an improbable mixture of factors that this demography was formed. Bad planning by a joker in the New York City Department of Public Housing, dire circumstances and good luck landed us in a planned ghetto at the center of so much that was virtuous and progressive about the city. Living there fed my aspirations and exposed me to the possibilities for success. Yes, even from this wretched place arose the worthy. If you have to grow up black and poor in America, you want to grow up in the racial demographics of the Amsterdam Housing Projects of the 1950's. If you're growing up black and poor in the Amsterdam Projects in the 1950's, you want to be in a crew that includes Brad Buffert and Ozzie Donaldson.

"If we did something and one of us got busted," Brad said, when we first started to hang out together, "that person's got to take the weight. That person's got to stay silent—no squealing."

"I'm down with that," Ozzie said, "and I trust you. But I don't know about Grady Lee."

I didn't like that Ozzie used my middle name, but I didn't respond to it. "I wouldn't ever give anybody up to the Man," I said.

"This is serious shit, you got to know how to keep your mouth shut," Brad said. "You cool with it Grady—for real man?"

"I'm down for real, man."

Brad slapped me five. Ozzie gave Brad five and then reluctantly, he slapped me five. Then we all smiled and slapped each other five again. This concluded our oath to achievements through silence and to the success of our triad. There did, however, come a time when it was not my silence, but my glibness that kept us out of reform school.

The Amsterdam Projects were built on the West Side of midtown Manhattan in 1947 and were intended to house the families of poor white veterans of World War II. The purpose was to do for poor inner-city working class whites what the Levittown development on Long Island had done for their more fortunate brethren—provide good affordable housing. This was in a time when the American government, to some degree, respected and leveled with poor white people. In those days, the white poor weren't used, politically, to prop up the white ruling classes without being, itself, rewarded. National and local governments still worked together to provide for poor whites. This was a way to thank the men who fought in the war, for their services in making the world free of the evil Nazi peril. The Levittown experiment went well for two generations and beyond.

Shortly after the Amsterdam Projects were completed, this joker in the Department of Public Housing, who must have been unaware of the separate, but equal doctrine of all things American, started assigning black and Puerto Rican veterans and their families to the Amsterdam Projects. By 1950 when my family arrived there from a one-room basement arrangement in Harlem, white families had begun fleeing to as far away as Levittown, but mostly to the Borough of Queens.

This was a time of flight. My mother, with her three children in tow, fled from my father and the South in 1947 to live with her sister, a cousin and her husband, in a crowded Harlem apartment. In time, they got my mother to apply for public housing, but although my mother was the spouse of a war veteran, the waiting list was years long. They eventually learned that the city's Housing Department caseworkers operated faster in placing a family if that family's living condition was desperate, so they had the four of us moved into a single room in the basement of an apartment house a few blocks away. We had a deranged neighbor who lived in the room next to ours. He was a short, stocky man who walked in tiny strides that made him wobble. He had a fat face and vacant eyes. He talked to himself and nursed a small Christmas tree decorated with peanuts and tiny bulbs that were tied to its branches. The tree was on a table by the door to his room in the basement. Each night that summer, he lit up his Christmas tree as he sang "gumble gumble, seaful, seaful/gumble, gumble, seaful, seaful." In two months, our caseworker had gotten us an apartment in the Amsterdam Projects. And in a few short years, the Amsterdam houses was sixty percent black, thirty percent Puerto Rican and ten percent white. Ninety percent of the people in the Amsterdam houses were happy to have arrived there from dilapidated homes and impoverish conditions in Puerto Rico, the South, Harlem and others parts of New York City. Ten percent of the population were white families simply too poor to move out.

Paul Neuman and his family lived in building 70, which was attached to building 60, where I lived. They were Jews. Jews too poor to move. Jews too poor to follow the dietary and other customs of their religion—it was simply cheaper to acclimate into secular society. Jews too poor to be Jews. The details of the circumstances, which prevented them from fleeing with the others, remained murky. It was never clear to me if the father was there or, if the mother worked, but my own unflattering family predicament curtailed my interest. Paul and his sister Ruthie grew up black. They were what today's youth refer to as wiggers. You might say that they were pioneer wiggers, but since there has always been whites who assimilated into black culture, it may be more appropriate to call them 50's wiggers. Paul Neuman played the trumpet and he mastered being black so well that he became an eminent figure among the community's musicians and jazz enthusiasts.

"Hey Paul," I yelled out across Amsterdam Avenue one Saturday morning while Paul was waiting for the uptown bus, "where you going?"

"Music lessons, got this cat in Harlem that's teaching me to read music and to play my ax. Gots to learn to blow my horn ba-be. Catch you later."

And there were other white youths, who hung out with their black neighbors, sang and danced to Do-wop, smoked reefer, chilled on jazz, and hustled in card games of Tonk and Black Jack. We were many people with one culture. Our pop heroes were their heroes. They dug Miles Davis, The Harlem Globetrotters, Willie Mays, Archie Moore, Dinah Washington and Dr. Jive. Some of the older white people stuck there in the Amsterdam Projects lived bitter, resentful and isolated lives—but they held on to the hope that they would one day make it out of there. In time, some did, others didn't. Most of those stranded there were elderly. They were people who always wore a bathrobe and slippers to the mailbox. They had few or no close relatives and no hope of ever leaving the projects alive. They were treated kindly by most of the adults, but often teased and harassed by the youth.

There was an old man who each day came down to the lobby floor in building 40, to check his mailbox dressed in a lounging coat. After checking his mail, he would step outside the door to catch some fresh air. The kids outside laughed and called him Elmer Fudd. "Here comes Elmer Fudd," one kid would shout out and all the other kids would chime in, "Elmer Fudd, Elmer Fudd, Elmer Fudd." There was one boy who was particularly mean; he would walk right up to the old man and point into his face. The boy laughed and circled the old man and called him Elmer Fudd repeatedly. The old man always hurried back into the building waving his arms in annoyance. That boy behaved as though the man's feelings were of no consequence, like he was indeed a cartoon character undeserving of empathy. And, yes, the old man did resemble the cartoon character Elmer Fudd some. Still, whenever I witnessed this event, I always felt sorry for the man, but I never had the courage to show my sympathy.

5

Besides Paul Neuman, and the other white youths who assimilated into the dominant culture of the project, there were also those who held on to their own identity while they allied themselves with the dominant culture for the sake of peace. These were, for the most part, street toughened white boys who would have preferred to live in Hells Kitchen, the neighborhood that bordered our own. They admired the Irish Westie's crime gang of Hells Kitchen, but the Westies were genuine gangsters who engaged in big-time felonies and had an association with the Mafia; an authenticity these white boys from the Amsterdam Project weren't down with. Some satisfied themselves with petty street crimes and others worked to finish high school and get into City College.

There was a white woman, Mary O'Leary, who may have been widowed or abandoned, who lived in building 238, which was in the rear of the projects across from the playground. She appeared to be in her late forties and she had two sons. One boy appeared to be normal and was seldom seen. He was a tall lanky boy named Tim, with brown hair and sad blue Irish eyes. The other boy, the one who was said to be the older of the two, was short and dumpy with unruly brown hair with gray streaks. His name was Dennis and he was widely known. His mother brought him to the playground every day in the summer and even during the winter months she sat on a bench while Dennis amused himself. Dennis had a jovial, fat face with Mongoloid features. It was clear that he had Down's Syndrome. In his early teens, Dennis had a vocabulary of maybe 20 words and the mental capacity of a 5-year-old child. Many of the children in the playground were awfully mean to Dennis in the beginning, but in time, he won some of them over. Some children played catch with Dennis using his basketball sized soft colored ball or ran around the playground with him in a game of tag. The teasing fell off and the other children left him alone.

In time, Dennis seemed to have charmed the people. Almost everybody spoke to him. Dennis would vigorously shake his head up and down, then say "Hel-low" his thick tongue made the word sound heavy. Then he would say "Mine," pointing to whatever toy he had brought to the playground. Dennis even fell under the protective eye of some of the neighborhood's toughest thugs. And, there were times when Dennis momentarily turned bully, and had to be pulled away from some boy or girl he was about to crush. His brother, a quiet boy whose presence in the neighborhood was stealthy, grew into a tall gangling boy who sometimes materialized on the basketball court in the playground. After he graduated high school, Tim joined the Army and never returned to the projects.

Although Dennis never seemed to age, he grew into adulthood living in the Amsterdam Projects. The only discernable change in Dennis over the years was that his voice grew deep and his body pudgy. His mother seemed to grow weary and exhausted. She had dedicated all of her being to the welfare of her retarded son. Over the grueling years, her labor of love had become overwhelming and although her devotion to Dennis and to his care was resolute, she had become feeble. One day while Dennis sat in the living room watching American Bandstand, Mary O'Leary fell dead on the kitchen floor. The fate she dreaded most; leaving Dennis to the mercy of others had come to be. She never had a telephone and address book so the police had to search the apartment for information about any relatives that could be contacted. An old letter was found with Tim O'Leary's return address on it. They saw in the letter, how Tim had implored his mother to bring Dennis and relocate to Texas where he had married and made a home. Mary O'Leary, a woman set in her ways and attached to attending Mass at Saint Paul's Church and visits with her few friends, never considered Tim's offer. After the funeral, Tim took Dennis to Texas and found a home for him in a facility for retarded people. Tim kept in close contact with Dennis as he made a new life bowling and playing team sports in the Special Olympics. Dennis loved rock and roll music from his days of watching American Bandstand on television and he became the prince of the ballroom at the weekly dances until his death at the age of 55.

In the early fifties, the Amsterdam Housing Projects quickly filled with a Puerto Rican population that totaled thirty percent of its tenants. Most of these people were fresh from the Island, with little education, no money, few skills; most didn't even speak English, but they had the emigrant drive to succeed. They got jobs in the garment center or as building janitors, enrolled their children in the public schools and started the climb up the long and slippery socio-economic ladder. The better educated of these new arrivals to the Amsterdam Projects, became policemen, transit workers, taxi drivers and shipping clerks. They enrolled their children in Saint Paul's Catholic School and their continued enrollment kept the school functioning for three more decades. Some were first generation New Yorkers who were well-acquainted with the racially motivated resistance to their presence, but they were steadfast in the hope that raising their families in this area would give their children the chance to join the better paying ranks of the work force. The American dream was no myth to these people.

Black tenants had been living in the neighborhood for longer than half a century before the projects were built. The four blocks of 61st, 62nd, 63rd, and 64th Streets between Amsterdam and West End Avenue were tenement buildings built before the Civil War and had become a slum neighborhood. This is where some of the city's black population was placed since the 1880's. This area became home to thousands of black families who were being displaced from their homes in Greenwich Village in south Manhattan and a few decades later, black families fleeing the South during the great black migration. Three of the blocks made a sharp decline from Amsterdam Avenue down to West End Avenue. White families lived across Amsterdam Avenue from 59th to 64th streets. The white residents lived on the hill where all the shops and bars were. The black residents lived on the decline toward West End Avenue. Blacks traveled to the hill to shop at their own peril. At the turn of the twentieth century, there were so many racial brawls on the hill that the neighborhood was dubbed San Juan Hill after Teddy Roosevelt's famous charge in Cuba during the Spanish/American War.

The Southern blacks that came to San Juan Hill were mostly Geechies from South Carolina. There was also a sizable West Indian population years before the time the old tenements were demolished. These two groups were thought of as ornamental servants and were given work in the homes of rich white families living on the East Side of Central Park. At the turn of the twentieth century, there was so much dissatisfaction with living conditions that blacks from the area began to move to Harlem as the Germans and Dutch residents of Harlem moved further north to the Bronx. The Phipps housing complex were built in 1908 in an attempt to stem black migration to Harlem and to keep a sizable domestic work force near by.

In the mid 1940's, all of the old slum buildings, in the four block area were demolished except the eight buildings of the Phipps complex—four buildings each near West End Avenue on 63rd and 64th Streets. These buildings were spared because they had been built less than 40 years earlier, each apartment had a bathroom and a kitchen, and the buildings had heating systems. The old pre-Civil War coldwater flats had a common bathroom on each floor and meals were cooked on hot plates. These were destroyed to make way for the projects. The new buildings on Amsterdam Avenue were built like three sets of thirteen story twins, attached at the side. Building 40 was attached to building 50. Building 60, where my family lived, was attached to building 70. At the end of the block, building 80 was attached to building 90. Behind the twins, down 62nd street, were four sets of six-story buildings on the left side that ran down to West End Avenue. On the right side, were four sets of six-story attached buildings that spanned to 63rd Street and down to West End Avenue. Across 63rd Street was the Day Care Center, back then a pioneering idea. A single building spanned to 64th Street, the community center, the playground, and behind that, the Phipps housing complex.

The Amsterdam Projects was built in a prime section of the city. It was near so many old immutable cultural institutions and new ones were being built in the area every year. Central Park was the Amsterdam Projects front yard, just three short blocks away. Riverside Park was its back yard. The Museum of Natural History and the Planetarium were in walking distance. The Columbus Circle

Coliseum was completed in 1953. Times Square was one station stop on the subway or a pleasant ten-minute walk. Manhattan's industrial section was close by. The old Madison Square Garden was a short walk away and near the famed jazz clubs of 52nd Street.

It was on a Saturday, sometime in the late 1950's, when Mayor Robert Wagner, Governor Nelson Rockefeller and President Dwight Eisenhower rode in a motorcade down Amsterdam Avenue to 64th Street. I remember the day because Larry Neslebum came running out of his shoe store screaming "Hey Ike, hey Ike" at the motorcade. The occasion was the ceremonial ground breaking for Lincoln Center for the Performing Arts that was being built across the avenue from the projects. Rockefeller had been pushing the plan and he knew that the Master Builder Robert Moses and his architects had designed the complex with its huge ugly back to the projects in contemptuous compensation for the mistake the joker in the city's Housing Department made in placing us there.

The Amsterdam Projects bordered the gateway to education, culture, glamour, power and wealth—all of this, and it was home to thousands of poor citizens of New York City. These were people who didn't have any precedent for prosperity—people who could be lured into a belief that there was no way out of this situation. It was like living in a place that was separated from the rest of the city by an invisible membrane—like living in a bubble, but many of the young people found that all they had to do to realize the possibilities was to step outside of that bubble. I learned to survive, even to strive in the bubble, but it was the life outside of that bubble that I ultimately aspired towards.

2

I first met Brad Buffert in 1954 at my friend, Willie Clark's home, at a time when everybody in the world was 13, or like myself, turning 13. He looked like the kind of kid I'd easily dismiss as inconsequential—he was chubby and wore thick eyeglasses. Brad's family, his mother, sister and brother, had just moved to the projects from Harlem. I had known Ozzie Donaldson from seeing him in the playground. His family lived in the Phipps buildings behind the playground. Ozzie had two brown-skinned brothers of average height, but his stunted height and light complexion mirrored that of his parents. Even at the tender age of 13, Willie Clark loved to gamble and had apparently invited them to his room for a clandestine session of Black Jack.

I happened to be there that Saturday evening. I had finished my newspaper route delivering the early editions of Sunday's papers and had stopped by to watch The Jackie Gleason show with Clark. Everybody called Willie Clark by his last name. Clark was tall, dark and ambitious. He worked after school at the cleaners on the corner across from my building. He made ten dollars a week and got paid on Saturdays. In a short time, I found out that this is why Brad and Ozzie were there. They were all classmates in school. Brad first met Ozzie in school, but Brad's building in the projects was across the street from Ozzie's in the Phipps. They liked each other and formed a two-man hustling crew.

"You got money—you want to play too?" Brad asked me as he, Ozzie and Clark positioned themselves to make space for the cards on Clark's bed.

"Play what?"

"Black Jack," Ozzie said.

"I got money, but I don't want to play no Black Jack."

"Okay, Tonk, we'll play Tonk."

"He don't know how to play Black Jack or Tonk," Clark told them. "Deal the cards."

That evening I watched them swindle Clark's week's pay away from him as his family's laugher at the antics of the Honeymooners filtered through his closed room door. I had come to watch the television show, but I witnessed something far more interesting and alluring.

My full name is Grady Lee Murrow. I was 10 years old when my family moved to the Amsterdam Projects. For the first few years, I spent my time with a group of friends; I secretly came to regard as squares. People who indulged in wholesome activities, obeyed the laws, played by the rules and were being taught to believe in the integrity of the system—losers. This isn't how I regarded them at first; this revelation only came to me after I became fully emerged into my association with Brad Buffert and Ozzie Donaldson and the world of the down boys. The social milieu of the hustlers, hipsters and those who understood the nature of growing up in a stacked deck colored my new perspective. Before my conversion, I was completely contented with trading baseball cards with Eddy Bishop, or going to the museum with Manny Black, or playing skullzie with Julio Otereo, building a box scooter with Crunch Collier, exploring Central Park with my brother, or talking goofy with Norman Brown. I still engaged in those activities after my conversion, but my main focus became learning how to be tough and hip, and how to pocket the unearned dollar—the hustle.

The summer is a lifetime to young people. Sarah always sent me to South Carolina to spend most of the summer with my grandmother. For reasons unknown by me, Sarah did not send me packing immediately at the close of school this summer. She hinted instead, that I would go later in the summer. After our first meeting, somehow, I started running into Brad and Ozzie more often. I was impressed with their renegade attitude towards life in the projects—it was the two of them against all the rest. They had a code of loyalty that didn't extend beyond them. Everyone else and everything else was fair game for them. Over the summer of 1954, I was drawn from my network of wholesome squares towards the dazzle of the down boys, although not completely. I can't say how or when it occurred, but early in the spring of 1954, I started hanging out with Brad and Ozzie rather than going to my regular group in an area we called "Down the Back."

Down the Back, there was another small children's playground where the girls and boys from that section of the projects hung out. The playground had concrete barrels; a boat made of bricks, swings, shade trees and a boxed in area of benches and climbing logs we called the "Bullpen." Evane Smith, a tall gregarious girl who had been in my classes since the third grade dominated the crowd back there. She was loud, audacious and overwhelming. We would develop what would be a life-long friendship. Evane lived with her mother and younger sister. Evane's mother was popular among our group because she was pretty and because she let us use her apartment as a kind of after school clubhouse and as we grew older she became one of us—nearly. Some of the kids called her by her first name—Ethel. I called her Mrs. Smith. There was Maggie Clark, Willie Clark's sister, who was my unofficial girlfriend for a period. Maggie had a pleasant face with a cheery smile and she grew into a ripe body in time. She liked me, but she later fell for Malcolm Tibbs. Deborah Black was a plain looking homely girl, but she was friendly, honest and smart. Shareen Mudd was from the avenue like myself, but hung out in the back. She was light-skinned and cute in an impermanent kind of way. Patti Smith, Evane's sister, was the youngest of the group. She was short and overweight and, at one point, was in an all girls singing group that sounded good enough to make it. Patti had an unpleasant talking voice that was transformed to a thing of beauty when she sang.

Some of the guys from the back included Willie Clark; a tall loner who acquired work ethics at a young age that allowed him little time to hang with the group. Clark always had money and he was always eager to risk it gambling. He saw the group in passing. When he wasn't in school or working, he was visiting with his girlfriend. Manny Black had two other sisters besides Deborah. His family had lived a block away from my family in Harlem although we didn't know each other. Manny and I spent many of our Saturdays together at the Museum of Natural History. Our favorite exhibits were the great whale hanging in the rotunda and the diagram of the women's reproduction system on the wall in the Human Anatomy section. The size of the whale overwhelmed us and the mystery of the diagram mesmerized us. Tommy Borden came from a large family of seven boys and one girl and they lived in the same building as Brad. Tommy and I had a fight when he first moved into the neighborhood, but we became very close friends in later years. Thomas Bedding and his two younger brothers lived with their mother, who was from the West Indies. The brothers were all smart boys who got into the better classes in school. Later, during the Black Arts Movement, Thomas moved to Harlem, changed his name and became an artist of durable distinction. Malcolm Tibbs was from the avenue, but he hung out in the back. He was a light-skinned, good-looking boy and it was he who Maggie Clark preferred over me—and years later married. Maggie chose the good-looking guy to fill her reproduction system with picture-book children over the plain-looking charming guy with nebulous potentials. Like I have done many times in my life, she chose style over substance. And, there was a satellite group that revolved around this core group. This was the circle of squares with which I spent my time before I started to run with Brad and Ozzie.

I have never been committed to anything completely—a characteristic that has impeded any success that I may have had foreordained for me. This has always been a complex issue for me. I realized early that being on the margins of the fractions afforded me a certain flexibility and accessibility to everybody. So although I, at that time, spent most of my time with Brad, Ozzie and the down boys, psychologically I still identified with all the fractions of my prior associations. That I never got solidly locked into *anything* saved me from criminality and jail, and, at the same time, obstructed my path to scholarship and a career as a writer—no wonder a future brother-in-law would refer to me as the *hip square.*

3

Brad Buffert had a charismatic personality and an innovative mind. He was a self-contained person who emitted the impression that other people were important to him. People felt special in his presence and valued his camaraderie. He was brown skinned and had a pleasant face. He wore thick eyeglasses and his eyes always squinted as though he was straining to see. He had an uncommonly pleasant voice and even back then, uttered the newest hip expressions. Brad had an innate coolness about him. He had moved with his family from a Harlem tenement block that was being turned into a public housing project. Once the projects were completed and the buildings were opened, they were promised to be placed back into their old Harlem neighborhood. Brad and I had lots in common. We were the same age. We each had a brother and sister. We were both, the oldest child. We were born in South Carolina. Both our mothers later fled to Harlem with three children. We were both fatherless. We both had an appreciation of our situation. Brad lived in Harlem until he was 13 and I until I was 10.

Harlem was a community of people with diverse survival traits back then. It's attributes ranged from aimlessness to nobility and everything in between, and you were what your group was. As I got to know Brad better, I'd think that he apprenticed under the brightest hustlers in his block in Harlem. Even at 13, Brad had already developed a knack to recognize the angles and the capacity to turn them to his advantage. Black children of our era, growing up in the North, developed an intuitive sense of the inequality of things from the actions of the grown people we watched. In the South, the lessons of inequality for black children were blunt and easily recognizable. North and South, I had had a taste of them both. As a community, we combated the affects of disparity by suspending whatever rules of the larger society we could. We sold goods we brought home from our jobs to each other, without fear of words going to the wrong ears. We developed an underground code of conduct to govern our relationships one to the other. As children, we developed an instinct for the unspoken rules of survival we saw practiced by the grownups. Some of us developed aptitudes to circumvent the wreckage of racism at a very early age. Brad excelled at all of this and he had the kind of audacity successful captains of industry are famous for—but he was a street-wise black kid. Where he lived, audacity usually led to a stint in the joint.

"Tell me," Brad once asked a counterman who had just brought us our bill, in a restaurant where we had finished eating steak sandwiches, "why is the bill always placed face-side down?"

"It's being polite to the customer, like we're not so eager for the money," he said. "Would you like a piece of pie?"

"Aha," Brad said, "it's so you can sell that piece of pie to people who didn't see how much they had already spent.

"Smart boy—apple, peach or blueberry?"

"No pie for me," Brad said as he turned his bill over.

This is the kind of sharp mind Brad possessed—nothing escaped his keen observation and curiosity. Brad always asked lots of questions of almost everyone. He once questioned me about why I always tried so hard to make people laugh.

"Because I can," I said.

"Especially when them cats are bullying you. You should stop that shit and stand up for yourself."

"What about you," I said, "every time Frankie Cane collar you up, you always mention your sister to him, 'cause you know he likes her. You ought to stop using your sister to save your ass."

"You think you're funny."

The upright among us waged the battle for equality head-on. Few people I knew thought that the time was near when the outcry for freedom would burst forth and the battle would be fully engaged. It was, in fact, this generation that Brad, Ozzie and I belonged to that would supply the ranks of the civil rights movement. Some of these street-smart kids were destined to become a part of the more aggressive cadre of the movement, but others had grown too selfish to get involved by the time the movement came. They sympathized with the goals of the civil rights movement. But many in the underground black subculture of hustling had the attitude that if something came of it—fine, but they also felt they were doing alright just as things were. All they wanted was to keep the Man off their asses. They were shadows in society; they would have to materialize to enter into conflict with the oppressor. If they surfaced, they would expose themselves to the sight of the enemy and lose a valuable advantage—invisibility. This invisibility, Brad, Ozzie and I discovered in 1954 and were now just in the initial stages of exploring.

Ozzie Donaldson was nearly a year older than Brad and me. He was short and puny, but he had many talents. He was a very bright boy, with the kind of singing voice that was popular near the end of the Do-wop era. He looked like Frankie Lymon and was often mistaken for the teenage singing sensation. The three of us once had lunch at the Times Square Woolworth and the counter lady refused to let Ozzie pay for our lunch thinking he was Frankie Lymon. Ozzie could have also been an artist; he could draw things to a life-like image. Ozzie had guts and nerves of steel. Ozzie Donaldson was also a kleptomaniac who delighted in surprising Brad and me by producing something he stole in a store we were all in together and even we hadn't seen him lift it. Ozzie loved to stump us and have us ask "How'd you do that?" His goal was not merely to deceive the shopkeeper or clerk, but also to beguile and seduce Brad and me with his sneaky proficiency. Ozzie Donaldson was a shoplifting artist.

Ozzie was also for a time, a musical artist. A shady young, white record producer pulled Ozzie from a failed neighborhood singing group that once included Ozzie's younger brother Chad and Norman Brown, a classmate of mine and two boys from the projects. Ozzie made a record during the end of the Do-wop period. The shady producer a little while later put out a version of Ozzie's record by a white singing group that was successful because the record producer pushed the white version on the radio and Ozzie made nothing from what turned out to be a minor hit.

Ozzie was egotistic and held himself high above everyone except Brad. His conceit may have come from his good looks or it may have been a way he compensated for his puny stature. Whatever the cause it made him difficult to get along with. Ozzie and I had very little in common. We really didn't even care for each other much in the beginning. We were each more loyal to Brad than we were to each other. Our attachment to Brad is what kept me and Ozzie in the team, but there would come a time when Ozzie's lack of self-initiative would keep him by my side and even under my leadership.

I was the third member of the three musketeers. I had none of the attributes Brad and Ozzie brought to our crew. I was a skinny boy, shy and timid. I had low self-esteem and a modest temperament. I saw myself as unattractive, with large lips, a broad nose and unruly hair. I was ashamed of my broken home and in a community of working class poor people, I was ashamed that my family seemed to have less then everyone else. So, I became imaginative, falsely aggressive and sharp-witted outwardly. I was funny, dumb and clownish. Deep down, I was analytical and perceptive. I was a walking contradiction. My true character was lethargic and my potentials would lie dormant for yet a few years. I liked reading because as a student at a Harlem elementary school I was exposed to literature in a program called "Story Hour," at the Cuntee Cullen library on 135th Street. And, I had a vague feeling that I would become a writer. My perception of the only positive quality in me that I was conscious of at the time was, as a quote from the bible goes, the size of a mustard seed. Although at this point I wasn't good at any hustle, I was accepted into the crew because I was down with any hustle.

There are many things one does not know about ones self at the age of 13. One of the things I didn't know about myself at 13, was that I would develop into a fiercely independent person—that I would take the lessons learned in the coming five years and turn them into my shield and my weapon. And, so armed, I would pierce out a tiny space for myself in the world where I could mature and grow. This is an account of the largely benign events of my life—but it is largely benign events that have filled America's jails with tens of thousands of young black men. I was headed that way before I made a major course correction. But first, I had to burn in the Potter's oven of experience. This is the story of that period in the inferno that hardens clay, makes steel pliable and shapes crystal.

San Juan Hill

CHAPTER TWO
So What, Jack?

1

Before we get to contemplate the events of the inferno, there is a preamble I feel necessary to an appreciation of the principal theme. The beginning is usually a good place to start. I was born in my grandmother's house in Charleston County, South Carolina on August 5, 1941, the day 10,000 Jews were murdered in Pinsk, Poland. The war in Europe was raging and was soon to be widened by the Pearl Harbor attack which forced America to make an all out effort using every resource it had to bring peace to the world. One of America's resources was my 21-year-old father, who became a soldier and went off to drive trucks in the Far East. The America military Dons of the time didn't believe that black men had the nerve and courage for combat. If black men did have the mettle for combat, these white commanders reasoned, they would be fighting us for their freedom and the freedom of black women and children right here in America. If the black man doesn't have the courage to fight to free his own, how can we trust him to fight for a cause that won't benefit him? The black man is cowardly. This line of reasoning led the military to assign blacks primarily to service and supply outfits. Because the heroics of black fighters in the Civil War, The Indian Wars, The Spanish/American War and World War I, had gone overlooked and unheralded and sometimes even covered-up—these generals misjudged the character of blacks of the 1940's.

The bold armored advance across France in 1944 by General George S. Patton threatened to collapse the American supply line to the frontlines of the fighting. An army without gas, bullets and food would quickly be defeated, so the Army Transportation Corps created a huge trucking operation called the "Red Ball Express." The name of the convoy unit came from the railroad phrase to "red ball" meaning to ship non-stop express. The unit was comprised of more than 75 percent black troops. The high commanders didn't want black troops to be a factor in any determinant role in the fighting war. But the allied supply line had grown so long that without the Red Ball Express transporting the 750 tons of supplies needed by the 28 divisions advancing across France and Belgium, there would have been no Allied victory. As fate would have it, it was the 24/7 three-month delivery of gas, bullets, blankets and food by my father and other black soldiers that made victory possible. The importance of the role black soldiers played in the triumph was never celebrated, but it was too enormous to cover up.

My father had left the Far East with his poem about kicking Tojo's ass and reassigned to the Red Ball Express where he would be given the opportunity to write a poem about the defeat of Hitler. Decades later, a few months before he died, he gave me those two poems. If my father had no other good quality, he had a propensity for writing poetry that describes conflict in a kind of "shit talking" way. The poems were a common man's ode to the defeat of tyranny. I had often hoped that he would have had a talent for poetry that nurtured family life instead.

For the first three years of my life, I lived with my grandmother and learned to address her as Momma Dolly. We lived in an unincorporated area of Charleston County, South Carolina, 25 miles from the city of Charleston. This place was hardly any different from other area of the state; impoverished, backward and raw with racism. The area was under the harsh control of half illiterate and fully hateful whites. Times were very hard during the war. My 17-year-old mother had to leave me behind when she went to live with relatives in Charleston. She worked in a cigar factory in Charleston and came home on the weekends. My grandmother's sister lived in the house behind her own. This woman was my great aunt. She had a daughter who had a baby a month younger than me. My grandmother would take me there to be nursed by her niece Viola. She would hold her own son and me on her knees and nurse us both at the same time. Everybody made an effort for the war. My mother's name is Sarah and as I learned to talk I'd call her what I heard Momma Dolly call her—so I grew up calling my grandmother—Momma Dolly, and my mother—Sarah.

People in the Hamlet where I was born spoke to ghosts and believed in the supernatural. People spoke of being ridden by ghosts while they slept. Some people even knew which ghost had ridden them and some even knew why—say, an unpaid debt or an unrepentant wrong deed. Ham Waller stumbled home late every Saturday night drunk. When he reached the old oak tree by the footpath to his house, he would stop, take his bottle from his hind pocket and lean up against the tree. This was where he and his Uncle Bink Waller drank their whiskey for over twenty years. Uncle Bink had been dead for five years, but that never prevented Ham from continuing to stop and share a drink with him. He could feel Uncle Bink's presence when the air temperature around the tree warmed up. He'd tell Uncle Bink how much the whiskey cost if it was store bought, and then he would pour a drink on the ground for him.

"Paid two dolla and ten cent for this here pint bottle of Canadian Mist. So you drinking high on the hog right now Uncle Bink."

And, they would drink and hold a conversation before Ham continued on his journey home. From time to time, people have disputed what Ham said about the cost of his store bought liquor, but no one has ever questioned that it was dead Bink Waller who helped Ham finish his many bottles.

This was a place where it was also considered disrespectful to the dead to point at a grave. To keep the spirit of the person who's grave had been pointed to from following them, children were instructed to turn around three times, stump their toes and spit. All of the adults had grown up in this tradition so they knew better than to point at a grave. All of the graves and headstones in the hamlet's one hundred and fifty-year-old cemetery are turned in the same direction, except those whose deaths were suspected to have been caused by foul play. These headstones and graves are slightly tilted to cause displeasure and retribution upon the gaze of the guilty. It is a way to let the culpable know that the details may be hidden, but someone knows the deed. These are people whose mythology and folk history go back beyond the Middle Passage. My people are the Gullah people of the Coastal Islands, whose habits, traditions, and customs were carried over from the door of no return in another time, on another continent.

One morning in October of 1945, there was great excitement in the house. Sarah was home from Charleston and dressed up pretty. And they had put my church clothes on me. Sarah's two brothers who owned a shoe repair shop in Charleston had come home for the occasion. Everybody was so happy, but I didn't understand any of what the excitement was about. Momma's house was right off the highway and every once in a while someone would go out to look down the highway. Finally, they moved the vigil to the front porch. We weren't there for long before the bus came. Soon as it was sighted and long before it reached Momma's house, Sarah grabbed my hand pulling me out through the gate and dragging me onto the road. The driver started braking by Momma's house, but by the time it stopped, it had traveled an extra hundred yards to come to a complete stop by Momma's brother's house. When the bus passed us, Sarah was dragging me on the ground. She was laughing and crying. We reached the bus just as the door opened. A man dressed in olive green army clothes came down from the bus. He hugged and kissed Sarah as a crowd of family members gathered around. He grabbed me up and kissed me and he kissed Sarah then me. The bus driver held the door open and everyone on the bus cheered. Then someone handed down two long bags the same color as his clothes. The bus door closed and the driver drove the bus off.

This man was Grady S. Murrow, my father. He was a towering figure to me, but actually, he was only five feet nine inches tall. He was a bright-skinned man with penetrating eyes and a wicked crooked-mouth smile. Everything about him and his belongings had the scent of mint; to me it seemed the scent was natural to the color of his clothes and the bags. This was one of only three really happy moments in our relationship. The next really happy moment came weeks after my father returned. While he was away at war, Sarah worked hard and saved her money. She bought some land a half mile behind Momma's house. This is where my mother and father built their house and when the house was completed, they got married. There was a wooded area between our house and the hamlet of houses that surrounded the highway. The night of the reception the tiny walk path that led to our house was lit with what was called flambos; soda bottles filled with kerosene and topped with a piece of cloth that burned slowly. That was a joyful day and evening.

My brother Ed Lewis and my sister Ann Ruth were born during the next 20 months—members of what is known in America as Baby Boomers. The last happy moment I can recall we had as a family happened on a Sunday afternoon. My father had planted a small vegetable garden. The vegetable garden was on the far side of a wagon path that ran by our house. After dinner that summer evening, Sarah and my father went out to the garden to pick a watermelon. They were in an especially playful mood and they tussled and laughed. I stood on the porch eager to taste the melon, but their gaiety fed my hunger and I waited patiently for the sweet delight. Later that evening as the sky darkened so did the mood and Sarah and my father had the first of many violent fights.

After the war, in the unincorporated section of Charleston County, where we lived, there was no great Levittown experiment like in New York—not even free flowing information of the benefits of the G. I. Bill was available to black ex-soldiers in our area. They came back to the same kind of life they'd left. There were no meaningful jobs, only demeaning work in the fields. These jobs paid so little, to work was pointless. Racism was rampant in the entire South and the crackers in our area at the time were as brutal as any white Mississippian. These returning black soldiers had been out and saw something of the world. They had been to France, Italy and Belgium and had been treated with dignity by the men and the women they met there. They had been half way around the world in the service of their government and, in my father's case, under constant danger, played a significant role in America's triumph. These men weren't looking for a hand out, but they felt they had earned the dignity of a job and a livable wage. A small taste of dignity never deminishes, but only creates a hunger for more. Crackers know this fact well and this is why they never treated black people with dignity—they know where this leads.

My father had some degree of pride—deserved or not. His own father was a proud man who owned land and refused all of his life to ever work for a white man. His name was Robert Murrow and his wife died when my father was a small boy. Robert Murrow raised nine children farming and he operated a small supply store. He knew that no one could give you dignity. It is something you give yourself. Fathers aren't always able to transfer their virtues to their sons. My father drank and thoughtlessly brought his bitterness that America was treating him unfairly into his relationship with Sarah and their children. My father had six brothers and two sisters. All of his brothers accepted the status quo of our area and farmed or worked in whatever capacity they could to earn a meager living for their families. None of them had been to war or had experienced what my father had in Europe, so it may have been easier for them to tolerate the racism. My father was known as "Big Joe," and his motto was "So what, Jack." He could out drink most men and would fight any *black* man in the area. Even before he went off to war, he was known for his drunken, rowdy loudness. Now his failure to find work had dampened his desire to live a family life. He drank and became more violent in the community and at home. He didn't care about anything or anyone.

"So what, Jack."

One rainy day my father came home drunk. He beat Sarah and threatened to kill her. He chased her out of the house and prevented her from taking us with her to Momma's house. When he was sure that she had gone, Big Joe left his three small children in the house by themselves. He must have known that this was wrong and dangerous because he made sure that people saw him on the road. He knew they would tell Sarah and Momma that he was out of the house. I was five years old, my brother was 15 months old and my sister was four months old. The wagon path that ran in front of our house hooked around to the highway bypassing all the houses in the hamlet. My grandmother, a Harriet Tubman figure with her apron and headscarf, revised the utility of the Underground Railroad. Knowing that no one would see her on this path, Momma came in the drenching rain to fetch us. She dressed us hurriedly, instructed me to hold on to her apron tail while she carried my brother and baby sister in her arms. It rained hard and the sky was haze gray as Momma walked as fast as she could and I dared not let go of her apron tail. We arrived at her house soaking wet, but finally safe from the turmoil.

The next day, Sarah's youngest brother, Uncle James, came from Charleston and made a complaint to the sheriff. When the sheriff arrived on the scene, they hauled me before him. The sheriff a fat red-faced man with an uncompromising look on his face sat in his patrol car. My father stood on the outside near the front of the car. My uncle stood in front of the car's open front window. He was talking in an agitated tone. My father stood silent. When I arrived, I could not imagine what I would be asked. I held my head down and trembled with fear.

"What'd you see boy?" The red-face sheriff asked. "Did he hit ya' Ma, boy?"

My father's eyes caught mine—his face-tightened stone like. His eyes did not hold a look that pleaded with me to lie. He shot me a look that terrorized me and has lain frozen in my memory for eternity.

"Well boy did he hit ya' Ma?"

"No suh"

Someone took me back to Momma Dolly's house. My disappointed uncle stayed by the police car talking. My father was freed. I had told the lie that would free us from him for good.

<u>2</u>

My uncle sent a telegram to my Aunt Dorothy in New York City and she arrived the next week. Aunt Dorothy was Sarah's unmarried sister who had been persuaded to move to New York City, a few years earlier, by one of their cousins. There were lots of preparations going on, washing, ironing, and buying me new shoes. I had no idea what all of this meant. A few days later, they prepared a big bag lunch of fried chicken sandwiches, fried sweet potato chips and big store bought cookies. My uncle drove Aunt Dot and me to the train station in Charleston. We were going to Harlem, in New York City. My mother, brother and sister would follow in a few months. My first image of Harlem was amusing and shocking. When we emerged from the subway, I saw a man walking with a dog—the dog was on a leash but it had a muzzle around its mouth. I had seen many dogs in my old community, but none with a leash and surely none with a muzzle. I once had a dog of my own, but it was killed on the highway in front of our church. After my move to New York, my dog would return to me in a reoccurring dream that I had until I was an adult. New York was a strange place where I had to learn to call what I had known all of my life as a biscuit—a cookie. What I had known as a bottle of dope in rural South Carolina, was a soda, in urbane New York City where everybody wore shoes—all the time.

Aunt Dot was a slender bright-skinned woman with splendid manners and high ambitions. She shared an apartment with her cousin Lacey and her husband Henry Brown on 134th Street between Lenox and Fifth Avenues. The plan was that as soon as they could find a larger apartment Aunt Dot would send for my mother and my brother and sister. School hadn't started yet and everyone worked, so I was left in the house alone. This was in 1947 and a television set would have been a luxury. Aunt Dot would make me a lunch before she went to work, which I'd eat early. I had nothing to do but sit or roam the rooms of the small apartment—it seemed the day would never end. I was frightened all the time, even at night when we slept. We slept with the window open and the shade up. The shapes and shadows that were made by the light that came through the window scared me. I was overwhelmed by this new environment and was having a difficult time adjusting.

One day while I was home alone, the people in the apartment above our own had a loud fight. At first, it was just loud shouting back and forth. This went on for what seemed to me a lengthy period of time. I went to the bathroom to hover in safety, but because of the hole that allows the heating pipes to run the length of the building, the noise of the argument made them sound nearer. Then, I could hear that they were tussling and things started to fall. The screaming became louder and then there was a thump. I became extremely alarmed. I didn't know what to expect. I went to the bedroom—it had a window that opened to the fire escape. I opened the window and crawled onto the fire escape. We lived on the fourth floor of a six-story building. I could see the back of the buildings on the next block and a great big open yard with lots of children playing. I started to climb down the fire escape, but a man's voice cried out for me to stop where I was. I was scared and obedient. Some men came and rescued me from the fire escape. Later that evening they explained to Aunt Dot that they were from the Harlem Boy's and Girl's Club that ran a nursery for the children of working parents and guardians. She could bring me there in the mornings and pick me up when she returned from work.

This arrangement went well. Only the other children teased me because I talked differently. I spoke in a Gullah dialect familiar to the Geechee people of coastal South Carolina. Soon they starting calling me "Country," something I know they must have gotten from their parents, who were themselves most often, from the South. The Geechee people of the Coastal Islands of South Carolina are African Americans closest tie to our ancestral homeland. We have maintained many customs that are traced directly to the country of Sierra Leone, the bright color of our homes, the markings in our yards and our patois. We speak a Pidgin English that can be traced back to West Africa. I really stood out from the other children and was made fun of. One day when all the children were dressed in bathing suits for the water sprinkler, two boys my age approached me in the locker room. We were all dressed in swim trunks. They called me names and taunted me. They threw me to the floor and one of them humiliated me by lying on top of me. They called me Country and threatened to beat me up if I told anyone. When that day ended, I threw the event out of my mind. That night I had the dream for the first time: I was alone on the subway platform at 135th Street waiting for a train. My brown dog I called Spot, although it had none, would appear and enter the train with me. Then Spot would do a curious thing—it would turn into a pretty girl with wavy hair. We would ride one station and the dream ended. I had variations of this dream for twenty years.

Soon we moved to number 16-18 West 136th Street, right across the street from Harlem hospital. More specifically, we lived right across from the hospital's kitchen. All of the aromas of each meal they made floated and hovered in the air near our building. The apartment had three bedrooms, a kitchen and a small dining enclave, a living room where cousin Lacey hung her picture of Jesus with a heart that was lit with a blinking red bulb, and a bathroom. In the hallway, there was a thing called a dumb-waiter where the trash was thrown out. I liked going to the dumb-waiter, ringing the bell for the attendant to send the box up. Then I would put the trash in it and it would be lowered to the basement. It wasn't long after we moved into the new apartment that Sarah arrived with my brother and sister. Cousin Lacey and her husband, whom I called Uncle Henry, had the master bedroom with two windows that looked out to the street. I slept in the center room with Aunt Dot. The room had a window, but a tall cabinet that held our clothes covered it. Sarah and my brother and sister slept in the room at the end of the hallway near the entrance door. This room had a window that faced out towards the vacant lot next to our building. Sarah was 23 years old. She had three children—no skills, and very little education. Aunt Dot could barely read herself. She had a job in the garment industry and she was a member of a local union that encouraged her to attend night school. She would help her younger sister to raise her family in the safety and dignity of Harlem, New York.

SAN JUAN HILL

Uncle Henry was hard working, hard drinking, quiet, charitable and kind. He took me to the barbershop and introduced me as his son. He loved what he called "Shoot 'um ups" and took me on Saturdays to the local movie theater where there was *Always a Western.* Some Saturday mornings he would hire me to sweep out his car and when I was finished, he'd give me a quarter for the movies. The nearest movie theater was one block away on 135th Street. It played three feature films, five cartoons, coming attractions and a serialized chapter film—all for a quarter. Plus they gave out door prizes mid-way through the showing. I went to the movies at noon and got out at 6:00 in the evening.

One Saturday evening, Uncle Henry and Aunt Lacey took me to a movie theater in Times Square. We took the subway to 50th Street and when we got up to the streets it was dark. The view down Broadway was magical. All the theater marquees were lit up and the lights all moved, blinked and made wizardry. Lights of all colors made the area festive and frolicsome. We went to see "Red River," staring John Wayne and Montgomery Clift, a romanticized version of the frontier white man's treachery towards Indians, Mexicans and the weaker of themselves. I was spellbound whenever the lean bodied Montgomery Clift was on the screen with his gun belt hanging at an angle near his trigger finger; his face holding an ever-present expression that pleaded for fair play. The young orphan boy grew up under the autocratic rule of Tom Dunson, but somehow he developed a sense for fairness and the will to bring it about. I respected Mr. Dunson, the cattle baron, but I feared him and even loathed him. Dunson would kill any man who interfered with his dream. He killed them on the spot and issued instructions to: "Bury him here, I'll say some words over him in the morning." The young man was forced to banish Dunson and take control of the cattle drive. In the end, the younger man got the cattle to Abilene and after a short fistfight, he won the tyrants respect. The younger man's triumph over the stubbornness of the older despot had a lasting impact on me.

That summer, some of the children in the building became friendly with me. I soon began to feel comfortable around them—I was becoming one of them though I talked funny they said. By accident, I discovered that I could captivate their attention with the three stories I knew. At night when we sat on the stoop before being called up for bed, they played a game where each kid told a riddle.

"Why did the man prefer an umbrella to his wife? Because he could shut up the umbrella, but he couldn't shut up his wife."

I didn't know any riddles so when it was my turn I'd tell a story. They became fond of my story telling, and instead of playing the riddle game, they would ask me to tell them one of the stories. They particularly liked the story my father used to tell me. It was about a time he and Sarah went fishing:

My father and mother went fishing in a rowboat. They fished and fished until it had gotten dark. In the dark, they could not find the way back home. They rowed and rowed and finally they saw a light in the distance. They rowed towards the light and as they got closer, they could hear loud music and laughter. When they reached land, they were greeted by a man who invited them to join in the party. They had never seen black people like these black people before. They were dressed in fine clothes, wore shoes and drank liqueur out of china glasses like white people. My father explained that they were lost and that they had three small children that they had to get back to. The host invited them to spend the night and said that they would help them find their way home in the morning. Then they were led to a room where they would spend the rest of the night. Early that morning, at the break of dawn, my father heard footsteps coming towards their room and he heard people sneering "We're gonna cut their heads off. We're gonna cut their heads off." Their voices sounded eerie as hags. And, as the footsteps came nearer, my father awakened my mother. "We gotta get out of here," he told her. "They coming to cut our heads off." They dressed quickly and when the people opened the door, my father and mother dashed out of the room and ran down a long hallway. They were chased by a horde of hags from the party all welding cleavers and hatchets. My father and mother ran and ran and finally they came to a door. They ran out of the door as the hags closed in on them. They came to a tall tree and climbed up it. The hags surrounded them and began to use their hatchets to cut the tree down. They chopped and chopped and when the tree was near ready to fall, my father called out to his three dogs; in a great voice, he called out Bozo, Battlemazo, Kazam. And, in one giant leap, three great dogs arrived on the scene and frightened the hags away. My father and Sarah went to get the fish that they had left tied in the water. They left the boat there; they would come for it later. They tied the fish in a sack to the back of Bozo, he rode Battlemazo, and she rode Kazam—home.

At the end of the story, my father would say that if I was ever in danger I should always summon Bozo, Battlemazo and Kazam. I always ended my telling of this story with the same admonishment. Everyone on the stoop felt that they had secret protectors lurking out there somewhere. One other story was about a fox, a rabbit, deception and their lunch. The third was about a contemptible white man and the vengeance of God's angels' way before the end of the world. I told those stories so many times that I became bored with them and started making revisions in them as I just did above, telling the story in plain English, something I couldn't do in those days on the stoop. Then I began to improvise stories of my own on the spot. Something was developing in me that astonished me.

During the hot days of that summer of 1947, I watched and helped my new friends make wagons from milk crates, odd pieces of lumber and discarded wheels from baby carriages. When we were finished, we would pull our creation 12 blocks down to Mount Morris Park, where we would climb to the top of one of its hilly walkways. Mount Morris Park is one of the highest points in Harlem. All of its steep winding walkways lead up to the Fire Watchtower that was built in 1857 to spot fires, in what was at that time, a fire prone section of the city. Then we would select three riders and their positions on the wagon. On two successive days, I was chosen for the front position on the wagon, when I really wasn't eager to be on the wagon at all. It wasn't out of fear that I didn't want to be among the first to experience the trial run—but, rather, not knowing what to expect, I wanted to watch first. But I was chosen and I couldn't chicken out. On each of those days, the wagon turned over on the second curve after we had gathered too much speed to control it. We were all thrown out of the wagon, but I got the worse of it each time because of my position in the front. The fall was great enough to bruise my knees and draw blood. My buddies would pull the wagon with me in it, wounded and acting the part, back up to Harlem Hospital. Oh, I milked the last ounce of sympathy from my comrades and I cherished the role of wounded martyr. They didn't take me home first to consult with my mother. They rushed me to the nurse's station with an unruly sense of urgency. There, a nurse would patch me up and send me home, without the need for an HMO card, and absent any fear of being sued for cleaning up and bandaging a little boy's scraped knees without the consent of his parents—no bill, no fuss.

The vacant lot next to our building, with all of its rubble and refuse, was the center of much of our activities. It was there that our wagons were constructed and it was there that we cooked mickeys. A mickey is a white potato cooked in a vacant lot over a fire made in an old metal trash can. Sometimes we would each bring a potato from home, but most often, a group of us would hunt discarded milk bottles and return them to the store for the three-cent deposit each bottle brought. Three milk bottles was exactly the price for a pound of potatoes. This lot was also the location where workers from the hospital's kitchen would bring us packages of mellow-roll ice cream without the cones. The hospital kitchen served the mellow-rolls in a dish and didn't order the cones; still we were always grateful for the wrapped ice cream, which we ate quickly and awkwardly. One day, a group of older boys brought a BB gun to this vacant lot we used as a playground and shot a boy in the eye. The boy was rushed to the hospital across the street, where he was treated, but the eye was lost. On another occasion, some older boys dangled a younger boy from the rooftop of our building overlooking the vacant lot. The young boy cried out in horror and just when the older boys were going to hoist him back on the rooftop, they lost grip of the boy's hands and he plunged to his death in the vacant lot. None of us were witnesses to either of these events, but the rumor of these incidences made them real to us and struck a fear in me that made me distrustful and anxious in large crowds of boys I didn't know well.

That summer, I learned to sneak on the subway by waiting for the train to come to a stop in the station. Then either running through the gate or ducking under the turnstile and through the closing doors of the train. A group of us would ride to stations with vending machines with loose peanuts and gumballs. Our leader was a boy who carried a hairpin with one end bent in the shape of a penny to stick down the money slot of the machines. This triggered a mechanism that then allowed the boy to turn the knob until the peanuts fell out. When we each had a pocket full of peanuts, it was off to the gumball machines.

I also learned to ride the bus for free. This was a dangerously open act of thievery of service. There was a groove lip just big enough for young fingers that ran along under the back window of the bus. While the bus was at a stand still we would grab onto the groove lip and rest our feet on the bus bumper as it took off. We had to ride in kind of a crouch to prevent the driver from seeing us through the rear-view window. Often if the driver knew that his bus was being violated this way he would speed up making the ride more hazardous for us. Or, sometimes the bus would be behind schedule and the trailing bus would be right behind it, the driver in the trailing bus would drive right up to the back of the lead bus as if he was going to crush the fare violators. This sometimes made us jump off of the bus before it came to a stop inviting the peril of jumping into a parked car. I was learning the ropes. I was becoming a young Harlemite and a New Yorker.

We had other family members who had been living in Harlem for years. One was Cousin Lonnie Wellstone. I called him Uncle Lonnie; in fact, I was always instructed to call all of my older relatives either Uncle or Aunt so and so. Uncle Lonnie was a large generous man. He gave me the first whole dollar bill I ever owned. Uncle Lonnie owned a candy store on 131st Street that was also a front for a numbers operation. When Aunt Lacey wasn't working, she'd pick up numbers for Uncle Lonnie. Aunt Lacey took me with her on the daily trolley rides across 135th Street to take the numbers to Uncle Lonnie's numbers banker. The reason I got treated to the trolley rides was because the numbers slips would be stuffed into my clothing somewhere even I didn't know. I knew that I was a part of a clandestine operation and that I had to behave without suspicion—and this gave me a mild rush of euphoria. Uncle Lonnie had two daughters and a son. They were named Dorothy, Willamette and Jesse. My two distant cousins, girls in their teens, took me to church on Sundays. They were pretty girls who had been in New York since their childhood and had acclimated well into Harlem's culture. Jesse had become enticed with the fast life; he was becoming a young street hoodlum, already headed towards the dead end.

Public School 89 was on Lenox Avenue and took up most of the block between 134th and 135th Streets. Each time we passed the school while on our covert missions, Aunt Lacey would point the school out to me and say that I would be attending there in the fall. In September of 1947, I started first grade again at P. S. 89. I had attended first grade in a school in South Carolina, but after verbal testing during registration at P. S. 89, it was determined that I needed to start first grade over again. Sarah had gotten a job working with Aunt Dot, so every day Aunt Lacey took me to school and picked me up after school. One day in October, Aunt Lacey took me to school and told me that I would have to come home alone because she had an appointment and may not be back in time to pick me up. If she wasn't home when I arrived, I was to sit on the stoop until she arrived, she instructed. All I had to do, she said, was cross Lenox Avenue at 135th Street then walk to 136th Street and then walk down 136th Street to our building. Simple. I was sure that I could do that. I had been this way many times before with my friends and with Uncle Henry when he took me with him to the barber for our hair cuts. She asked me if I could remember how to get back home; I assured her that I would. I wore a white shirt and tie under a wool sweater, knicker pants, plaid knee socks, a pee coat and a wool pie cap with pull down earflaps. The sky was an ominous gray.

Each morning all the first and second grade children assembled in the first floor lunchroom and were escorted to their classroom by their teacher. About mid way through class that day, all the children got up from theirs seats and went to the window in a noisy rush. I remained seated afraid to move without permission. All the children were jumping up and down and pointing out of the window. Even the teacher, a woman who was otherwise pretty strict, rose and went to the window. Finally, I worked up the courage to leave my seat. I went to the window and stood behind two girls. The sky outside the window was white as cotton—billions of small flakes of cotton blew in the wind and made everything white. The street below was covered with white cotton; the car tops were covered also. What a strange place I thought, I had been in the field with Momma Dolly when she picked cotton and put it in a sack on her back—but never had I seen cotton fall from the sky.

"It's snowing," all the children shouted. "It's snowing."

The teacher regained control of her class and instructed everyone to return to their seats. "You'll be out in it shortly," she said. At the end of class, our teacher escorted us down the stairs to the large exit doors on the 135th Street side of the school, not to the front entrance where I was accustomed to entering and leaving. Everything had a different look than I ever saw before but I thought nothing of it and began to walk in the direction I thought would lead me home. This thing that in my mind resembled cotton and the children called snow was cold to the touch and was everywhere. It was difficult to walk in it, and the wind blew it into my face making it difficult to see. I crossed a street and continued to walk, but I didn't see anything that was familiar. It was white everywhere. I crossed another street and continued to walk. Finally, I realized that I was lost. I started to cry—not out loud, but my tears mixed with the wet cotton on my face. A black policeman noticed my bewilderment and came over to investigate the situation.

"What's wrong son?"

"I can't see my house," I said after a moment of hesitation.

"That's no reason to cry, I'll get you home. What's your name?" The police said bending down and removing one hand of his glove.

"Grady Lee."

"Is that all of your name Grady Lee?"

"Grady Lee Murrow."

Where do you live, Grady?"

I looked around. I didn't know where I lived because I couldn't see anything that I could recognize. I said nothing.

"Where do you live," the policeman said putting his hands gently on my head.

"I don't know."

"What grade are you in?"

"First."

The policeman realized that I had come from the school at 135th Street and if he returned me there, he could get my address. A woman in an office at the school found a card with my address on it. As the policeman walked me across Lenox Avenue, I begin to realize what happened. The snow had disorientated me and I had walked up Lenox Avenue, rather than crossing it—anyway it was special having a policeman escorting me home on the first day of what became known as the blizzard of 1947. Aunt Lacey had returned. The policeman advised her on the importance of my knowing my home address and even suggested that she write it on a piece of paper and have me carry it in my pocket.

I attended school at P.S. 89 until mid-way through the third grade, but before I left, I was introduced to something that would forever enrich my life. P.S. 89 had a partnership with the 135th Street branch of the New York City Public Library. Together, they developed an after school program called "Story Hour." Children from the school were invited to the library after school where pretty librarians would read these wonderful stories of adventure, enchantment and discovery. A whole class of children would crowd into a space around the librarian. We would sit in tiny wooden chairs and on the floor. No one would say a word unless the librarian prompted us to and that was mostly to ooh or ahh at some picture we were being shown from the book. There was among these dedicated women, a librarian whom I can still picture in my mind's eye all these decades later. She wore a blue suit and a white ruffled blouse. Her hair was jet black and wavy and looked like she went to the hairdresser every day. Her face was bright, her eyes sparkled and always seemed to be beckoning me—and as she read, the words seemed to form on her lips so that I could see and touch them. Her voice must have been angelic because I never heard it. When she read, my eyes grabbed the words from her lips and I was completely awash in their meanings. I don't remember her name, I may never have known it, but her image and her kindness shall forever remain with me. Story Hour was held three days a week. I never missed a session. After that experience, whenever I moved to a new community, the first thing I'd do is to join the local library. I love libraries and I love librarians.

By the time I reached the third grade, the grown ups around us had finally figured out how to use the system to get us our own apartment. They had Sarah quit her job and they moved Sarah and the children to a dark and dingy small basement room so that she could apply for welfare and an apartment in public housing. When the caseworker saw our living conditions and the mad man that lived next door, all haste was made to get the children out of that situation. Sarah was notified that we would be moving to the Amsterdam Projects in a month's time. Then, my father arrived in Harlem. He had come to persuade Sarah to return to South Carolina with him. They met at times and at places where I was not present, so I don't know what was said between them. Big Joe was only in the city for a few days. One of those days he took me on a walk down Lenox Avenue to one of his cousin's apartment.

"How you like this place, boy?"

"OK suh."

"Don't you miss home, boy?"

"Don't know."

"I come to get you children and your Momma."

"Suh."

"Don't you wanna go back home with me, boy?"

"Don't know, suh.'

"Your Momma been seeing some man, boy?

"No suh."

"That's all you can say, 'suh?'"

"Suh?"

"So what, Jack."

Then just like that he was gone and we were not to meet again until I was a soldier in the 82nd Airborne Division. Sarah did tell me once he left, that he had come to take us home, but we were about to get our own apartment and things were looking up. While he was there, they went to some older relatives for mediation, but Sarah was adamant in her position that she would not return to the abusive situation she'd been helped to escape. Besides, even the worse condition in New York was better than what we had in South Carolina.

Sarah, Aunt Dot and Aunt Lacey saw the apartment before we moved. It was on the first floor. It had two bedrooms; a bathroom, a kitchen and living room all neat and new. It had a new style refrigerator and a modern stove. Once it had been painted it would be prefect for the four of us. The three of them worried about the location—downtown with all those white folks. They told Sarah that maybe after she had been there for a while; she might be able to transfer to a project back in Harlem. It didn't take long for Sarah to realize that this spot in midtown Manhattan was even more important to the needs of her children than her need to be near relatives in Harlem. In the summer of 1950, we moved into an apartment at the building on Amsterdam Avenue. We were living in the same place where white folks lived—in the same building as white folks, though they were fleeing everyday.

2

There was a white family who lived directly a top our apartment with a son named Eddie Ryan. Eddie was a scrawny, red-faced boy with red hair and really blue eyes that made a bizarre contrast with his red complexion. The father was a New York City Police detective who could often be heard arguing with his wife. Eddy attended Saint Paul's Catholic School. Eddie and I became acquainted, but they moved within a year of our arrival. Another boy, Vincent Giovani, was tiny for his age. His family lived in an E apartment five floors above us. Vinny, as he was called, was always buying something. I thought his family might have been rich—twice a day Vinny would call upstairs to his mother from under our window. "Maaa throw me down a quarter." And, in under a minute's time I would hear the coin hit the pavement. I often rushed to the window to see Vinny hunt after his money—if I saw it from my angle upstairs, I'd point it out to him. Vinny Giovani's family stayed in the projects for years and when they did move it was somewhere near-by in the community. Vinny later hung out with Paul Neuman and a group of young black jazz musicians in the neighborhood—his final destination, the rooftop shooting galleries.

I got enrolled at P. S. 141 on 58th Street near Tenth Avenue. Amsterdam Avenue and Tenth Avenue are the same, 58th Street divides the two. I was in the third grade; my brother Ed Lewis was in kindergarten, my sister Ann would start school that next year. In the beginning some of my friends from the old building in Harlem would come downtown and spend a night with us. I was proud to show them our sparsely furnished, but clean and brightly painted apartment. That winter I showed off the long hill on 61st Street where all the kids went sled riding when it snowed. I didn't have a sled, but the custom was for kids without sleds to wait a quarter way down the hill and jump on a kid's back as he sped by—the extra weight would increase the speed of the sled down the hill and everybody was happy. The hill ended in a sharp left curve and at an angle that brought most of the sleds to abrupt stops. One Saturday morning, a kid from building 40 reached the bottom of the hill with such force that he was able to turn his sled around so that he was facing the oncoming sleds. The sled that was immediately behind him was now in front of him and one of its runners pierced his right eye. It happened so fast. It was what people explained away as a freak accident. He lost that eye and his family soon moved away. For the rest of us, this incident gave the ride down the hill a new sense of danger for years to come.

Patrick Henry was in my third grade class and he lived in a tenement building across the street from the projects. I got to know him even before Eddie and Vinny. He was the first white boy I ever knew. We became friends and walked home together from school. After a while, I'd meet him across the street and we would walk to school together. One morning, he called me into his building. He and some other white boys stood behind the staircase smoking a cigarette. He told them my name and when it became his turn to puff from the cigarette, he handed it to me. I took one puff and gave it back to Patrick. He wiped off the part of the cigarette that had touched my lips before he took a puff and gave it to another boy who then refused it. The smoke from the cigarette produced a sickening taste in my stomach, which I thought came from having my lips touch the same spot on the cigarette as white boys. I wiped my lips and did a lot of spitting as Patrick and I walked to school. P.S. 141 was being quietly integrated by the change taking place in the neighborhood and the people who were the most perturbed with it were the white teachers, not all—but most. I would often hear them in the halls referring to the black and Puerto Ricans students in derogatory terms—they didn't hide their feelings.

It was in this third-grade class that I had a Zen experience decades before I became aware of the existence of the practice. I would sit at my desk and daydream about the sensation of being on the crest of time. I saw time occurring in waves and I realized that everyone and everything rode the crest of time together. We each experienced the present moment together. No one could move ahead of others, we were all in the present moment and received the next wave of time simultaneously. The rich and the wise, the poor and the displaced, the weak and the powerful, the ruled and the rulers, all experienced the uncertainties of the next wave of time together. There was something equalizing about this revelation. It was the state of being where every person and all things were coequal and parallel. I later found out that to attempt to live in the moment was one of the principle concepts of Zen Buddhism. What a strange notion to fly into the mind of a third grade child. Another thing I did in that third grade class was to figure out how old I would be at the turn of the twenty-first century which was, at that time, fifty years away. I figured that should I live, I would be 59 years old in the year 2000. That seemed old and the year 2000 seemed so very far away. But I decided that I should make it there. Then I wondered how much further I would last realistically. I came up with the year 2022. I can't say what it was in this class that inspired such esoteric speculation, but there they were.

There was a tall white girl in my third grade class. Her name was Mary Ann. She had just recently come to America with her family. They were refugees from Northern Ireland who came to America to escape the centuries old war between the Catholics and the Protestants. Mary Ann had been traumatized by the violence in her village. She had witnessed bombings and her home was once set on fire. She was nervous and panicky all the time and always looked down towards the floor when she spoke. She played with her hair constantly and even in the relatively calm setting of our classroom, she was uneasy and shaken. She had a heavy Irish accent and often nervously repeated herself. Her chatter always seemed disconnected to what was going on at the moment.

"And what do you think of that Mary Ann," The Teacher once asked her, after explaining to the class that we would be making a field trip to the Central Park Zoo to see some of the animals we had been discussing in class.

"Oh I, feel, feel bad for them, them."

"Mary Ann, dear you'll see some animals that you're familiar with from your homeland like lambs and sheep. Won't you like that? Won't that be grand, dear?"

"I don't like, like it when they hurt, hurt me."

"Anyway," Mrs. Hoffman continued "I'm giving you all a note so your mothers can pack you a lunch."

The children mocked and teased Mary Ann because of how she sounded and her agitated manner. Our teacher spent lots of her time trying to make the class understand what Mary Ann had gone through, but no one in our class could make sense of a war between religious factions that did to children what had been done to Mary Ann—I know I didn't. But I could relate to what Mary Ann was going through here with these kids. I knew how it felt to be teased because you were different, I empathized with her, and I was kind to her in small ways that she recognized. The teacher assigned her a desk next to mine.

"Why do you chew on your pencil?" I'd asked her.

"I don't know," she'd say taking the pencil from her mouth and looking away from me. Then in a minute, the pencil would be right back in her mouth.

I didn't want to become too chummy with her because of what the other kids would think of me. During lunch recess in the yard, all the children would be running around playing, but Many Ann sat alone and twirled her fingers. At the end of lunch recess one-day, we passed on the staircase and I kissed her on her lips. She pressed her lips back against mine, then ran up the stairs to our classroom. When class was over that day she ran home happier than I had ever seen her.

It was during this time that Evane Smith, my lifelong friend, started sending me love notes in class that suggested grownup acts. On Saturday mornings, Manny Black and I used to take our mother's shopping carts to the supermarket to carry shopper's groceries home for a tip. Whenever Evane went shopping with her mother and sister, she would point me out and plead with her mother to let me take their groceries home. Evane would eventually raise her standards, but not before making me popular among the girls down the back.

4

A little while after we moved downtown, Sarah became friendly with a woman, Mrs. Magaleane Collier, from South Carolina who had just moved into the projects with her family. She had three daughters, five sons, and a second husband. She was a happy woman who made no distinction between grownups and children—she treated everyone the same. In people, she only saw what God saw. Our families became very close. Her oldest son was four years older than I was, so he became like a big brother to me. We called him

Crunch Collier. Although Crunch had several younger brothers, he preferred having me as a kind of sidekick—all cowboys had a sidekick back in those days and Crunch viewed himself as a cowboy. Crunch Collier was a teenager, he had the fastest bike, he made peerless soda-crate scooters and all the girls admired him. That I was the sidekick of such a kid was it's own reward.

Crunch Collier worked part time in Al and Ben's Luncheonette and Candy Store. They needed help to collate the different sections of the Sunday newspapers. New York City had nearly a dozen or more newspapers back in the 1950's and on Sundays, they all carried three or more sections. Crunch recommended me to the two Jewish merchants from the Bronx and they hired me. Crunch would knock on our door at 4 o'clock Sunday morning to get me up. This was my first job. In a short time, I became the stock boy at Al and Ben's Candy Store. My duties were to keep the candy counter and soda cooler well stocked. I'd attend to that chore after school. Near closing time, I'd come back to sweep and mop the floor and restock again. On Sunday mornings after collating the newspapers and checking the stock, I stayed to serve the kids coming from Sunday School and morning Mass who bought candy with the some of the money they were supposed to put in the collection plate. After two years, I was making seven dollars a week; I gave five to Sarah and kept two for myself. I worked there until I was nearly 13 years old.

It was Crunch Collier, who first took me to the community center at Haaren High School, where I developed a talent for playing basketball. I was good right from the start and I enjoyed it immediately. As I got better at basketball, my popularity rose. Basketball gave me a certain sense of power and creativity. I played against guys who were bigger, smarter, tougher, better looking and came from a more typical background, but none of this helped them on the court where I reigned supreme—not even Crunch Collier. Word got out about my game and I came to the attention of a neighborhood man who liked working with the community's youth. Mr. Ronald France had formed a team to play in a league at the YMCA. He wanted me to play on the team. Sarah would not let me go out at night by myself, so I had to refuse Mr. France's offer. On the evening of the team's first game, Mr. France came to our apartment with the entire team to ask my mother if I could go. He promised to pick me up for each game and bring me back home. Sarah was impressed that this man thought me so essential to his team that he would go through this bother and finally said yes. I was embarrassed, but happy to be on the team.

For a while, basketball took over my life. Most Saturday morning I would go to the gymnasium on 60th Street and play basketball with Duke Reeves and his younger brother Truman. And, whenever there was a Harlem Globetrotter movie playing at the Tivoli Movie Theater, I would watch it all day. I admired the smooth efficiency with which Reese (Goose) Tatum directed his team. For me, The Goose, was more than a clown performer, he was a wizard of movement and details with eyes in the back of his head. He knew where each member of his team was and where each of his opponents was at all times. He had the essentials on everyone and always made the right choice when it was time to pass the ball. I thought that that was a talent that should have qualified him for the presidency. After being inspired by the Harlem Globetrotter movie, "Go Man Go," one winter day, with snow piled up everywhere you looked, Truman and I wanted to play basketball in the worse way. The gymnasium closed at 12:00 noon and the outdoor court at the playground had a foot of snow on it. The playground attendant, whose job it was to shovel the snow away hadn't done it. He never did, nor did anyone expect him to. Truman and I approached the attendant about the snow on the court and he loaned us his shovel. We shoveled a spot large enough for us to act out our Globetrotter fantasies around the perimeter of the pole that held the basket. Others soon joined us and with another shovel and enough manpower, we cleared half of the court. We chose up sides and played some three-man games with a wet basketball. Later the sun came out and dried the water on the ground, but it snowed again that night.

I was making friends and adjusting to my new neighborhood. My brother and sister made friends and adapted even more quickly than I had. My family was doing swell and I thought we were all happy. Young children never consider the age and needs of a parent. When we moved into the project, Sarah was only twenty-six years old. Once in a while, she and some women from the project would go to dances at the Harlem YMCA. At one of these dances, she met a man named Matt Harmon. They had an affair that lasted a decade and produced my second sister. Beatrice was a beautiful baby, but she cried a lot. Ed Lewis, Ann Ruth and I loved to watch over her. Sarah was working part time and we were often left to care for Beatrice for long hours on Saturdays. Sarah left us Saturday mornings watching cartoons. Beatrice would be in the bedroom. Whenever she started to cry, we would change her diaper, feed her and warm a bottle for her, but that seldom stopped her crying. The three of us would sit on the couch, with me in the middle holding Beatrice and we would improvise a song to her.

"Go to sleep Beatrice, you know we love you.

Go to sleep Beatrice you know we love you.

Momma's coming back home, because she loves you.

Momma's coming back home, because she loves you.

Go to sleep Beatrice, you know we love you."

Beatrice's eyes would dart around our faces, a faint smile would illuminate her face and she would coo—as if all was right with the world. As much as I loved my new sister, I missed going to the gym on these Saturday mornings—I was also in love with basketball.

It was during this period of time that Aunt Dorothy married a man from the Bahamas named Bertram Strong. They moved into a railroad flat on upper Park Avenue in East Harlem. They were two industrious people, working, saving and helping Sarah provide for her family. Aunt Dot was barren and years later, they would adopt a baby. But in her younger years and in the first years of her marriage to Uncle Bertram, we were their children. It was if we had two mothers and a dad. Aunt Dot bought me my first bicycle and my first wristwatch. Uncle Bertram often took us to the Arcade on Broadway and in the summer, he took us to Coney Island. Before Sarah got a telephone, every evening she would give me a dime to go to the corner drugstore to call Aunt Dot with this or that message and to let her know that we were all doing well. I called that number so many times it is burned into my memory ——AU5-2858. Many Saturday mornings I took the bus to Aunt Dot's apartment to pick up something she bought for us. She often sent food to Sarah that she bought from the 116th Street market. Uncle Bertram insisted that Aunt Dot keep a fruit bowl that was always filled with mangoes, grapes, apples and oranges. I would eat two pieces of fruit before I left.

Because of the war, I didn't know my father until I was four years old and when he returned we lived together for only a year, so it was easy for me to forget him. All the major figures in my life had been women except for Uncle Henry and now Uncle Bertram. Still, I was getting along fine, adjusting and making a way for myself. It was my story telling ability that won me approval in my first New York community, now my talent at basketball was paving the way for my acceptance in the Amsterdam Projects. I was learning something useful about how personal ability could open doors of approval, consent and patronage. I was doing well in acclimating to my, now, not so new, environment. My diction was improving, from the point of view of my acquaintances and I was developing a citified persona. It wasn't until I had nearly forgotten my Southern country roots, that Sarah started sending me back South to spend the summer with Momma Dolly. These are the major events that formed my ambiguities, and my uncertainties, my knowledge base and my ignorance pool before the establishment of the trinity with Brad Buffert and Ozzie Donaldson. A trinity that hardened my behavior, endangered my freedom and took my intrinsic nature on a long ride in the wrong direction.

San Juan Hill

CHAPTER THREE
Three for Two

It was during this summer that we started to drink wine. We started smoking cigarettes a short time later and by summer's end, we were smoking reefers. We were imitating the older boys who would parade around the neighborhood reciting the street slogan of a cheap wine called Thunderbird.

What's the word?
Thunderbird.
What's the price?
Thirty twice.
Where you cop?
The liquor shop.
What's the motto?
Empty bottle.

We thought this was cool and on Saturday evenings a group of as many as eight of us would linger near the whiskey store on 64th Street until we found someone whom we could entice to purchase a bottle of Thunderbird for us. Then we would find a secluded location near West End Avenue to go through the street ritual. Someone would open the bottle and pour some of the wine to the ground and sounding much like a priest giving Communion say "This is for the boys upstate." This was our ghetto salute to ghetto boys who were incarcerated in reform schools and to young men who had started their penitentiary careers. We had seen the older boys' sacrifice what amounted to a tablespoon of wine to the ground in this sacrament, but our first times; we wasted nearly half of the bottles, "This—is—for—the—boys—up—state," mainly because we were afraid to drink the stuff. After the ritual, we passed the bottle around, each of us taking tiny sips until the bottle was empty.

There was an older boy in our neighborhood whose name was Dylan Taylor, but he drank so much Thunderbird that everyone called him Wine. His lips had turned red and his eyes were sleepy. He usually drank a whole pint bottle by himself and was even seen on the week days carrying a bottle of "Bird" with the brown paper bag wrapped around the neck of the bottle to ward off moochers. Wine was a respected member of the tough crowd, but he was also a nice guy who didn't bully the younger boys, as did most of the older boys. He had also once been a scholar who obtained awards and high grades in Catholic elementary and high school and, for whatever reason, was now letting his tough wine-drinking image suppress his scholarly self. Wine had the demeanor of a person who had reached some high pinnacle to discover a reality that repulsed him into oblivion and he had reconciled to it. He behaved like he knew some dark secret that some of us would some day encounter. Wine was particularly stingy in the ritual for the boy's upstate. He developed the skill of being able to turn the neck of the bottle over so quickly that only a small bead of wine the size of a tear drop would fall from the bottle. "This is for the boys upstate," Wine would say almost in a disdainful manner.

Gene Anderson lived on 64th Street in the Phipps complex right past the playground. Every evening he could be seen hurrying to the whiskey store. Moments later Gene returned with a fifth of wine. Gene carried the bag containing the wine in front of his genitals holding the bag with both hands as he switched walk down the street. In the winter, he would half conceal the bottle under his unbuttoned coat like a pregnant woman covering her belly. As he walked, his head moved from side to side and he dragged his feet like he was wearing slippers. Gene always behaved as if he had to return posthaste to something that had been interrupted but would continue on with the arrival of the wine. There was always groups of people sitting on the benches in the playground and when Gene passed someone from the first group that spotted him, would call out ritualistically "What you got in the bag Gene?" Gene always answered the question with a question that was a word play on the answer, "Must-I- Tell." Gene would then throw his head away from the people he spoke to and without breaking his stride continued on his way. Everyone would feel amused and laugh. Gene and his gay friends at the end of the block didn't drink Thunderbird. They drank Muscatel, but Gene would never *tell*. Lots of people in our neighborhood drank wine or liquor and that summer we were making our rites of passage under that kind of influence.

There were also families who were actively directing their children away from the habits that could be picked up in the streets. The number of straight kids didn't seem to match the number of street-wise hip kids, but there were even more of them—they just weren't as visible. Even at an early age, they were making their character known. Gerald Reddish from the back of the project got elected president of the student body of our junior high school, P. S. 17, at a time when I didn't even know the meaning of the word politics. His mother, a single woman, was head of the local PTA and started to guide Gerald towards achievement at a young age. It was mostly from this group of straight and narrow people that the neighborhood's success stories arose. They held faith that they would receive a fair shake from the system although, in America, there were tens of thousands of black college graduates working at the Post Office or some other blue-collar work. But this generation was being educated at the same time the civil rights movement was beginning to coerce some changes from America.

As the civil rights movement ram down some of the doors of discrimination, those that were educationally prepared, walked in the doors to file for the benefits of equality. Out of this environment, there came a professional cadre. The generation that lived in the Amsterdam Projects during the fifties produced judges, politicians, entertainers, priests, psychologists, a District Attorney, actors, teachers, artisans, and entrepreneurs, pilots and bankers—a complete professional class. And, mailmen too. They brought distinction to that area of San Juan Hill. This group of people doing the things that laid the foundation for their success didn't make a big impression on me at the time. Studying and making good grades in school didn't seem to matter to me during those years. I was attracted to the instant gratification being a player in street life gave me.

But, even without this success, the neighborhood's most famous son, the great pianist Thelonious Monk, already distinguished the San Juan Hill neighborhood. Monk grew up in the Phipps complex and was often seen around the neighborhood when he wasn't on tour. Monk had helped to pioneer the new sound of Be-bop jazz at the same time as Charlie Parker and Dizzy Gillespie, and was an inspiration to many of his neighborhood contemporaries. Many of the men in Monk's generation, who still lived in the neighborhood, had tried their hand at music. They grew up at a time when jazz was a way to fame and a little money. Many of them were talented musicians, but they didn't make it because they sacrificed their talent for the security of a job at the Post Office. Monk used to tell them in his dark foggy voice "You can't play music and work at the Post Office—you gotta choose one or the other."

2

The first week of August, Sarah announced that I would be going south to spend the final weeks of summer with Momma Dolly. Aunt Lacy and Uncle Henry were driving down and I would go with them. I didn't mind going. This was the best situation of all. I get to spend part of the summer in both places. I looked forward to seeing all of my many cousins in South Carolina and spending some time with Momma Dolly.

My grandmother's name is Emily Sanders. She was short and thin. Her skin was wrinkled dark and leathery. She always wore an apron and had her hair tied up in a handkerchief. Momma Dolly was a very spiritual person who knew instinctively that there would come a time when the black race in the South would rise. During my summer stays, I heard her make this assertion many times in conversations with her guests. She couldn't read or write, but she had an inborn intellect and she could count money. One of Momma's cousins, who lived way down in the gorge that began across the road from Momma's house, would visit with her once or twice a week. My grandmother was born in 1895 and this woman was older than my grandmother. Momma Dolly addressed her as Cousin Gally. She looked like she could have been born during the final days of slavery. Her skin was old and ruffled. Her face was pallid like she was part Indian, or once been light skinned. Her eyes watered and were a faded gray and gave me the impression she saw into another dimension. Snot always hung from her nose. Her teeth were rotten. They would sit on the porch and talk. I was allowed on the porch during their conversation as long as I didn't look either grown up in their eyes.

"The white man ain't gwen rule we fer all da days of da earth," Momma Dolly told her visitor.

"Cos'n Dolly, I sho da hope and da pray fer da ruination of da white man's power over we, but it ain't 'gwen happen fer we da see."

"All the same, Cos'n Gally, I 'leive in a God in he'bin and He ain't gonna let one race da rule da o'der into da end of da earth. So it da happen whetter we da see it a not."

"The white man da clever beast da work fer da debbol and da debbol da make he mo' clever fer he work."

"Sho' you right, Cos'n Gally, but da last act da come from God. God da rule da earth. And only He truth da suhvive in da end"

By then, I would be looking straight up at both women.

"What you da look at boy. Ya see gro'n folks da talkin'. I betcha I da spit in ya eye ya don' mind."

After her guest had gone, Momma Dolly would give me a bowl of hot blueberry dumplings and a glass of milk.

"When I da die, I jes wantta be buried next to ma bertha Johnny," Momma Dolly often lamented. There was an old Civil War rifle and sword that stood in the corner of her sitting room. They occupied that corner across from the fireplace for so long that they were regarded as part of the décor. I later learned that the rifle and sword had once belonged to her older brother Johnny Sanders who fought in the Spanish/American War. He was attached to the

24th Negro Voluntary Infantry Regiment that made the first charge up San Juan Hill in Santiago, Cuba. Racism never takes a day off; even then, the black regiments were issued old weapons from the Civil War, while the white regiments were given the more modern weaponry that had developed in the thirty years after the Civil War. The Negro Company was comprised mostly of buffalo soldiers from the Indian Wars who never seemed to tire of adventure and the opportunity to prove themselves to the white man. These men were fighting for the honor of the black race and to remove themselves from the threat of lynching and the stigma of segregation. When Grand Uncle Johnny returned home, he gave Momma Dolly his rifle and sword. He moved to Brunswick, Georgia, where he got a job as a stevedore, married an unfaithful woman and lived out his life. Whenever Momma Dolly spoke of being buried next to her brother Johnny it was obvious that she was proud of him; that his bravery was directed toward her hopes of the black race standing on an equal footing with all other Americans—North and South.

Momma Dolly's husband, a mysterious man from Nassau, Bahamas, took their two young sons, to live in Charleston and left her with their two daughters. His name was Reginald Frank Morrison and besides the fact that he was a very industrious hustler, who operated a fruit and vegetable cart that he pushed through the cobblestone streets of Charleston harking his wares, his existence is muddled with mystery. He came back home to the countryside in 1949 sick, and died shortly after. One son, Uncle Leroy, eventually moved back, married and built a house next to Momma's. The Korean War was being waged and her other son, Uncle James, was drafted into the Army.

When I was younger, during my summer visits, Momma Dolly used to take me to pick blueberries and to the creek to catch crabs. Sometimes I went to the fields with her to pick string beans or cotton and to listen to her communicate her concerns to God through her sorrowful field songs. This visit, I felt too old for such things and I was now knowledgeable enough to make some reasonable comparisons between the two life styles and hip enough to make what I felt were the more mature choices in both worlds. I opted to spend most of the time with my cousins.

My two favorite cousins were Bannie and Tuffy. Our fathers were brothers and our mothers were first cousins—so we were related on both sides of our family. Bannie's real name is Clarence Murrow and his father was an automobile mechanic. Tuffy's name is Arthur Murrow and his father was a farmer. Their brother, who was my father, was never there when I came back for summer visits. He was always seeking work out of state, so we never got to meet during any of my visits. There is a four-month age difference between the three of us with me in the middle. It was Bannie's mother who nursed us both on her knees when we were infants—we even look alike. Tuffy got his name from the fact that no one could out wrestle him. He was even able to throw some of the older boys to the ground. I would spend nights at their houses and they would spend nights with me at Momma's house.

One day while we played in Bannie's yard, word came that his father was too busy to come home for lunch as was his custom. He worked a mile away at the Chevrolet auto-repair shop in Hollywood. Aunt Ola made up his lunch and told Bannie to take it to him in the old pickup truck. I went along with Bannie on the ride to Hollywood. Although Bannie was only thirteen and unlicensed, he was taught to drive at an early age and drove like an experienced driver. When we arrived, Uncle Clarence was still at work on a vehicle that was impaired with a particularly vexing problem. He explained the problem to Bannie and had him hold a wrench for him.

He gave me two dimes and said I should go across the road for two ice cream cones—Bannie would be ready to leave when I got back. Across the road from the shop was a restaurant. All the times I had visited South Carolina, I had never transacted any business anywhere other than the local grocery store between Momma Dolly's house and the church. All of its patrons were black although the owner was white and lived in the neighborhood in a house besides the store. At that store, we always walked in the front door and I had never thought of the store as a store for blacks. Whenever Momma Dolly sent me to the store, I frequently came upon one or another of my cousins and would be delayed returning home, so Momma sometimes would spit on the ground and demand that I return from the store before her spittle dried up. It was either that I was too much of a meddler or that the environmental change was so overwhelming that I missed some dangerously obvious differences.

I walked into the restaurant, a big ice cream smile on my face. White people were sitting at the counter and at tables eating, but somehow they all noticed me. They all looked at me as if I was a creature from another planet. I instantly knew something was wrong. I was paralyzed with fear. I stood right there, not knowing what to do.

"What you want boy," the white waitress asked.

"Two vanilla ice cream cones."

"Well you better march your ass out that door and come 'round the nigger side," she said pointing to an opened outside pick up window. I turned around and walked outside and around to the rear of the building to the window where the waitress looked through the pick-up window and again asked me for my order. When I returned I told Uncle Clarence what had happened and I could see the fear in his eyes. He sent us home immediately. A year later at a small grocery store in a place called Money, Mississippi, a young black boy my age from Chicago, named Emmett Till, had a far more tragic drama with southern customs.

3

I got back to New York the weekend before school started up again. That Friday evening I hooked up with Brad, Ozzie and the group of fellows who always chipped in on the wine. There was going to be a back to school party at the home of a girl whose family lived in building 70. We were going to get our *heads bad* before we got to the party. As we stood in a group, Brad began collecting what I thought was wine money from everyone. Brad liked being the collector, so in the times when more money was collected than needed, he didn't have to put in any of his money. We split up for a while and met up again in the courtyard at the Phipps complex. I didn't see a bag with any of the boys who went to the store.

"Where's the wine," I asked.

"Be cool," Brad said.

Ozzie produced a skinny looking cigarette and lit it. He took a deep pull and made a fizzing sound. I was reminded of the sound a lit firecracker fuse makes.

"Oh snaps," I said, "its gonna blow up."

They all had a good laugh and then proceeded to coach me on how to hold the smoke in. In the short time that I was gone, my crowd had gone from wine to marijuana. I didn't have a say; I just automatically joined in. I didn't feel any of the affects of the reefer the first time, or the second time I smoked it, but having reefer money quickly became our main focus. Soon we were introduced to a man who drank in the Green Gabriel Bar on Amsterdam Avenue. He sold five and ten-dollar bags of marijuana discreetly from his booth at the bar—but he also sold marijuana in an amount that we could sometimes afford. These were his three joints for two dollar sales. People of drinking age who smoked pot met him there to make their purchases, but we were too young to go into the bar. This man was in his thirties and was known as "Fatman." Under the dark of night, we waited outside of the bar. We sent messages with anyone who went into the bar to let Fatman know that we wanted to see him. He would emerge from the bar.

"Whose dealing?"

"I am," Brad said.

"Walk with me."

"What you want?"

"Three for two," Brad says as he hands Fatman the money.

"What that you got in your pocket there boy?" Fatman asks as he drops the three joints in the pocket of Brad's windbreaker. When Brad returned to the group, we went to our former drinking spot to smoke two of the joints. When the reefer took effect, we'd ask each other if we felt *it*. Norman Brown, who didn't stay a pothead for long, would say "Fatman's joints done fucked me up," and we all knew that we were high. The third joint was saved for a booster later when the effects of the first two began to wear thin.

We were at that age when change was rapid. Our environment was molding us, but our introduction to marijuana had an influence on the tilt of our change. We started to reject some of the behavior we formally admired. The older boys would get tightened-up on wine and liquor and get into arguments and fights. As we started smoking pot, we found this kind of behavior brutish and loathsome. Our individuality started to set in. Brad started paying an inordinate amount of attention to clothes; Ozzie started listening to his father's jazz collection. I gave up comic books—some. And, I began to read Alfred Hictchcock mystery novels. We became more analytical and our taste in music changed. We were evolving with Miles Davis into the era of the cool.

In September of 1954, I was to start junior high school. Brad, Ozzie and even Clark were a grade ahead of me because I had to start first grade all over again when we first came to New York. Public School 17 was on 48th Street between 8th and 9th Avenues in a notorious neighborhood called Hell's Kitchen. It is a neighborhood that grew out of the slaughterhouses and breweries of 1800s Manhattan. Hell's Kitchen had been home to the white underclass for two centuries. It is the site of the worst of the 1863 New York riots against the Conscription Act that, through a lottery system, consigned white men to the Union Army during the Civil War. Outraged, white people in Hell's Kitchen went on a three-day bloodthirsty riot against blacks in the bordering areas. The neighborhood was made up of Irish and German immigrants and had been infamous for its street gangs since the close of the Civil War. Now, there were also some Italian and Jewish families in the area, but they were not prominent in the gangs and mostly ran the small mom and pop stores and eateries in the area. It was a community of squalid tenements, street waifs and sensational multiple murder cases. Remnants of these half centuries old gangs were still there in 1954 when I started attending J. H. S. 17. The founders of the

Westies, the bloodiest of Hell's Kitchen's modern street gangs were enrolled at J. H. S. 17 during this era.

Students from the projects who were enrolled at J. H. S. 17 were issued transit passes to ride the city buses and subways to school. The number 11 bus stopped on 48th Street at 9th Avenue, so there was only half a block to walk to school. Going home, we had to walk to 10th Avenue to wait for the bus in the heart of Hell's Kitchen. We always walked in groups to discourage incidents and to protect each other. Norman Brown lived in the Phipps houses. He was short and stout. He had a heavy voice and laughed in a bouncy baritone. We knew each other causally until we landed in the same seventh grade class at J. H. S. 17 and became close friends. We often walked to the bus stop together.

I learned right off that because of Norman's slow-wittedness he was going to need my looking after and guidance. Norman would fall for it all and buy the Brooklyn Bridge. "Georgette said that if I bought her a soda in the movie," Norman once told me, "she would meet me in the court yard on 63rd Street when we got home."

"So did you buy the soda?"

"And a bag of pop-corn too."

"Did she meet you?"

"Haw, I ain't seen her in the court yard yet. She said that her mother won't let her come to the court yard because boys hang out there."

Norman liked me and he trusted me and over all the years that he floated on the fringe of my activities I never betrayed his trust. When we had money, we ate lunch together at Romeo's Spaghetti House. And when we had extra money after lunch, we would chip in to buy a bag of peanuts at Mr. Planter's and share them out, one by one, on the way back to school. It was easy to be in Norman's company, there was no pretense of hipness or on the edge hustler— we were just kids. We enjoyed Abbott and Costello, Martin and Lewis, The Dead End Kids and the comedy/horror movies. "So you want'a fight do you?" Norman was fond of quoting this line from one of the Dead End Kid's movies, "So go join the army." Then his baritone laughter would bounce in the air for a moment.

Being with Norman Brown was a respite from all the complexities and tensions of the down boys although he was jinx. Few things went right for Norman. It was seldom by any one thing he did that failure occurred. It was that fate just had it in for Norman Brown. Once we were all playing basketball in the new community center on 61st Street. A fast break situation materialized and Norman was spotted all alone at the half-court-line. I sent the ball sailing to him—no one could catch him. All he had to do was to dribble the ball to the basket and make a lay up. Norman dribbled the ball in such a hurried clumsy fashion that he lost the tempo of the ball's bounce and when he leaped to shoot his lay up there was no ball in his hands—the ball was just on its way back up from a dribble. Everyone roared with laughter. Even Norman laughed, although I could tell that deep down he was terribly disappointed.

Brad Buffert and I started our relationship with a struggle for supremacy. I didn't think that I would play second banana to a chubby kid with thick eyeglasses, and I didn't readily get caught up in his charisma. All the chubby bodied, thick speckled kids I'd ever known were unpopular and had esoteric interest, or were unpopular and had no interest, so I resisted Brad's sway. Brad Buffert was nothing but a tough street-wise cool kid who, later as an adult, developed the demeanor of the social upper class. Still, in the beginning, I was judging him by his superficial qualities. Our struggle for domination took the form of determining who was toughest. In junior high school, we would sneak up on each other and whack each other in the back as hard as we could—then run off before the other guy could recover from the blow. I never hit Brad with all of my power fearing that I might hurt him, but he let me have it whenever he caught me off guard. He showed no pity. Our contest had an underlining psychological aspect to it and that was to find out who was also the toughest mentally—who had the tenacity to overpower the other. After a week, I caved in. I called a truce that cryptically signaled Brad's leadership. It was then that I fell under the spell of his charisma. Ozzie had no leadership ambition, he was eager to acquiesce to the allure of Brad's camaraderie and saw me as competition for Brad's allegiance.

We were always thinking up schemes to enrich ourselves with other people's money. There was always a card game going on in our neighborhood, in the playground, in back of the staircase in some building, or at someone's home. We came up with a method to cheat at cards by secretly passing each other cards. We knew that it would be dangerous to get caught passing cards in a game with the older boys in our neighborhood, but if we could perfect our system gambling with them, it would be easy sailing in the school yard games with white boys. We practiced our techniques at Ozzie's parent's apartment, listening to jazz and smoking reefer, while they were working or at the bar. We found out that Ozzie was best at the sleight of hand and I was the clumsiest. "Do that shit again," Brad asked Ozzie once when he palmed a card while he was shuffling the deck. "That would work in Black Jack."

"Yeah," Ozzie said, "but I got to figure how to get the card back into the deck."

"Let Grady fool around some to get their eyes away from you." Brad was the intended receiver of palmed cards most of the times while I clowned around as a distraction. The system worked well and we went undetected for a long while.

4

Teddy Hughes was an older boy who had quit school and had a job stocking and delivering groceries at the local supermarket. It was a full time job and he was paid twenty-five dollars a week plus tips. Brad goaded Teddy into the first of their one on one games of Black Jack and took his entire paycheck from him. Teddy delivered groceries through out the neighborhood on a tricycle with a storage box up front. Brad was holding some money he was to take to the bank for his mother when Teddy rode through the playground on a delivery. Brad showed Teddy the money and said it was over fifty dollars and that he'd play Teddy head to head when he got off from work. When Teddy arrived after work, Brad had only three dollars in his pocket, one of which he had gotten from Ozzie. Teddy did not know this. They played on a bench in the middle of the projects before a large group of onlookers, while the sun was just going down. Brad won the cut of the cards to become the banker. Brad flipped the deck, planted face cards and took clues from Ozzie. Brad didn't have to worry about any spectator who might see one of his trick plays because street etiquette demanded the kind of silence that amounted to complicity. After Brad had conquered Teddy in the first game, he made a gesture of magnanimity by offering him two dollars. Teddy accepted the money but wanted to use it to restart the game, Brad refused. Teddy made such a fuss that Brad demanded the two dollars back—Teddy refused.

"Gimme a chance to win my money back," Teddy asked.

"Man I was trying to be nice to you—let you have a few bucks to walk with."

"I don't care about that—let's play cards."

"That's my two dollars," Brad said. "I'm not going to play against my own money."

"Your money—that was my money."

"It ain't no more, now why don't you just be cool and walk with the two bucks."

"I ain't playing you again. You don't give a man a chance to win his money back. That's shit—don't come looking for me to play cards with again."

"Okay, lets play. High card for banker."

Brads cuts a ten. Teddy cuts an eight. Brad is the banker. He shuffled the cards and had Teddy to cut them.

"How much?"

"Fifty cents."

"Fifty cent? You can't get your money back like that. One hand for the two dollars, " Brad offers.

"Fifty cents."

"One hand—bet the two dollars," Brad insisted, all the while using the distraction the dispute caused to arrange the top cards in his favor. Brad looked at Ozzie and on cue, Ozzie told Brad that his mother was looking for him.

"I gotta go," Brad said, placing the cards on the bench.

"Okay, two dollars," Teddy said.

Brad confidently dealt the card out without lifting the deck from the bench. Teddy had a ten showing. He peeked at his facedown card and seemed pleased. Brad had a king showing. He lifted up his facedown card and slammed it to the bench face-up. It was an ace for blackjack. Brad picked the two dollars up. Ozzie and I walked off with Brad. He gave Ozzie three dollars and he gave me two. The crowd of other kids went about their business.

That could have been all there was to that, but Teddy was a prideful boy. He was seventeen and thought he had a reputation to protect. Teddy associated with some of the toughest of the older boys in the neighborhood and he had their respect. He didn't want it out that he was taken by a thirteen-year-old kid. Teddy had only lived in the neighborhood for a few months and gained his acceptance among the older boys merely on the fact that he had moved from Harlem. For black kids in New York City, living in Harlem was the ultimate learning experience for street smarts and toughness. So, black kids who lived in Harlem received unearned and unproven respect from other black kids around the city. Brad had come from Harlem also, and he had lived in the neighborhood for only a short time also, but the transferability of the Harlem myth was more active among the older boys and young men. Teddy had more to lose if he didn't redeem himself. So every payday for the following two weeks, Teddy met Brad on the bench and encountered the same results. On Teddy's pay evening, Brad never had more than three dollars he had put together during the day, but he'd always manage to show Teddy a couple of tens and a twenty sometime during the day. The lure lasted until Teddy found out that Brad came to the games with far less money than he did. Teddy devised a scheme to rescue his image and stand Brad down. Brad was sitting on the bench with an unopened deck of new cards. A crowd had gathered to witness the slaughter.

"You ready," Teddy said.

"Yeah," Brad said. "You owe me half on the new deck of cards."

"That so?" Teddy said. He picked up the cards, opened the box, and pulled the cards out. He placed the joker's back into the box and he counted the cards face-up. Then he put the cards on the bench.

"Put your money on the bench," Teddy said.

"What," Brad said.

"Put your money on the bench. We gonna play one hand for it all." Then Teddy took two tens, a five and five dollars in quarters on the bench. "Put your money on the bench."

"Let's cut to see who is gonna be the banker."

"You can be the banker," Teddy said.

Brad shuffled the cards and had Teddy cut them.

"How much?"

"Thirty dollars."

"What?"

"Thirty dollars. Can you cover it?"

"I got you covered."

"Lemme see it. Put the money on the bench where mine is. Don't deal the cards until you put your money on the bench."

Brad looked at Ozzie and he looked at me.

"Man, lets go to the Diner and get something to eat," I said.

"Yeah," Ozzie said, "you might as well give me my ten dollars back. This dude don't want to gamble."

"Put your money up," Teddy said loudly.

Brad walked away from the bench. Teddy took the cards and started a game with three other guys around the bench, who were offering bets of 25 and 50 cents. We walked down the sled-riding hill to go the Market Diner feeling a little humiliated. Brad had taken three weeks of Teddy's paychecks, but Teddy had won the showdown that would be talked about.

The Market Diner on Eleventh Avenue and 59th Street was opened around the clock. After the card games we went there for french-fries to take out or we sat and had scrambled eggs and home fried potatoes in the diner. The diner was shaped like a large art deco trailer from the 1930's—it was shiny and clean inside and outside.

It was a popular eating place for many of the workers in the area and for taxi drivers. The diner was a block east of the Hudson River where there were docking piers for cruise ships and tugboats. Foreign sailors from the ships ate at the diner. There were a few bars in the area that were hangouts for prostitutes that catered to the sailors. There was also a major sanitation refuse processing plant that took up a whole block. The sanitation workers from the plant ate at the diner. But for me, the most interesting industry in the area was the slaughterhouses that lined both sides of Eleventh Avenue. Everyday, even Sunday, the howl of the animals going to their death could be heard even over the clamor of the refuse processing plant. The railroad rail cars that brought the animals in alive and later carted the carcasses down to the meat processing plants on 14th Street, were between the Hudson River and 11th Avenue, underneath the Westside Highway. Many of these workers ate at the diner. I walked down the Avenue many times listening to the shrieks and I feared to even imagine what was taking place in those huge gray buildings of horror—all so that the people of this city could eat.

There were always taxicabs doubled parked outside the diner. One day after we all had steak sandwiches for lunch at the diner, Ozzie noticed that many of the taxis drivers left their cigar boxes or coin changers in their unlocked cars. The front of the diner was nearly all glass. You could see out to the street from every booth. Only patrons who sat at the counter would have their backs to the streets. We reasoned that the cabbies probably each sat in a booth where he could see his car. We decided to hit them at night. Brad and I would be lookouts as Ozzie wiggled between double-parked taxicabs taking moneychangers and cigar boxes of money. We got fifty-five dollars from three cabs our first night. We were smart enough not to go back immediately. We let a few days go by before we struck again. When we all worked together it was always on Brad's insistence, but there were also times when Ozzie struck alone. Then, a weakness that plagued me throughout my youth destroyed our hustle—I let it out about the money left in the open cabs to some other boys in the neighborhood and as the word spread, there was a rash of stealing, both during the day and at night. The cabbies became aware and stopped leaving their money in the unlocked cabs. Not only would they take their money with them into the diner, but they also locked their empty cabs. Whenever we went to the diner or walked by it going somewhere else, we always eyed the inside of the cabs for cigar boxes or money changers and on rare occasions there would be one left by a hurried or new driver.

One day Brad and I had walked home from school. We were on 61st Street and Columbus Avenue when we ran into the Rudland brothers. Jack and Leroy Rudland hadn't been living in the projects but a short time and didn't fit into any group yet. Jack was sixteen and the older of the brothers. He often bragged about once being shot in a Harlem street gang war. Leroy was quiet and reserved. Their family moved to the projects from Harlem, and they were eager to return to Harlem. The brothers had come from the 59th Street subway station. The four of us walked together. We crossed the Avenue at 61st Street in front of a small restaurant that was another favorite of cab drivers. A taxi was double-parked by the restaurant and its window was rolled down. Jack looked in the cab and saw a cigar box on the seat. He grabbed the cigar box of money and ran. We ran after him. As we ran, Jack stuffed the money from the cigar box into his pockets and threw the box away. No one was chasing us and we thought no one had seen us, so we stopped running. We turned the corner at 63rd Street and walked towards Amsterdam Avenue. Brad and Jack were into an immediate argument of how the loot would be shared up. Brad wanted a four way even split, but told Jack that he would agree to giving Leroy and myself a lesser share as long as he got an equal share with Jack. Jack had counted the money. It totaled twenty-seven dollars mostly in change. Jack would have none of Brad's sharing ideas. He took the money—it was now his and his alone.

We arrived at the end of the block with the argument still raging between Jack and Brad. Finally, Jack agreed to give us one dollar each, but before he could dole out the cash, we walked right into an awaiting police car, two policemen and the taxi driver from the restaurant. The taxi driver was pointing at us and telling the policemen that we were the ones he saw taking his money and running off. Someone saw us running and noticed which block we turned into. That person then made an inquiry in the restaurant and along with the taxi driver alerted the policemen who raced silently to wait for us on Amsterdam Avenue, at the end of 63rd Street. The taxi driver had not seen us himself and was, at this moment, lying. He was seeing us for the very first time. The policemen loaded us into the back of the patrol car, rejecting our pleas of innocence. They drove us to the 54th Street police station. They made us empty our pockets. Jack was the only one who had any money. He also had an empty pack of Bamboo cigarette rolling paper. The Bamboo brand was popular among pot smokers for rolling their joints. The rest of us had wallets and house keys; I also had a rubber band and a half-used pencil. They questioned us all in the same room. We denied taking any money from the cab. When they asked Jack about the money he had, he said he had saved it. They didn't believe him or any of us. Jack asked one of the policemen if he could buy a pack of cigarettes. The policeman took all of Jack's money, but he did return with a pack of Marlboro. They put us in four individual cells until it was time to take us to the Manhattan Detention Center, known as the Tomb, for arraignment. Jack was in the first cell, next was his brother Leroy. Brad was in the third cell and I was next to him. The cells on the other side of my own were empty. Jack lit up a cigarette and the scent drifted down the row of cells.

"Share out the cigarettes," Brad asked Jack.

"Yeah lemme have a cigarette," I joined in, wanting something to ease the tension and fear. Jack said nothing.

"Lemme have a cigarette," Leroy asked in a timid voice.

Jack passed us each one cigarette.

"Motherfucker," Brad said, "if you don't share out that pack of cigarettes evenly, I'm gonna call the police and tell them you took the money."

Jack passed us each four more cigarettes.

That evening we were taken downtown to 100 Centre Street—

the Tomb, and placed in a large holding cell with a hundred other people. We were the first case to be called. The night court judge heard the charges against us and set a date for a hearing before a judge in six weeks. Our parents were sitting in the courtroom and upon our release they set out on us. They were angry and flustered. Uncle Henry drove Sarah and Aunt Dot down to the Tombs while Aunt Lacy stayed at our house with my brother and sisters. As soon as Sarah could reach me, she grabbed my ear and led me out of the courtroom under a barrage of questions. On the car ride home, I told them what had happened. Brad and I were coming home from school when we met the Rudland brothers. I left out any reference to the taxi driver's money and Jack taking it. It was easy for me to declare my innocence—I hadn't taken anything from anyone. When we got home, they all warned me that this was serious business. I could go to reform school. This one incident could ruin my entire future. I had never had my future discussed before so this was new and interesting talk.

"I don't know what we gonna do with you," Sarah said. "I ought to ring your neck."

"That won't do no good," Aunt Dot said. "Grady, you got to keep away from them bad boys. You hear?"

"Grady is a good boy," Uncle Bertram said. "We just need to watch over him and give him some guidance. I feel he gone be alright."

"Go take your bath," Sarah ordered.

"Sarah, let him eat something first," Aunt Dot pleaded.

"Then you fix it for him, I'm too mad."

"Sit down son. Let Auntie fix up a plate for you."

I was hoping to get a glimpse of what kind of future they had envisioned for me, but the nearest the conversation came to that was a vague offer by Aunt Dot to finance college for me if I stayed out of trouble.

I had never thought about the future myself. What kind of an adult would I be? What I'd be doing to earn a living? Would I be married—have children? These thoughts had never crossed my mind. The future was this vague thing in the far distant by and by. It wasn't a thing I needed to plan for, or try to direct—it would come in time, and wherever I was in life when I met with the future—there I was. It wasn't just that I had low expectations for myself. I had no expectations for myself at all. The most I had ever heard in the way of guidance was to stay in school. That wasn't enough to build my confidence for the future. My future would unfold with the roll of the dice of chance.

5

That weekend, early on Saturday morning, Brad and I met in a section of the projects called the "Bullpen." It was called that because it was boxed in with these wooden climbing logs like those we had seen at the rodeo at Madison Square Garden. We were getting our story straight for when we had to return to court. We would give up the Rudland brothers, if necessary, to save ourselves.

"Fuck this," Brad said. "I ain't going to the slammers for something I didn't do. Plus, that motherfucker didn't want to share none of the money with us—we ought to give his ass up just for that."

Yeah," I said, "but we were with him when the bust came down. We gotta stick to the story."

"I know," Brad said. This shit is playing out like those silly fucking books you read."

"You must have read one?"

"Yeah. You left one at Ozzie's house and I found it, took it home, and read it. Alfred Hitchcock Mysteries, weird stuff, all the stories end crazy. What you see in that shit?"

"It's like a puzzle. I can never figure out the endings until I get there. I think I want to write like that one day."

I remembered the contents of the book I'd left at Ozzie's house. It contained one of my all time favorite stories. It was about a French woman imprisoned in a French colony somewhere in Central America, who plotted her escape and enlisted the prison's undertaker, himself a prisoner, in the endeavor. When a prisoner died, Jose, the prison undertaker, would take the wooden coffin with the dead body to the prison's Potter's Field where he and two other inmates would bury it. The French woman and Jose concocted what they thought was a realistic and achievable scheme to set her free. The next time a prisoner died, under cover of darkness, she would enter the hut where the coffin would be and crawl in on top of the dead body. They didn't waste nails to fasten the coffin's top, so getting into the coffin would not be a problem. Jose and his two gravediggers would take the coffin by horse drawn cart and bury it in Potter's Field. Then Jose would sneak back to dig up the coffin and set her free.

A few days later, the French woman heard that someone had died. That night she loaded her pockets with as much of her small belongings as she could and went to the coffin hut. She had a small compass, a hand drawn map and some matches. She quickly got into the coffin on top of the dead body and pulled the top back over the coffin. Early that morning, before the break of dawn, she could feel the coffin being lifted and placed on the cart. She felt the bumpy ride to Potter's field. She felt the coffin being lowered into the hole in the ground. She heard the dirt hit the top of the coffin as they covered it. Then they were gone. She knew that it would take an hour for Jose to return to set her free. Time passed by. She didn't have a watch, but she knew that far longer than an hour had passed. Then that length of time passed again and there was still no digging—no Jose. She became concerned that Jose had betrayed her. The time had doubled again and she could tell that there was less oxygen in the coffin. She fumbled around to reach the matches in her pocket. She brought a match up to where she lay face to face with the corpse and lit the match only to see, in her horror, that it was Jose whom she laid atop. He was the only human on earth who knew she'd be in that coffin. Now there would be no one coming to set her free.

"I'm gonna be a writer one day," I said.

After I said that, it didn't sound like a cool thing and it sounded far from being a realistic expectation. What I said was just a fantasy and Brad pretended he didn't hear it

"Ah man, it's just something to read," I said stepping back into the fold.

"How are we gonna make some money today?"

Right then, I remembered something. I had been in Rococo's delicatessen early one Saturday morning to buy a pound of lard for my mother who was going to fry fish that evening. It was how I learned that the old lady opened the delicatessen on Saturday mornings to cook the sausages, meatballs and tomato sauce. Each night they left a bag of change on the cash register right above the punch keys. The old lady had to go to the back to get the lard from the refrigerator. If we could get there soon enough, she wouldn't have had time to put the change into the cash register yet.

"You got any money?" I asked Brad.

"No,"

"Not even a quarter?"

"No. Why?"

I told Brad about the lard being in the back of the store and that just the old lady would be there right now. And, I told him about the bag of change. Brad got excited about the possibilities.

"Go get a quarter from your mother," Brad said in a commanding voice.

"Get one from your mother," I replied.

"You guys out here early in the morning playing the dozens," a voice said. It was Clark; he was on his way to work at the cleaners.

"Hey Clark," I said, "where you going?"

"To work—gotta make that money."

"You wanta make some quick money?" I asked.

"Always," Clark said. "How?"

"You got a quarter?"

Clark looked at Brad and me like he was being ensnared in some scheme where he was going to come out a loser. He knew that in all of his dealings with Brad, he lost, but he trusted me.

"What you gonna do with a quarter to make money?" Clark asked.

I explained the situation once again and Clark gave me the

quarter. We all walked up the hill to Rococo's deli. The delicatessen was on Amsterdam Avenue between 60th and 61st Streets. 60th Street was the only solidly white block in the neighborhood. Al and Ben's Luncheonette and Candy Store was at the end of the block. Brad and Clark stayed outside the store unseen. I went in the deli, said good morning and ordered a pound of lard. The old lady went unsuspectingly to get the lard. The bag of change was right in place. I gently lifted the bag and put it into my jacket pocket. The old lady returned; put the lard into a bag and handed it to me. I gave her the quarter and she rang up the sale without noticing, just then, that the bag of change was gone.

Now the Rococo family was the largest Italian family in the neighborhood. The Rococo's had five beefy sons and three daughters. All the sons were in their late teens and early twenties. These were baseball bats, heads beating, no shit taking Italians. In a situation like this, they could easily get away with murder. My two companions kept an eye on me as I walked back to the projects, but they didn't risk rejoining me until we were back safely in the bullpen. We sat on the bench and I counted the coins.

"What we got," Brad asked.

"Twenty-five dollars," I said.

Clark put his hand out and said he had to get to work. I counted out eight dollars and gave it to him.

"You my man," Clark said. "The quickest eight dollars I ever made."

As Clark was walking off, I counted out eight dollars and gave it to Brad.

"You a dumb dude," Brad said, "you didn't have to give him that much. You could have given him his quarter and two bucks—you're stupid."

I though about it and concluded that Brad was right—but I didn't have to give him eight dollars either. There was a lesson here that I filed away in my mind for future references. Later that day, I lost my money playing blackjack with Brad, Ozzie and some other boys in the back hallway of one the Phipps building.

After dark, Brad and Ozzie chipped in together to buy a five dollar bag of reefer from the Fatman. There were still old tenement buildings on 64th Street, east of Amsterdam Avenue with common bathrooms on each floor. We found an unused one on the first floor. We latched the door and sat on the tub as Ozzie rolled up the bag of marijuana. There was only one other fellow in our neighborhood that rolled a neater joint than Ozzie. He was a short dark-skinned boy even younger than we were. He was known as "Little Moe," and people enjoyed recalling the time a policeman happened upon Little Moe and two other boys while Moe was rolling reefer. They ran and the policeman took out after them. Moe quickly stashed what he had already rolled, but he ran with the joint he had in his hands and when they had lost the policeman, the other boys assumed that Moe had thrown the half rolled joint away in case he got caught. Little Moe produced the joint. He had finished rolling it while he was running from the police and it was even more perfect than the others. People liked to say "Little Moe can roll a perfect joint even running from the police." A lot of people hired Moe, and paid him in joints to "twist up" their bags of reefer. "Roll'um like you running from the po-lice, " they teased.

Brad counted the joints as Ozzie finished rolling the last one. The total came to 27. Back then it was acceptable if you got between 24 and 29 joints from a five-dollar bag. Anything less then that—you got ripped off. Anything more then that—you were going to switch dealers.

"I'll tell you what," Brad said, "Let's make 2 three for two sales in the playground to get back four dollars of our money."

"I'm down," Ozzie said.

"That's for you," Brad said as he handed Ozzie 10 joints. He put 10 joints into his jacket pocket. He held up the 6 joints that would be sold and handed me the last one on the side of the tub. "Light that up."

Brad was right too, about those Alfred Hitchcock mystery books I liked with those unpredictable and bizarre endings. This day, for me, was playing out with the eerie feeling of one of those stories in Hitchcock's anthologies—where logic is enticing, but deceptively dressed. I didn't complain about the breakdown on the smoke—I filed it away. I began this day being generous to Brad in the breakdown of the loot from the deli and here he was ending the day by slighting me on the sharing of the reefer they bought with the money they swindled out of me in the card game. Brad was learning to be innovative in a field that would later help him to realize the American dream.

Court day came soon. We all arrived at the courtroom in separate groups. The Rudland brothers were dressed in dark suits, white shirts and ties. Jack Rudland even had a pocket-handkerchief peeking out from his jacket breast pocket. Brad wore a striped suit made from a material that shooned, white shirt and tie. I wore an old brown wool jacket, brown wool pants, white shirt and tie. When our case was called, we were directed to stand before the judge's bench. The taxi driver and one of the arresting policemen stood across from us. The judge was impressively dressed in a black robe and sat high above everyone. He had clear blue eyes, gray hair and almost tan skin. The charges were read out to the judge.

"What's your side of the story?" the judge asked no one particular.

"My friend Brad and I," I spoke up, "was coming home from school and we met Jack and Leroy on Columbus. We all was walking home together. When we reached Amsterdam the cops were there and they arrested us."

"Were they running when you arrested them?" The judge asked the arresting officer.

"No," the policeman answered.

"Did they all have money?"

"No sir."

"Did any of them have money?"

"No sir." The policeman said because the policeman at the station on the day of the arrest had pocketed the evidence for a pack of cigarette and didn't make a report of the money.

"Oh that's enough of this," the judge said irritated to see

what he imagined was yet another group of black boys so easily railroaded. This judge must have known the system. He must have heard hundreds of stories of black boys being sent up the river on shaky or non-existent evidence. Blacks didn't stand a chance once they got ensnared into the system. This was a fiasco this judge was determined not to be a part of. Before him were four fine looking, well dressed and mannered, black youngsters with concerned parents equally well dressed and mannered. These boys looked like they might develop into upright citizens and make a contribution, such as the Negro sometimes does, to society—now the system wanted him to send these boys to reform school.

"Case dismissed." The judge said. "Next."

That night I dreamt about my dog Spot. We met on the downtown platform at the 135th Street station. The train groan into the station, hot and crowded. By the time the doors closed and the train began to move, Spot had turned into a pretty girl. All the years I had this dream, I could never describe the girl, I only could see that she was pretty.

6

The new community center opened up in the fall of 1955. The city government let the Board of Education fund a program that provided teenagers a safe place with wholesome activities and responsible adult supervision. Every neighborhood had one. Our new community center opened in the newly built elementary school on 60th Street. There was already a community center in our neighborhood, but it operated out of the basement of a building next to the playground. It had small, cramped rooms with exposed pipes and wires and the other equipment that made that upper building function. The lighting was dim and depressing. And, it had few popular activities. The new community center gave us access to the gymnasium where there was a weight lifting room and a basketball court. Rooms used for arts and crafts classes, whist games, checkers and chess were on the ground floor. There was a music room where people listened to jazz, and rhythm and blues records. The large cafeteria had two ping pong tables and in a corner by the entrance doors was a television set. All of these activities were popular and well attended.

On the second floor, there were rooms where kids could take remedial classes in school subjects. I was up there once—it was quiet and like a ghost town up there compared to the noise and reverberation of the other used locations in the building. Community centers were a good thing for the youth of the city and it was a good thing for many teachers who signed up to work the additional five nights a week to earn extra cash. The teachers who supervised at these centers were mostly men—the tougher the better. They weren't allowed to supervise at a center in the school or neighborhood where they taught daily, so extra travel was involved. These were people dedicated to more than just the extra paycheck, they really wanted to help shape young people's lives.

Once in a while, the community center sponsored special events like talent shows and movies in the school's auditorium. Once they had a concert with Louis Armstrong and I got his autograph. I gave the autograph to my sister. I was too hip to be seeking autographs. The community center gave two dances a year. One at the start of the season and another near the end of the season. It was at a dance at the beginning of the season that I almost got shot. The dances were held in the cafeteria. All the dances were big crowded events—every young person in the neighborhood was there, and sometimes guys in their early twenties came crashing. I was talking to an older boy named John Mack who offered me a drink of wine. He had it in his belt, but we needed to go outside to drink it. There were double sets of exit doors and between the sets of doors, there was a small lobby. We were at that spot when a guy called Jamaica Hip came into the lobby. Jamaica Hip was a short West Indian boy, much older than I was and even a little older than John Mack. Jamaica Hip came up to me and pointed a small pistol in my chest. I froze. John grabbed Jamaica Hip's arm and attempted to protest his interference. Jamaica Hip took the pistol from my chest and pushed it into John's stomach. John shoved Jamaica Hip's arm and the pistol went off. John fell forward and his head touched my shoes. He was groaning in pain, grim agony on his face. Jamaica Hip went out of the outer door with the pistol in his hand, looking pretty much like he was in a daze. He paced up a few steps and then back a few steps not knowing what to do. I ran into the music room where I told one of the supervisors what had happened. After the police interviewed me, I went home and went to bed. I couldn't sleep—the event kept replaying in my mind. If I could have slept that night, I'm sure I would have dreamt about my dog Spot and the comforting pretty girl.

During the next week, I heard in the streets that it might have been the bottle of wine that saved John Mack's life. The bullet remained in his body, but they said that the bottle he held in his belt might have directed the bullet away from any vital organs. John was in the hospital for several weeks and when he was released, he returned to a hero's welcome. Jamaica Hip spent the night in jail. There were never any charges made, so he was released and the incident was written up as an accident. Jamaica Hip was free to continue his fascination with firearms and played up his willingness to use them. He knew that this incident made him a major neighborhood figure—some people even feared him. Now he had a street resume that listed the fact that he shot a person and suffered no consequences. This all elevated his image in the minds of many in the community and in his own mind.

Jamaica Hip's enhanced street credentials were not long lived. He later got into a fight with a tall slender boy called Duck. Jamaica Hip was a show-off fighter; he didn't fight to defeat his opponent, he fought to impress the spectators. He danced a fancy footwork. He held his hand in an unorthodox boxing position and even looked off from his opponent, but none of this worked for him. Duck was whipping his ass badly. Throughout the fight, Duck hit Jamaica Hip at will with walloping blows to the face and chest. The spectators began to laugh. Jamaica Hip got frustrated. He disengaged from his boxing stance and distanced himself from Duck. He knew that he was out-matched. He would have to use the myth of himself as a shooter to salvage some dignity.

"You wait here," Jamaica Hip said, "I'll be back." We all knew what that meant. Jamaica Hip turned and started to walk away. Duck took a few quick steps to head him off. He grabbed Jamaica Hip's shirt in the chest area.

"If you're gonna come back," Duck said, "I might as well kick your ass right now." And he whacked Jamaica Hip in the jaw. "I'm gonna fuck you up so you won't be able to come back." Duck hit Jamaica Hip again in the face. Jamaica Hip put up no resistance.

"You coming back?" Duck asked shaking Jamaica Hip by jerking his shirt back and forth. Duck raised his hand to strike another blow. Jamaica Hip's body went limp as he succumbed and shouted out that he would not return to continue this fight. Saliva and blood were coming from his mouth.

"I'll fuck you up now," Duck said, and he made Jamaica Hip repeat his surrender over several times.

"It's all over man, it's all over," Jamaica Hip said in a really believable manner and tone.

Duck taught us all a lesson that day; never let a potential threat develop. "Out da Fire," Jamaica Hip's Island people would say. Duck was one of New York's Finest before he joined the organization that flaunts the slogan. A few years later Duck became a New York City policeman, moved away from the projects and although he still had family there, was seldom ever seen in the neighborhood.

The community center was a great place to spend the winter nights from seven until nine. It kept us from hanging out in hallways or sneaking into the neighborhood bars to keep out of the cold. Some of us had the face and physical appearance to fake up our ages in the bars where the bartenders didn't know us. But, as soon as they found us out, they kicked us out. When the community center closed at nine o'clock, many of us went to Al and Ben's for candy, an egg cream or a comic book, before we went home. Once a month I bought the latest issue of the Alfred Hitchcock Mystery anthology. Then most of us went home to watch some television before bed and school the next morning.

7

In New York City when there is a warm day deep into the fall people call it "Indian Summer." This was a bright sunny day that blocked the autumn chill from the streets. This day was suitable for a feast not available in the school cafeteria. So, Norman Brown and I had spaghetti. When we returned the schoolyard at J. H. S. 17 was crowded with girls jumping rope, boys playing stoopball and other crowds of young people mingling around near the end of lunch recess. Norman Brown and I had just returned to the schoolyard from Romeo's Italian restaurant where we each had a twenty-five cent plate of spaghetti and sauce. We were next in line to play the winners of a stoopball game. We watched the game as we waited our turn. All of a sudden, Mr. Glick, the gym teacher roughly grabbed me by my shoulder and shoved me towards the entrance door to the lunchroom. I was puzzled and though I offered little resistance, I repeatedly said that I hadn't done anything.

"Why you grabbing me?"

"Keep moving."

"I didn't do nothing."

"I said keep moving."

Finally, he had me alone in the lunchroom.

"So you like to hit girls huh?"

"What are you talking about? I didn't hit no girl."

"You threw an orange into a crowd of girls singing and hit one of them on the head."

"I didn't have any orange to throw."

"I got people who saw you throw it—don't you lie to me you little shit."

"Mr. Glick, I didn't eat lunch at school today. I had spaghetti at Romeo's."

"You do this again and I'm gonna crack your head open, then get you suspended—you hear me."

"I didn't do it."

Right then, the bell rang and it was time to go to afternoon classes. The gym teacher let me go. Later I found out that someone had hit Charlotte Monk, the niece of the famed piano master, in the head with a rotten orange. Someone thought it would be fun to blame me by lying on me to Charlotte. The next day Mr. Glick got a visit from Polly Wolly. Polly Wolly was a major figure in our neighborhood. He was, perhaps, the dominant leader of our neighborhood's tough guys. He had gone to reform school at the age of ten and been back time and again. All this was in preparation for a life stuck in the revolving door between freedom and incarceration. Going to jail was an acceptable thing in black communities all over America. And back then, as it is today, many black men went to jail. Only back then, black men weren't judged in the black community for having spent some time in the slammers. Black people considered the oppressive nature of white society and the restricted opportunity for black folks. Under these conditions, it was almost honorable to have been in jail. Young men wore the completion of a six-month sentence with a holy reverence. Polly Wolly was fearless and he was feared. He was merciless and remorseless in his ill treatment of people. He was thought to be capable of anything. Polly Wolly had appointed himself my guardian angel or the devil that watched out for me. He was a brown-skinned boy with bright roving eyes. He had full lips and a crooked mouth smile that reminded me of my father's smile.

When I was in the sixth grade at P.S. 141, my teacher, an old Jewish woman whom I liked, once punished me for making a bomb sound during a fire drill. I don't know how word of this got back to Polly, but a day a so later the teacher told me that my brother had threatened her over the incident. I had to convince her that my only brother attended school there and was in the third grade. She checked my family records to confirm that I had told her the truth.

"Well, he looked like you," she said.

I never mentioned anything to Polly and he never spoke to me about it.

The day after Polly's visit with Mr. Glick, I was summoned to the vice-principal's office. Mr. Glick sat in a chair to the side of the vice-principal's desk. The vice-principal, a huge man with thick eyeglasses and a stern look, spoke first.

"So you like to hit girls with rotten oranges and get your thug family to threaten teachers, huh?"

"What I said," in complete surprise about the second part of his accusations. "I didn't hit anyone with anything."

"Young man, you've turned a boyish prank into a serious charge. I could suspend you and call the police for threatening a teacher."

"What? I didn't threaten anybody and I didn't hit any girl either."

"That's enough from you—you little punk. Mr. Glick tells me that your brother came into my building and threatened him about disciplining you for throwing the orange. This is a serious matter. No ones comes in this building and threatens my staff. A report on this whole incident has been written up and will go into your records. Next time I hear anything bad about you—out you go. Is that clear?."

"But…"

"Is that clear?"

"Yes."

"Now what's your brother's name."

"My brother is nine years old and he in the forth grade at P.S. 141."

"Then who was that you sent here to threaten Mr. Glick?"

"I didn't send nobody here—honest," my demeanor turned morose and my voice struck a sincere tone.

"He said his name was Polly Wolly," Mr. Glick said.

"Who is this Dolly Lolly," the vice principal ridiculed, "or whatever it is you people call yourselves."

"I don't know any Dolly Lolly."

"Don't be a wise guy. Who is Polly Wolly?"

"Mr. Glick," I pleaded, "I told you I never threw the orange."

"Who is Polly Wolly," the vice principal demanded in a raised voice.

"I don't know," I lied. I thought of Polly by his real name and repeated the lie. "I don't know,"

"That's enough of this," the vice-principal said. "Here, sign this. He turned two pages face up on his desk. "Sign next to your name."

He handed me a pen from his desk and I signed the bottom page of the document next to my name without reading it—although I did glimpse the words Polly Wolly several times on the page that I signed. Then he took a sealed envelope that was on his desk and handed it to me.

"Have your father sign the note inside and return it to me tomorrow."

"My father don't live with us."

"I'm not surprised. Have your mother or whoever is your guardian sign it and return it to me tomorrow."

The vice-principal didn't tell me to leave; he used his hand to dismiss me with a kind of degrading sweeping motion.

Polly Wolly's name is Robert Mule. He lived in a building in the rear of the projects with his mother and three sisters when he wasn't locked up. I don't know what he did to get his first stay in the reformatory, fact is, I don't know the details of any of his crimes that sent him to the home for wayward boys in his early years and to jail from the time he was seventeen. He has been a repeat offender for a period of over fifty years, and though in the latter years he cast himself as a political prisoner, his arrest in the former years involved stick ups and drugs. I do know that today he has an arrest record that could weigh several hundred pounds. Also that he is now known by the name Abdullah Kawnza. I've kept in touch with Robert through all of his name changes and each phase of his life they represented. When he was an associate of the Black Panthers, he introduced me to some of the New York leaders of the Panthers who were headquartered on the ground floor of the defunct Theresa Hotel in Harlem. It was they who got me to submit some articles for their national newspaper that got the attention of someone who tapped my telephone.

I first met Robert when I was sidekick to Crunch Collier. Robert was seeing Crunch's older sister and when he was out of the slammer, he was often at the Collier household. Robert and

Crunch were the same age and had a mutual respect for each other. They didn't hang out much because they were complete opposites. Robert was roguish and treacherous. Crunch was industrious and considerate. Robert knew that Crunch Collier was capable of acting crazy himself, so there was never any noticeable friction between them. Through his years in reform school, Robert had learned the art of intimidation. His behavior was impulsive and explosive. He could lull a person into thinking everything was fine and dandy then bang—he would explode either physically or verbally. This never happened with Crunch Collier in my presence.

During his final term in reform school, before he started to go to adult jails, a guy at the reform school put Polly Wolly in touch with a guy in East Harlem. This guy in East Harlem was a leader of the Sportsman street gang and he had the authority to commission Polly to start a division of the gang in our neighborhood. Upon his release, Polly gathered a group of the neighborhood's toughs to make a pilgrimage to the kingmaker in East Harlem. This group later formed the upper echelon of the Amsterdam division of the Sportsman. They recruited boys in the 15 to 19 age range. Then they started practicing their war tactics by beating up groups of boys my age in our neighborhood. It began to be hazardous for the younger boys in the neighborhood to congregate on the weekends. Polly and his gang would divide into raiding parties, swoop down on groups of younger boys, and beat them up, then run off laughing. They were rehearsing for future battles with their real enemies. The Sportsman was, from time to time, at war with the Dragons, a Spanish gang based in East Harlem and the Chapmans in Fort Greene Brooklyn. All three gangs were in a perpetual war with the white gang from The Bronx called the Boston Stompers. Then, the gang gave the younger boys an option: continue to get beat up or organize yourselves into the junior Sportsmen. Lots of us went around calling ourselves junior Sportsmen, but there was nothing formal about our group. There were no initiation or membership dues like in the senior gang—we didn't even have a list of members. Still, whenever senior gang members approached any group of younger boys, they would declare their membership in the junior Sportsmen and avoid being harassed.

Polly Wolly was the Supreme Leader of the Amsterdam Sportsman. Wine was next in line and was the warlord. Jamaica Hip was a captain along with thugs with names like Superman, Graveyard, and Dittybop. Stonewall Jackson, a particularly vicious neighborhood bully and repeat offender was an associate of the gang, but not an official member because he was uncontrollable. Stonewall Jackson was a big boy with the muscular body of a heavyweight boxer. He had a voice that sounded like Popeye the Sailor Man and he stuttered. His eyes made him appear just a tiny bit retarded. He was cold hearted, cruel and easily provoked to violence—just the sight of him made my spirit sink and my mind fearful. One day I was walking down Amsterdam Avenue eating an ice cream cone I had just bought when I came across Stonewall Jackson.

"Gim, gim, gim, gimme that ice cream," he stuttered.

I wanted my ice cream. It was just unbelievable that I would have to give up my ice cream cone. I had already licked all over it. I took another lick to convince Stonewall that he might not want it after all. He gave me a look that suggested I had better comply with his demand.

"I said, gim, gim, gim, gimme that ice cream," he said, this time reaching his hand out for the ice cream that was quickly moving towards his hand.

Twenty-five years later, I met Stonewall Jackson on Amsterdam Avenue. He was lying under the flagpole by the school at 61st Street with a can of beer in his hand. He had been in and out of jail continuously for all of those years. He was homeless and dingy, a mental and physical mess. He had had the kinds of jailhouse experiences that sap the desire to live and drives men insane. As I looked in his face in passing, I could tell he recognized me. His eye rolled up in his head then went vacant, but he smiled and mumbled something incoherent.

"Gim, gim, gim, gimme that beer," I said in appreciation for this real life version of a Hitchcock scenario. Stonewall Jackson's mouth formed a half smile and he closed his eyes.

Crunch Collier was one of the few boys in our neighborhood, in that age group, who was able to resist the lure of the Sportsman without reprisal. You had to be tough to resist their solicitation or you had to be protected by someone high up in the gang. I suspect that Polly Wolly insulated Crunch from the vengeance of the rest of the gang. Beside that, Crunch Collier was too busy working and helping his family to survive. Crunch Collier wasn't often seen in much of the neighborhood—he was found mostly at Al and Ben's Luncheonette or in front of his or his girlfriend's building.

It might have been that Robert was envious of the relationship Crunch and I had. He may have wanted a younger brother to guide. And, this may have caused him to want to protect me. He lived in a household of females who had no use for him. This may have been the source of generosity towards me as well as the source of a rebelliousness that kept him in a perpetually revolving situation. I'm not sure, what it is that kept me connected to Polly Wolly. I'm sure it's more then the fact that he looked out for me. It may be that his story has unfolded like one of those I've read about in the Alfred Hitchcock Mystery anthologies and I can't figure what bizarre event will bring it to a close. So, I hold on for the ending—his or mine.

At the end of the school year, many of my friends graduated from J.H.S. 17 and would be going to high school in September. Clark and Tommy Borden went to a vocational school downtown. Thomas Bedding went to a technical clothing design school. Brad and Ozzie went to Machine and Metal Trades school, which told me where I would be going that next year when I graduated. I wouldn't be going there to learn a trade in the fields they taught—I didn't know what they offered. I didn't know what any of the high schools offered. I would be going there because that was where my boys went.

San Juan Hill

CHAPTER FOUR
Hustlers

I met Katherine Russ through her cousin Joan who lived on 53rd Street and attended Junior High School 17. In the fifties, there were still many black families living in the blocks surrounding the popular jazz clubs on 52nd Street, just east of Hell's Kitchen. Joan and many of the black kids from her area hung out in the Amsterdam Projects. There was a public swimming pool on 60th Street that was a popular summer attraction. This is where I first met Katherine. She was with Joan and two other girls from 53rd Street. Katherine lived in Harlem and during the summer, she would spend weeks at a time with Joan. Everybody called her Butchie and I liked her on first sight. She was sixteen. She was light skinned with reddish hair. She had a comely body still developing. Her eyes were bright. Her face was soft and pretty. She had full lips and a lovely smile. Her set back was that when she laughed out right, her rotten teeth were revealed. Those rotten teeth told more about her than all of her other features. She was a person of unbridled excess and bad dental hygiene, and, perhaps, faulty family genes. But I was still taken with her.

Whenever Joan and Katherine came to the projects, they hung out with my old gang down the back. They would go to Evane's or Maggie's house. By the time I got wind that they were in the area and got down the back, they would be outside in the small playground behind Evane's building. Katherine had a worldly manner and it wasn't long before I found out that she smoked reefer. At the time none of the other girls down the back smoked weed. Butchie liked to hang out with the boys because she knew we would be getting some wine and that I would hustle up a joint or two.

Maggie was my girlfriend in a kind of on again, off again relationship. I sat up late at her house on the weekends watching television and we went out to the movies. I once took Maggie to a dance at a ballroom on Broadway and 96th Street. Sometime during the dance, we went to the bar to order a drink. Maggie was a good-looking girl and she was well proportioned. This night she was radiant. At the bar I felt an arm on my shoulder. I turned to see who it was and when my eyes focused, I could hardly believe it.

"Hey how you doing. Long time, no see," he said, his eye fastened onto Maggie's smile.

I picked up on what he was doing right away. He was helping me to impress my girl for a shot at her.

"Hey Frankie," I said. Then I introduced them. 'Maggie Clark meet Frankie Lymon." They shook hands, our drinks came and we walked back to the dance arena.

"I didn't know that you knew Frankie Lymon," Maggie said excitedly. I had never seen Frankie Lymon before in my life except on his album covers, on television and in the movies.

"Yeah, we're old Harlem buddies."

I could see that Maggie was impressed. But when I was not around, she was with Malcolm Tibbs and I suspected that their relationship had gone beyond the kissing and petting we engaged in. So, I kind of encouraged them on. Besides, Butchie was hip and from Harlem, so I began to pursue her.

Joan was cute too. She too was light skinned. She had a freckled pretty face and eyes that sparkled. I introduced her to Ozzie and she liked him. Ozzie always had a sort of difficult personality. He didn't get along with people very well. He was too into himself. Guys found it hard to communicate with him and girls found it even more difficult to connect with him. He was blunt, aloof and arrogant with almost everybody. Ozzie always made girls feel like he was the center of attraction and not them, so he never showed any clear feelings for Joan. But he liked the idea of smoking reefers with girls and showcasing his knowledge of jazz to them. I started dragging Ozzie down to 53rd Street when I knew that Butchie was at Joan's house. When Joan's parents were at work, we smoked reefers and listened to jazz records. Joan and Butchie loved John Coltrane and Joan's father had a great collection of Coltrane and Miles.

Joan soon started to complain to me about how difficult it was to get Ozzie to show her some affection. She described him as a conceited egotist. He was even reluctant to kiss her she said. One day when we all returned to the house from an outing in Central Park, Joan put on some records and suggested that Butchie and I go into her room and leave her and Ozzie on the sofa. It was obvious that they had discussed and planned this surprise. Ozzie objected, but Butchie grabbed my hand and pulled me to Joan's bedroom door. She immediately started to kiss me. Joan rose to close the bedroom door. Butchie and I never said a word. We communicated through passion, instinct and telepathy and found ourselves half-naked on Joan's bed. It was all a clumsy event for me. It was obvious that Butchie had more experience, but it was nevertheless a defining moment for me. One of life's mysteries had opened up and revealed its essence to me. An hour or so later, Ozzie and I left the girls and walked back up to the Projects. I was bursting to tell him what had taken place, but Ozzie is a funny guy and I could tell he didn't want to hear my story or talk about his.

I saw Butchie again a few days later. She and Joan were down in the back of the projects. There were lots of people around, but they were to the side talking to Willie Clark and Manny Black. I expected her to approach me when I got near, but she ignored me. Joan said hello and asked me about Ozzie. I told her that I would be seeing him later in the evening. Then I said hello to Butchie. She acknowledged me almost grudgingly and immediately said something funny to Manny. When he laughed, she playfully pushed him. I had taken what happened between us in Joan's bedroom the wrong way. I knew we hadn't taken an oath of fidelity or declared ourselves involved in a special relationship, but I believed that we were bonded in some way. She was all I had thought about since that afternoon. I had an after-glow that lasted until this meeting. It became clear to me that Butchie had done Joan a favor. She had gone in the bedroom with me to give Joan a chance to seduce Ozzie. Because she was a person of excess, she went all the way—lucky me. Her flirtation with Manny was to show me that that was all there was to it.

Manny and Clark didn't know what had happened, but they sensed my awkwardness and embarrassment. Willie Clark had always been a fellow who spoke his mind. "Hey, you want to talk to her in private?" he asked me.

I hesitated. He caught me off guard, but before I could think of how to respond to his question, Butchie spoke.

"He ain't got nothing to say to me," and she grabbed Manny's arm and walked off.

I needed to recover.

"I don't have anything to say to her. I gotta go."

Joan took my arm and walked with me a few steps. "I'm sorry," she said.

"For what?" I said, and I began to walk off alone.

"Are you going on the boat ride?' Joan yelled out.

2

There were several types of social clubs among the community's adults. Most people called them Circles. There were susu clubs where its members gave a certain amount of money to a collector each week and each week the collector turned the total over to a member of the club in turn. There were clubs for rotating gambling parties that were known during the Harlem Renaissance period as rent parties. The two major clubs in San Juan Hill were The La'Grande Social Club and the Royal Lions Social Club. Both of these clubs sponsored summer boat rides and winter dances. These were major events in our neighborhood that nearly everyone attended. Among my peers, the boat rides were the most popular events. Our neighborhood was like a ghost town on boat ride day.

One club gave a boat ride that started early in the morning. The boat went up the Hudson River to Bear Mountain where most people got off to picnic and enjoy the recreational facilities at the resort. The boat went on to West Point Military Academy with those who stayed aboard, then it turned around and returned to retrieve the people at Bear Mountain. The highlight of the day was the evening trip back down the Hudson River. People would break out what was left of the libations, liquid and smoke, the band would play in an all out fashion and the females wanted to dance up close. The other club gave an evening boat ride. The boat left the pier before sundown and made several trips just up the Hudson beyond the George Washington Bridge and back down to the Statue of Liberty—this boat ride had the party feel of the returning trip on the day boat ride for the entire time. Everybody was lit and ready to party from the start.

The boat rides all started and ended at the 125th Street piers in Harlem, where decade's earlier the crippled ships and boats of Marcus Garvey's failed Black Star Line moored. Garvey, a Jamaican, was going to build a fleet of cargo and passenger ships to prove the black man's business competence and then used those vessels to transport blacks back to Africa once a location for a new country had been negotiated. I imagine that because they knew the ship's purpose, the sight of those ships must have made black folk's hearts thump. There was also a ferry at the 125th Street piers that took people and cars to New Jersey and Palisades Amusement Park. Marcus Garvey's dream, the ferry line, even the amusement park and the 125th Street piers are long gone and belong to the memory of history.

Both clubs always hired the popular calypso band led by another West Indian; a man named Fats Greene, for their winter dances and for the boat rides. Fats Greene had a wide following in our neighborhood and throughout Harlem, parts of Brooklyn, and Queens. When we reached our mid-teens, we would go to a dance just because we saw Fats Greene's name on a promotion flyer. Fats Greene recorded one or two records with his band that had a cult following, but his main appeal was his live appearances. During this period, there were many calypso bands that flourished. The steel drum bands were popular and The Mighty Sparrow flew all the way from Jamaica to make appearances, but for me and for the people of San Juan Hill, there was no other like Fats Greene.

The boat ride Joan asked me about took place on a Saturday evening in the third week in July, 1956. Brad, Ozzie and I had our tickets and were prepared for a week. We bought special outfits to wear, practiced our calypso dance steps and bought an ounce of marijuana to roll up and sell on the boat as individual joints. We chipped in five dollars each to purchase the ounce. When Ozzie finished rolling, we each had 50 joints. We also bought a bottle of Beefeater's gin for ourselves. The boat left the pier at 7PM. People started arriving as much as two hours before. They carried folding chairs, food, booze, blankets and card tables. They moved up and down the gangplank searching each other out; giving out tickets held for a relative or a neighbor. Almost all of the Amsterdam and the Phipps complex black residents were there; even many former residents of the community still attended the boat ride. This was such a big thing that Harry Goldberg, the owner of the Century bar closed his bar, gave his two brothers the day off and was on the boat seated with some of the more prominent members of the community and the organizers of the boat ride.

While the boat sailed down the Hudson River during the last two hours of sunlight, The bands played mellow sedated music as people set up in their area, settled down and enjoyed the scenery. Everyone anticipated the fall of night when everything picked up. The mood just kind of built up as people moved about greeting each other and making offers of food and drink. And, there were those who were seeking out the reefer dealers. All three of us were mostly sold out before dark. I wore white seersucker pants, a blue and white striped shirt, white low-cut sneakers and a blue cap. Every time I went to the rest room, I'd count the money I'd made and admired myself in the mirror. It wasn't until after dark that I saw Joan and Butchie. They were on an upper deck. The boat was making one of it's many turns near the Statue of Liberty and the two girls leaned on a rail looking at the monument. I walked over to the rail and said hello. They both greeted me with a kiss on my cheek.

"Who y'all with?"

"We were supposed to come with Clark and Manny," Joan said. "But Clark got off from work too late and Manny never bought a ticket—so here we are alone."

"Y'all want something to eat?"

"No, not yet," they answered simultaneously.

"Y'all want something to smoke?"

"You got smoke?" Butchie asked.

I had a joint in my pocket, what I had left was stashed in my secret spot. I lit it up and handed it to Butchie. She took three drags and handed it to Joan. Joan took some and handed the joint to me. I refused any and pointed to Butchie. When they were finished, we went down to the level where the band was playing. I told them to wait there. I returned with three cups of gin and soda. I reminded the girls that there was a concession stand on the lower deck if they wanted something to eat or I offered to get them something from the table of any of the older folks I knew on the boat. They both declined. I asked Butchie if she wanted to dance. She handed her cup to Joan and we went to the dance floor. Fats Greene and his band were playing an in-between tempo, rhythmic tune that brought on inspired dancing. The bass kept the meter while the drums pounded a repeated image around the bass. The horns flared off in another direction and the crooner sang something about seeing a devil whose head was red as fire. Butchie and I danced apart holding on to one hand and when the music suggested it, we embraced and danced pressed close together. Butchie was a good dancer. She was soft and graceful and as we clung to each other, I imitated her movements and felt like I would melt away. When the music was over, we walked back to where Joan stood.

"Is Ozzie here?"

"Yeah. He's with Brad somewhere."

"I knew you wouldn't be here without him."

"We're not always together."

"You're not gonna dance with me?" Joan said as the music started up again. I took her out on the floor. This was a dance free from romantic notions floating about in my head. After the dance, I set off to locate Ozzie. He was in a crowded, poorly lit corner of the boat watching some guy hustling some kind of card game—I didn't pay much attention to it. Ozzie said that he would come and hang with us after he sold the rest of his joints. Brad was hanging out with a crowd of older girls and boys at a table full with food and drinks. Ozzie never did come to where Butchie, Joan and I were and I wound up spending the rest of the boat ride in this threesome.

Wherever you find a crowd of people, you'll find a hustler. Somebody trying to pick your pocket—one way or the other. On the boat rides there would always be a team of hustlers in a secluded spot or even in the restroom, set up to play what is called three-card monte—a game where the hustler holds three similar cards in his hands. It is often three aces—two of one color and one of the other color. The hustler is betting all comers that they can't find the card of one color after he has shuffled them around a little. It looks easy and it looks tempting. What the spectator doesn't know is that the hustler is usually working with two rustlers who at different times come out of the crowd and make easy wins to further heighten the spectator's temptation. It is the rustler's job to make it look easy to find the winning card and together the hustler and the rustlers convince many in the crowd to try their hand and eyes for five or ten dollars. Besides having rustlers, the hustler has to first have swift hands that can create the illusion that a certain color card has been thrown to a certain spot. The hustler holds one card in his left hand and the other two cards in his right hand, one on top of the other. The lone card, say a red ace, is on the bottom and is the one visible to the spectators. After the hustler has assured all eyes that the winning card is the bottom card in his right hand, he has to use his thumb and pinky finger to switch the cards in his right hand so that the winning card is on top when he throws them out. This is done in the quick movement he uses to turn his hand and the cards over face down in the wink of time before he positions them.

On one such boat ride, Ozzie watched the hustler's hands for hours until he was sure that he saw how the illusion was created.

Then he practiced the move for weeks before he even told Brad that he had it. Ozzie came up with the idea that he and Brad worked the Garment Center with the three-card monte hustle on paydays. He wanted to leave me out of the scam, but Brad persuaded him that it would be more convincing to have two rustlers, plus one of us could look out for the police. When we started working the Garment Center we were expecting to attract some of the guys who were hauling tailored goods on push carts and rolling racks from factory to showroom for thirty bucks a week—the guys who bought a bottle of wine or whiskey before they took the subway back uptown. To our surprise, it was the white fair wage earners who were most interested in our enterprise. These were people who went to Las Vegas once a year and maybe once a month they'd attend a floating mob casino. They played the horses. They had the number of their dentist and doctor in a personal telephone book, but their bookie's number was in their heads. These were people who couldn't resist the lure of chance and had the money to gamble.

In the beginning, Ozzie would set up shop on the stoop of a building or on the sidewalk near parked cars—right on the ground like dice shooters. We came to learn that this made our high priced players feel awkward that they were engaging in a crude activity. Once while I was positioned in the crowd in my role as a rustler, I heard two well-dressed Jewish men who chewed on fat cigars make comments about how Ozzie was situated.

"So Murray, you gonna get on your knees in such a nice suit to watch the boy handle the cards," one said to the other.

"On my knees," the other guy replied, "I should give you the money to bet for me and let you watch the cards for me—your suit is not so nice as mine."

I repeated this conversation to Brad and Ozzie one day when we were up at Ozzie's house listening to his father's new Art Blakely and the Jazz Messengers album. Together we came up with the idea to have Ozzie set up on a fold up serving tray, the kind that was so popular in the TV dinner era. I came up with the idea to cover the serving tray with some kind of cloth. We later agreed on a white pillowcase. We chipped in and bought the serving tray. Ozzie donated the pillowcase from his mother's linen closet. Now we were in business—big time.

In time we learned the best period to set up operations was from ten in the morning until two in the afternoon. People went back and forth for coffee and lunch during those hours. We also learned that because the lunch period is so limited, people didn't have much time to give to our enterprise—they had to eat and run. This was to our advantage to have a crowd that was constantly changing. Brad and I could make several confidence-building appearances. We no longer fished for the lower end cart pushers who killed time in between deliveries drinking wine in spots on Ninth Avenue. We were emboldened enough to set up in the heart of the garment center looking to attract the guys with money and an irresistible weakness to place a bet. We worked 8th and 7th Avenues from 34th street to 42nd street. Ozzie would find a spot, unfold the tray and cover it with the pillowcase. Then he would take out two black aces and one red ace. He'd bend them slightly and begin to shuffle them around on the tray. "Find the red ace for even money." he'd say trying to attract a crowd. "5, 10, 20, I place 'um you, find 'um. Even money for the red ace." If a crowd began to gather at the tray but no one took the bait, I'd go into the crowd with two or three five-dollar bills in my hand. I'd watched the cards go down on the table and to make myself conspicuous to the crowd, I'd asked that the cards be thrown out again.

"You gonna bet?" Ozzie would ask.

"Yeah, I'm gonna bet."

Ozzie showed the cards, the red ace in front of the black ace in his right hand. Then he thew them out. I placed five dollars on the center card.

"Anyone else?" Ozzie asked the crowd. "Anyone else?" then he flipped over the card to the right on the center card. It was a black ace. Now with just two cards left, a fifty-fifty chance, Ozzie asked "Anyone else? Do we have a winner." I could feel that there were many in the crowd who wanted to place a bet, but first wanted to see how my bet came out. Ozzie feels it too, but he knows that no one will bet this time. So, he milks it a little longer. "Place your bet. Never too late. Bet with this five dollar better and you too may be a winner. Last call." Ozzie sounds like the barkers at Coney Island. Then he takes the five-dollar bill off of the card, folds the bill and uses it to flip the card over. It's the red ace. Ozzie taps the five spot against the tray in mock disgust, and then he reaches into his shirt pocket and removes a roll of money. He peels off a ten-dollar bill and gives it to me. He adds the five to his roll and returns the whole thing back to his shirt pocket. Then he shuffles the cards out on the tray again. I place a ten dollar bet on the middle card again and this time Ozzie shows the winning card quickly and without offering anyone else a chance to place a bet. It's the red ace again. He pays me. I look at my watch.

"Lunch on you," I say and walk off.

Many in the crowd are now confidant and they step up to bet. It's Ozzie's turn to do his thing. I did mine. Over the next five or so tosses of the cards, Ozzie brings in fifty dollars. Brads moves unnoticed into the crowd. When the betters get a little hesitant, Brad moves to the tray with bills showing in his hands. He places a bet and comes up the lone winner. Many in the crowd begin to think that they know what's going on here. Ozzie hold the card in plain sight of all the spectators. Calls out his spiel and throws the card to the tray. Brad places twenty dollars on the center card. Ozzie brings it to the crowd's attention that the ante has been upped by calling out, "Big money on the center card." The crowd senses a turning point—two, three, and then four bets totaling eighty dollars are made on the center card. Ozzie turns over the card to the right of the center card. It is a black ace. He looks into the crowd with a worried frown on his face. He lifts the money from off of the center card. Folded it all in half and uses it to flip over the center card. It is also a black ace—there are no winners.

We ran our hustle for months before the police started to hassle us. It wasn't bad though, it may be because it was mostly well-dressed white men that made up the crowd, and the police would just break us up. Most of the times they didn't even get out of the car. They would just stop and call out to break it up. Sometimes when someone a block away spotted a police car, they would yell up to us that they were coming. Ozzie would call off the bets, fold the table up and start to walk away. One day while we were smoking reefer and discussing our routine, we decided to work the threat of the police into our advantage. Once in a while we suffered big loses by a winner who got lucky or may have learned the tempo of Ozzie's routine. We didn't use it often but the few times we did, it worked fine. One of the times was when a fat Jewish man, gnawing on a cigar and holding an expensive looking woman's fur coat that hung over his arm, placed a hundred dollar bet on what Ozzie knew was the right card. Ozzie called out a certain spiel that was the signal for us to yell out that the police was coming. People hustling to get away from the table quickly caused the confusion Ozzie needed to grab up the cards and the money—making sure to hand the bet back to the better as he folded the table up and quickly disappeared. The gambler had his money back and he really couldn't be certain that he had the winning card, so he was happy.

This was the routine we played over and over in every section of the garment center. We mixed up elements of our routine quite a bit, but the only real change we made was to buy a wooden folding table, which eliminated the need for the pillowcase. Ozzie said the table was too heavy for him to carry. Brad and I took turns carrying the table to and from our work site. We made a split at the end of each day's hustle. We often ended up with three hundred dollars. Ozzie gave us seventy-five dollars each; he ordinarily kept half the take for himself. I found out later that Ozzie made another split with Brad when I was not with them. In a three hundred-dollar day when his share was one hundred and fifty dollars, Ozzie would kick Brad another twenty-five dollars. What was I to do?

Now we were making real money. Brad could really indulge his affection for clothes. Among the street kids of our era, there were only two cool ways of dressing. There was the Ivy League look of plain front pants, penny loafers, and button-down shirts. And there was the Hustler look: pleated pants, wingtip shoes, white on white shirts. Another name for the Hustler look was "conservative," but everybody used the term Hustler. These things were basic to each look, but then there were variations on each look and clothes that embellished each style. Alligator shoes were one of the many enhancements to the hustlers look. A blue blazer was emblematic of the Ivy League look. We became familiar with the better stores. We bought Clarks of London shoes from McCreedy's & Schiebers on 47th Street, sweater-shirts from AJ Lester's in Harlem; Caps from Brooks Brothers on Fifth Avenue, sportswear from Macys and marijuana from Jimmy's Bar on Lenox Avenue.

Brad chose the Ivy League style of dressing and I followed. Ozzie didn't have a taste for fashion. It might have been because of his tiny size. His waistline was small and he had to make a hole in his belts to make them fit. At sixteen, he still had to shop in the boy's section to find things his size, while the rest of us were shopping in the men's department or at men's shops. Ozzie wore things like pullover shirts with string ties that I once saw on a Roy Rogers' poster for the rodeo, and bellbottom pants. Lord knows where he found his funny looking shoes. The only distinction about Ozzie's sense of fashion was that he was partial to the color black. Brad and I spent most of our money on clothes. Ozzie bought a reel to reel tape recorder for his singing group to record their practice sessions on. And, he bought lots of jazz records. Every week, he went to Sugar Ray's barbershop in Harlem to have his hair processed. All the boys in his singing group, except Norman Brown, had their hair conked. Ozzie conked their hair and he would talk his brother through the process of doing his hair. Ozzie still conked the other three boys' hair, but now he went to Sugar Ray's.

3

There were really great dressers, male and female, in our neighborhood. Fine clothing was not the sign of success, it was success itself. We didn't aspire to the kind of concrete success a professional person might have, but we wanted to look the part. We chose style over content. The barriers to becoming a professional success were so formidable that we settled for the more superficial aspect of achievement—being well dressed. The people of our neighborhood put on a fashion show parading up and down Amsterdam Avenue on Easter Sundays that would rival those that went on in Harlem during the Black Renaissance. On Easter morning, many of us went to the shoeshine hut owned by an Italian man named Salvador Pasquale. We all called him Mr. Sal. The hut was a small little building attached to a tenement house at the corner of 64th Street. Many New York streets had them; they were used as newspaper stands, shoeshine parlors, or flower retailers. Salvador Pasquale was an old immigrant who lived, with his wife, in the building that his hut was attached to. Easter and Mother's Day were his two best days of the year and though they were Sundays, he worked all day. "Only gangsters and blacks shined their shoes," Mr. Sal often said.

The two best dressed boys in our neighborhood held the spotlight from their late teens until their mid twenties. Some people referred to them as Mutt and Jeff because one was small and the other was stout. The small fellow's name was Jerry Palmer and his partner's name was Willie Jeffrey. These fellows defied any description of either of the excepted styles of our sub-culture's dress code. Their style was not clearly Ivy League or Hustler in appearance. Like most people who reach the top of their field of endeavor, they became innovative.

Still, I think that Jerry retained more of the Hustler look and Willie leaned more towards the Ivy League look. On a Sunday, Jerry might be hooked up with gray pleated trousers. The cuff broke for an inch over brown, entirely alligator shoes. He might have on a gray jacket with a black pattern that ran through it. He would definitely have on a white on white shirt and a colorful tie that locked the whole outfit together. He would accessorize with a silk breast-pocket handkerchief that was barely seen. That Sunday, Willie Jeffrey would meet Jerry on Amsterdam Avenue wearing his double-breasted blue blazer with buttons that were purchased separately and sewn on. His white linen trousers, a powder blue shirt with an ascot sticking from his neck, a blue and white ship captain's cap, white tennis shoes and a white silk handkerchief hanging from his breast-pocket. They would each be carrying horns in cases. Jerry carried a trumpet and Willie carried a saxophone. I never heard either of them play a note, so it may be that the instruments were as much a part of their outfits as were their trousers. Nemsie Brothers, the Jewish tailor shop on the Lower East Side, made much of their wardrobe.

Willie Jeffrey once told me how he and Jerry got interested in playing music. They were both big jazz fans and visited all of the hot jazz clubs. One evening they were at Birdland to hear the music of trumpeter Donald Byrd and alto saxophonist Jackie McClean. They were sitting at a table with the famed radio disc jockey Symphony Sid. During the intermission, they all went backstage where they were able to enlist the headliner musicians to tutor them on their instruments. Willie explained how kind and patient the musicians were with them. Willie took lessons from Jackie McClean until McClean went to Europe for an extended stay. Donald Byrd coming to the projects to pick up Jerry in a red MG really impressed Willie. Willie remembers the time as heady stuff, two teenagers hanging out with *real* musicians, and he confesses "We couldn't play a lick, but we looked good carrying those axes."

I once smoked hashish with Jerry Palmer. It was a rainy Sunday afternoon and I was on my way to the apartment of a young woman who had been deserted by her husband. She had two small children, but still, she turned her apartment into a hangout for teenagers and young adults. There was always a crowd there listening to records, drinking and getting high. Jerry lived on the second floor of the building next to mine. That Sunday he was in the window of his room eating his dinner and he saw me about to pass.

"Hey Grady," he called out.

"Hey Jerry."

"Where you going?"

"To Liddia's."

"Want some smoke?"

"Yeah."

"Come on up."

I knocked at the door and Jerry's sister showed me back to his room. He was finishing off a plate of fried chicken, red rice and collard greens and listening to a Charlie Parker record on a small record player in his room.

"So what be going on at Liddia's?"

"Nothing much. Just some place to hang."

"I hear she 'pose to be fine. You fucking that woman?"

"No man, that's Ralph's girl—when he's home." Ralph was Ozzie's older brother and he was in the navy.

"I ain't never been there so I want to check it out. I'm gonna crash down there with you. Hey, while I put on some clothes, roll two joints. Jerry handed me a matchbox half full with brown marijuana and went to the bathroom to bathe.

"Light up," Jerry said on his return.

"I lit up a joint and took several drags before I handed it to Jerry. It had a deep pungent aroma I was unfamiliar with.

"You ever smoked hash before?" Jerry asked with a mischievous smile on his face.

"No," I said, thinking that there was no great difference.

"How you like it"

"It's strong."

"Wait until that fucker hits you."

Jerry dressed and I replayed the Charlie Parker record.

"So you dig Bird huh?

I really thought the music was antiquated. I wasn't yet aware of the evolution of jazz, so I didn't see that the music Bird played was an important link to the music I liked. I was into the cool mood of Miles Davis. I dug the funky jazz of Cannonball Adderley. I admired the smooth riffs of Ahmad Jamal, the chaos of John Coltrane and the well thought out compositions of Lee Morgan. I even understood and liked some of the music of Charlie Mingus, but right at this moment, I was smoking Jerry's reefer.

"Bird is cool."

"I got high with Bird on a bench in Harlem way before he died. Bird was a down dude, you hear me—and he could blow his horn," Jerry said as he finished dressing.

"Light up the other one," Jerry said.

I could feel the rush of air all around me. I became aware of the diminutive size of Jerry's room. The rain outside seemed clean and healthy, but loud. I was able to choose the sound of the raindrops that blended most melodiously with the sound of Bird playing "Scrapple from the Apple." I became aware that I was high like never before.

"No more for me. You smoke it."

The full impact of the hash didn't affect me until we changed environment and got outside into the air. As we walked, Jerry was talking about some of the famous jazz musicians he knew and got high with, but all I could do was watch his feet, which seemed to me, at the time, not to be touching the ground. He was floating down the block and I surmised that if Jerry was floating I must me floating also. We floated our way to Liddia's apartment talking about music. Music was important to us all, because it had been demonstrated that music was a way out of poverty and the projects.

There were three good Do-wop groups in the neighborhood. The better of the three groups was a group composed of five over-the-hill guys who had modeled their group after the outmoded style of older groups like the Ink Spots. They were in their early to mid twenties and were into that ghetto famous antidote for failure that produces certain doom—heroin. But they could really sing and dance, and put on a good show. They had a stand out guy named Joe Reed who was a real showman. Joe Reed could sing, tap dance and clown up a storm. The other two groups showed great promise. The Cleartones, with Ozzie, his brother Chad, Norman Brown, and two other boys and another group called the Emersons. The Emersons made a novelty record called "Hungry." The record received good playtime on the radio and the Emersons played the Apollo Theater for a week. Brad, Ozzie and I went to the show twice. We paid once and got in through the back door once. The Emersons never made it to the big time, in fact, they never made another record that was released, but they were stars on San Juan Hill. Ozzie's group had a manager who made many promises. He was a fly-by-night guy who was barely connected to the music business. He was a hustler trying to make a killing for himself off of the backs of talented young black boys. This turned out to be the story of the Do-wop era. The vast majority of the talented people who created the music that is called rock and roll made untold billions of dollars for the white managers, producers and people who controlled the music industry and nothing but fleeting fame for themselves.

The manager of Ozzie's fledging group once pulled him aside after a studio practice session to tell of a deal he had for him. Ozzie was to be paired with a young female singer and they would be recording in a few months time. He could have a contract for Ozzie and his parents to sign in a few days if Ozzie agreed to leave the group and pair-up with the girl—her name was Darlene. They would record as "Ozzie and Darlene." Ozzie agreed. All the members of his group except Norman Brown condemned him. Ozzie's brother felt the betrayal most. The Cleartones tried to rearrange their repertoire, but in a few months the members drifted apart. Over the next several months, we saw very little of Ozzie. He was always in the studio rehearsing. Even when school started back up, Ozzie would rush from school to the studio. During the first months of school, Brad saw Ozzie more often than I did because they frequently traveled to school together. The group of boys my age had gone on to high school—another source of irritation for me. I was now a senior at J. H. S. 17.

4

The black and Puerto Rican students from the projects were an overwhelming majority in the school. The white students came from Hell's Kitchen and the surrounding areas. I went through junior high school in learning disability classes. These classes were loud, disruptive and unproductive. My classes were composed of mainly black and Puerto Rican boys, some white boys, and a few black and Puerto Rican girls. I never had a white girl in my class. Oh, I'm sure there were white girls whose grades merit the lack of attention received in a learning disability class, but I suspect school officials had constructed overriding mechanisms to prevent that kind of exposure to young white girls—no matter how dumb they were.

Most of the white boys dressed the way Marlon Brando did in the "Wild Ones." They wore black leather motorcycle jackets, black boots, and Lee dungaree jeans with wide belts. The belts had big silver or gold buckles that were sometimes sharpened for battle. In gang fights, the belts would be wrapped around the hands a few turns and the buckle would be swung as a weapon. One morning in school a dispute broke out between one such white boy and me. I don't remember what the dispute was about, but the white boy proposed that we settled it after school in a vacant lot on 47th Street near 10th Avenue. I agreed, even though I knew that this was in the heart of Hell's Kitchen. I was pensive all day during classes. I hadn't been in a fight since sixth grade and that was mostly a prancing match with few struck blows. I worried about this white boy who was brave enough to challenge a black boy to a fight even knowing that we ruled the school.

Some people may have been on the scene when the dispute occurred and heard our agreement. I may have told some of my friends about the fight, but I'll never figure out how word of it got back to the older boys in the projects—and to Polly Wolly. When school was finished that day, and I went down to the exit, a large crowd of black and white kids had formed. Apparently the word had gone out in the Hell's Kitchen neighborhood also; my challenger had a large assemblage of his gang at the school. Someone took charge of my opponent and the white group and started walking the one and a half blocks to the lot. Polly Wolly took charge of our group and we followed. Each group was hyping their fighter on. Someone carried my books and all I could hear from the mob were angry shouts—his mob and my own.

We reached the vacant lot. It was fenced in with a part of fencing large enough to climb through torn out. My opponent and his seconds were already in the lot. Polly Wolly and two of his boys climbed through behind me. It was a chilly day and I was wearing a windbreaker. My adversary had already removed his jacket and stood near me huffing and beating his chest. I moved a step back and stood by the building bordering the vacant lot to remove my jacket. As I got my jacket half way off, he jumped on me and hit me twice in the mouth bouncing my head off of the brick building. I moved away and quickly threw my jacket to the ground. Everything was dark for a second. My head was hurting and I could feel warm blood in my mouth. I touched the right side of my top lip where it stung and felt a wide split in my lip. He came at me again and I danced from side to side trying to clear my head. He held his hand in front of his face like Rocky Marciano and he moved, shuffling in an awkward up and down motion. The crowd outside the gate was howling. Our seconds eyed each other ready to join the rumble if one side or the other moved first.

I didn't know this boy's name and I don't think he knew mine. Our dispute was probably about space and dominance which all seemed trivial now because we were both slaves to a higher class. But just as we do today, we were fighting each other over the remnants of reality they leave to us. When will it end?

He moved in again and we made an exchange of blows that I got the best of. My confidence was building and the fear was gone. I stopped dancing around and stood still. He lumbered in again and lunged at me, I stepped to the side and hit him on the head. He bobbed up and down, I was timing his rhythm so I could pop him on the up stroke, but he switched up on me, charged in throwing blows from an up-right position. I backed up fast to get out of the way of his punches. We now faced each other from different positions. I stood still again. He charged in and I sent a blow to his temple hard as Brad might have. I didn't hold anything back from the punch. He went down and the crowd howled even louder. He didn't move and for a moment, I had bad thoughts. "Stomp him," Polly Wolly hollered. "Stomp him," and the black part of the crowd joined in. "Stomp him, stomp him." The white boy's seconds looked disappointed enough to be in agreement that he should be stomped. I stood there above him with my tongue feeling the split in my lip. Then someone yelled out that the cops were coming and I could hear the sirens blaring. Everybody started running. I didn't know what to do, the boy was still lying on the ground and he hadn't moved.

A boy called Little Charlie and another boy named Bill Chapman climbed through the hole in the fence. Charlie grabbed my jacket and the both of them led me through the hole in the fence. We started running up Tenth Avenue. Once we had gotten two blocks away, they looked at my lip and decide to take me to the hospital. There was lots of blood coming from the wound; Bill Chapman gave me his handkerchief. I went to the curb to look in the side mirror of a parked car. I have large lips and the right side of my upper lip was split wide open. We only had another block to go to reach St Claire Hospital.

St. Claire's was a Catholic hospital and many of the nurses were also nuns in the church. A nurse took me into a room and cleaned the wound up. It wasn't long before a kind doctor came to take a look.

"This is going to need stitches," he said

"I know," I said and nodded.

"What happened?"

"I was in a fight."

"I know that," the doctor said, "and I should see the other guy—right."

I said nothing about the other guy to the doctor, but I wanted to tell him that he was exactly right. He should see what happened to the other guy. The nurse brought in a metal tray with the instruments the doctor needed to stitch up my lip. I received four stitches from the doctor and a lecture on the evils of quarrels and brawls from the nurse, who had now turned to her role as a sister of the church. I agreed with her sincerely. She sensed my honesty— after all, I was a hustler, not a brawler. My lip was swollen and covered with gauze and tape. On our way home, Bill Chapman and Little Charlie lavished me with compliments for knocking the white boy out. They had never seen a person knocked out in a street fight before and felt privileged to be with me.

Little Charlie lived in a building behind my building. I knew him well, but we didn't associate much. Bill Chapman lived in the building next to mine. We were once in the same singing group.

After all the good singers in the neighborhood formed their groups, the non-singers looked on with envious eyes. We felt left out and without a dream, so we formed our own singing groups. And held dreams—it was something to do. Bill had skin that lacked pigment. He looked almost like an albino. His hair looked like it had been bleached and he sucked his finger, but he was good looking and a true friend to me. Bill's father was black and his mother was second generation Cuban/American. She spoke flawless English and was as generous as she was kind. She gave me a sixteenth-birthday party that summer when Sarah couldn't afford to. Bill's parents were separated. He had a sister who spent most of her time with their father in Harlem. Bill and I were close and I spent a lot of time at his home, but he was to me what I was to Brad—a gullible dupe.

Little Charlie told me that he would retrieve my books from whoever had them and bring them to my house. Bill Chapman walked with me to my door. He was really concerned about how I felt. I didn't want him to actually bring me home, so I told him that I was okay. I thanked him and said that I would see him later that evening. Sarah was not home when I arrived. She had taken Beatrice to the clinic. Ed Lewis and Ann Ruth were home. They had finished eating a snack and were doing their homework. They were both alarmed by the sight of the bloody gauze and my taped up lip.

"What happened to you?" Ed Lewis asked. Ann Ruth ran up to me and put her hand on my lip.

"You're hurt," she said.

"I'm okay, I had a fight at school." I sat down on the couch and they sat beside me, the way we used to sit on those Saturday mornings when we sang to Beatrice.

"Who did this do you? I'll get him." Ed Lewis said with a mean grimace on his face. And I could tell he meant it. Once when we lived in Harlem and Ed Lewis was only five years old he hit an older boy in the head. The boy had bullied me earlier and word got to Ed Lewis about it. He was wearing a popular Roy Rogers' saddle ring that had a point that drew droplets of blood from the bully's head. Although, in years, I was the length of World War II older than he was, Ed Lewis was more courageous and often viewed himself as my protector.

"I knocked him out," I said.

The door pushed open. We only locked our door at night back then. It was Beatrice. She entered through the door a few steps ahead of Sarah. Beatrice was eating what was left of an ice cream cone. My mother was carrying a package with the night's dinner in it. Beatrice saw my bandaged lip and it must have frightened her. She dropped her ice cream cone. Then she picked it up and gave it to me. I put her on my lap, ate off the section where the ice cream fell and gave the cone back to her.

"What happened to you?" Sarah asked as she put the package on the table.

"I was in a fight at school with a white boy." I put all the emphasis on the words "white boy," knowing that to Sarah, as with many black parent's, those words would make my part in the occurrence more permissible. Black parent didn't send their children to school with instructions not to get into fights—except with white kids. But because of their own experiences with white people, they were relieved when their children stood up to white children. It was a sign of progress.

"What happened to your mouth?"

"My lip got spilt. I went to the hospital. The doctor stitched it back."

"What was the fight about?"

"He pushed me in the hallway."

"Lord, all this over a push. Is your mouth hurting?"

"No, not much."

"You want some tea?"

"Yes, thank you."

The following week, I found out that the fellow I fought was a boxer with the Police Athletic League and that he was hoping to go on to the Golden Gloves. When I saw him in school he complimented me on the punch that put him away and asked if I wanted to join the P.A.L. he belonged to. I declined. We were respectful of each other, but I was clearly the superior personality. Near the middle of the school year, I signed up to attend Machine and Metal Trades High School where Brad and Ozzie started the previous year. I finished my final year at Junior High School 17, a member of the admired unofficial student hierarchy.

5

The winter went smooth in school and in the neighborhood. The harsh weather put a damper on the Sportsman's gang activities, but ushered in the spring of heroin usage among gang members. A large fragment of the gang found heroin more interesting than diddy-bopping. They had been junkies in our neighborhood all along, but nothing like what sprung up in the summer of 1957. These were guys who had reached their upper teenage years and early twenties—the transitional years. They were out of school and many were jobless. Hardly any of them were prepared for any kind of work other then general labor. Many of them had dropped out of high school and were now entering those transitional years ill prepared. Many of them hadn't even developed good hustling skills. They could bust into a parked car for the contents on the seat, trunk or glove compartment. They could knock someone over the head for his wallet or stick up a liquor store—they could steal. They shot heroin into their veins and stole to get the money to buy more heroin.

They lost the unity and social structure they once had as a gang and splintered off into small competing cliques. They used the rooftops of the Phipps buildings to shoot up and this was where they would hide their works. Works are a needle, a spoon, a tie, and maybe a jar of water. There were two or three sets of works hidden on the rooftops. They all knew where the works were kept and they all used them. The one problem that occurred repetitively was that many of them didn't refill the water jars once they shot up. Water was needed to cook the heroin in the spoon. On 64th Street, one group was always asking another group if there was any water on the roof. The phrase "Any water on the roof" became to mean that the inquirer had scored and was about to take off. Guys who used to harass and beat us up now spent half of their time on the heroin merry-go-round, and the other half nodding off in a drug induced stupefied numbness.

Here is where we parted company with the older boys. Brad, Ozzie and I made a pact that we would never use heroin. We didn't have any respect for the adult junkies in our neighborhood and we derided the older boys for going from street thugs to street junkies. We shunned the myth that smoking marijuana led to shooting heroin. In our minds, marijuana just made you cool—and analytical enough to recognize real danger. We didn't know that all minds wouldn't work like that. For many people, smoking marijuana would be the first step that would develop into an inquisitiveness that would lead to the hard stuff. We were even cultivating our penchant for drinking wine. For us, it had become brutish to drink wine straight from the bottle or to drink what we called Sneaky Pete street wine—the 60 cents a bottle kind that came with a slogan. For us, Thunderbird was no longer the word. We went to the liquor shop for Duff Gordan's Nina Sherry. We were developing a higher class of street sophistication. This was something that was taking place in black neighborhoods throughout the city as young people began to mix and hang out in different neighborhoods.

Our music was jazz. It was hardly sufficient, in our crowd, just to know the major names in jazz. A complete knowledge of the side players was required to illustrate an understanding of the personnel who made the music. It was also necessary to have a store of knowledge in the trivia surrounding jazz. We collected this information the way other youths collected baseball cards. We studied the mix, blends and flourishes sidemen brought to the lead players the way other kids studied the statistics of baseball players. We knew that Paul Chambers provided the steady bass tempo on "Kind of Blue". Or, that Sonny Rollins' playing on the Williamsburg Bridge was the sign that he was working things out. This would hasten his return to the real world and the business of making music. Or, that Afro-Cuban jazz was born when Dizzy Gillespie discovered Chino Pozo in Havana, Cuba. We even had a special etiquette for listening to jazz music in a group. Silence. Absolute silence was required. There could be as many as eight or ten boys in someone's house listening, most likely, to his dad's jazz records and the only time there was talk was in-between records. We all sat around in chairs or on the floor. Many of us closed our eyes as we listened. I secretly wondered if we all heard whatever was playing in the same way—did everyone appreciate Horace Silvers' riff on "Song for My Father," or make the repetitive mental flight with Ahmad Jamal playing "Poinciana." A joint always heightened our listening pleasures, but we also loved the music without being stimulated.

"We're moving back uptown," Brad told us one day while we were watching a basketball game in the playground and listening to The Jazz Messengers on the radio of a man called Sleepy Willie. Our hearts sank. I don't know who was the most disappointed, me or Ozzie.

"When?" Ozzie asked.

"Where?" I asked, before Brad could answer Ozzie.

"In two weeks. We're moving back to 125th Street."

Brad had been seeing an older girl from the Phipps buildings for almost a year. It was rumored that the girl was pregnant. People were saying the baby could be Brad's. I had heard the rumor several times, but I didn't know what to make of it. I didn't think that Brad knew what the implication of this situation was because he continued to see the girl. She was four years older than Brad and lived in an apartment with her two older sisters. The young woman's baby was due around the time Brad and his family would be moving back uptown. It was as though the perpetrator was leaving the scene of the crime before the evidence had arrived. Brad's family cast the roles in this predicament differently, he was only 15 when the 19-year-old girl became pregnant and rumors had them pondering whether to pursue her for statutory rape.

"I'm getting out of Dodge right in time," Brad said.

"Why?" I asked.

"That chick told me she was having a baby and I don't want to be mixed up in that shit."

"But you have been popping her," I said.

"Every weekend, but I used rubbers."

"All the time?" Ozzie asked.

"Almost all the time. There was a few times when the drug store was closed—but she's got an old man she goes with. That's got to be his baby."

"Brad you're gonna have a crumb snatcher," I said and we all laughed.

As it happened, the baby came the week before Brad's family moved. The whole neighborhood was abuzz about it. The girl had some grown cousins who lived in the Phipps houses on 64th Street. They were Asian looking, husky black guys named, Tootie, Boogie and Ching. It was rumored that they were going to take care of Brad if he didn't own up to his responsibilities, but the girl must have explained the situation to them about the possibility that she could legally be charged for statutory rape. The next week, Brad and his family moved back to Harlem. Brad continued to hang out with us for that summer until he met a new crew. I often went up to Harlem to hang out with him. Ozzie was always too busy and seldom went with me. The new projects on 125th Street were 20-story structures built to resemble the shorter cooperative buildings that housed the faculty of Columbia University. The buildings had three elevators that ran at twice the speed of the old ones in the Amsterdam Projects. These buildings were built in a style that counteracted the stigma of public housing.

Brad quickly established relationships with some of the more prominent street-guys in the new project on 125th Street. Zip Jackson was a tall boy with an independent spirit. He was a great basketball player with a fancy Harlem style. Once after walking ten blocks of Harlem with Zip, I felt like everybody in Harlem must have known him. On every block, there were people who spoke to him. Even people from across the street hollered out "Hey Zip." It was like taking a walking tour with a politician or walking with a beloved celebrity. Ross and his brother, Harris Blake, were sharp witted and sharp dressers—hip street kids who also did well in school. Years later, Ross and I struck up a friendship and hung out together. Things happened to Ross in spectacular ways. He lost a leg in an accident in the subway and he married the sister of a famous black author. His brother, who became an accountant, had a more one-sided fate and spent some time in the joint. Stanley Sellers was a quiet guy. He was unexcitable, he spoke calmly and his movements were rhythmic and deliberate. He was very bright and ambitious. As Stanley developed close contact with bulk marijuana dealers, he became Brad's main man and they created an alliance that brought them financial success at an early age.

These guys formed Brad's essential circle of friends. Their relationships with each other were more like Ozzie's and mine when we were Brad's main cohorts. What they had in common was their attraction to Brad's charisma. Brad associated with other groups of boys who were involved in the kinds of criminal acts that warranted heavy jail time. One of these was a boy named Lem Suttleton. Lem was nineteen when Brad took me to his house. He lived with his mother in a tenement building across the street from the projects. After Lem and Brad talked for a moment, Lem took out a bag that had lots of money in it. He started dividing money into spending piles. "Fifty dollars for today," he said to Brad pointing to a stack of tens, "a hundred for tomorrow, and the rest for next week." He stayed high on marijuana, was steeped in the occult, owned two pistols and was clearly a psychotic person. Brad never brought all these people together at one time, but juggled his relationship with them as his needs dictated. Zip and Ross were the two of Brad's uptown crew that I got to know best. I admired these hip Harlemites and I would sometimes go uptown to hangout with them.

5

Right at a time when financial stagnation had set in on me, the cleaners across the street from my building opened a new branch in Greenwich Village. Willie Clark, who had worked at the cleaners for several years now, chose to work at the new branch downtown. He recommended me to take his place at our local branch and I was hired. The inside work was easy. My job basically, was to match clothing to their ticket numbers. Once in a while during the week, I went out on a delivery. On Saturday, I made deliveries all day and the tips nearly equaled my salary for the day. Old Dutch Cleaners was next to the Green Gabriel bar on the corner of 62nd Street on Amsterdam Avenue. I had to be at work at six on Saturday mornings. On many of those mornings, Ned Burner, our neighbor, would be hanging on to the lamppost at the corner outside of the bar, which had been closed for an hour. He was drunk and waiting for someone to help him cross the street that was, at that time in the morning, empty of traffic. I would walk him to the entrance to our building and return across the street for work.

Ozzie had been spending more and more time in the studio. He was meeting popular artists who were also rehearsing for upcoming releases. He met the girls group The Bobbettes from East Harlem several times. The Bobbettes were five young girls who had been together as a group since before their teens. They were ready to record and make themselves stars. All of the girls thought Ozzie was cute. Two of the girls were sisters. One of the sisters found Ozzie beyond cute and wanted to get something started between them. One Saturday the two sisters came downtown to the projects. They found Ozzie in the bullpen. It was evening and there were many small groups of people drinking wine, smoking reefers and talking. I was in a different group than Ozzie when the sisters arrived. It was my habit to move from group to group telling jokes and making people laugh—a roving jester sharing in their bounty.

Ozzie called me over to his group to introduce the girls to me.

"This is Grady Lee," Ozzie told the two sisters. Ozzie knew that I hated both of my names, but I hated my middle name most. The name Lee identified too closely with the South and even though a large proportion of black people in New York had Southern roots, no one wanted to admit it. Ozzie only used Lee when he wanted to disparage me. The four of us finally formed yet another group. We found a bench far off from the others. The conversation started up with them talking about their work in the studio. Then the taller of the two sisters asked Ozzie where he lived. We could see his apartment in the Phipps houses from the bench we sat on.

"It's the apartment on the second floor with the lights off," Ozzie said pointing in the direction of his building.

"The lights are out, let's go up there," she said in a suggestive manner.

"For what?" Ozzie snapped.

"You don't want to take me to your house?"

"It's not that."

"You don't want to be alone with me?"

"I have to be somewhere soon."

"I have to use the bathroom."

"Grady Lee can take you up there," Ozzie said handing me the key.

"Come on Mr. Lee. We'll be back," the tall sister said as she took my hand and led me towards Ozzie's building. We walked down the long tree-lined corridor until we got half way to the building. She stopped walking and we stood there in silence for a moment.

"That lame dude. I thought he would come after us. I don't really need to go. I was just testing him."

Then she turned to look back in the direction where we left her sister and Ozzie. Ozzie wasn't even looking in our direction, but the shorter sister was. It was too dark and we were too far away to tell if they were talking—but if they were it would have been without looking at each other. She started to walk back and I followed. When we reached them, the girl looked at Ozzie with a frown on her face.

"So you wanted to play games," Ozzie said. You said you needed to use the bathroom—what happened?"

"Let's go," the tall girl said to her sister without looking at Ozzie.

"Bye Mr. Lee," she said

"Bye Mr. Lee," her sister said.

Later that spring Ozzie and Darlene's record came out. It was called 'Candy Pop." And right about the same time the Bobbettes came out with a record called "Mr. Lee." The Bobbettes' record was a big hit and put them, for a while, on the map. I went years thinking that the song was named for me—for my willingness to be gracious and as a means at getting back at Ozzie for acting like a cad that night. During the weeks that the record was hot, I didn't mind so much being named Grady Lee. Then I read somewhere that the song was written for a teacher that the girls despised. The song was originally filled with derisive lyrics and that the girls were persuaded by their producer to change the lyrics to avoid a possible libel suit.

"Candy Pop," didn't do so well. Not for Ozzie and Darlene anyway. I was at Brad's house the first time I heard the record on the radio. I was eating some beans and franks Brad made. When the record began to play we looked at each other but said nothing. We listened. The record had kind of a white sound to it. The musical arrangement missed the mark—any mark, and the lyrics were childish. I didn't close my eyes listening to it because I feared I'd see white kids frolicking at Sheep's Meadow in Central Park.

"Candy Pop, candy pop
Ooh candy candy pop."

Our good friend and partner had achieved this great accomplishment. He made a record that was being played on the Dr. Jive radio show and all we did was finish eating our beans and franks. I'm sure that in our hearts, we wished him well, even if for selfish motives, but we didn't know what there was positive to say about this record. We weren't looking at this through the eyes of snobbish jazz enthusiasts. We recognized that money and fame were involved here. Still we had to follow the edict: If you can't say anything good, don't say anything at all.

I later found out this was destined to be a one shot deal. Darlene was a white girl. They couldn't appear on stage together anywhere in the United States. Ozzie, without knowing it, had made history by being in the first mixed-race musical duet in segregated America. We never saw a promotion picture of the duet and Ozzie never spoke about her. Certainly, he never mentioned that Darlene was white. Still, the song did fairly well in certain demographics areas. Well enough to be covered by an all white group that could make public appearances. This group added their own flair to the arrangement and turned the song into a chartered hit. The song was even re-recorded by European groups and did well in Europe. Over the summer, Ozzie waited for the start of his next recording project, but the call never came.

6

In September, I started high school. I was once again reunited with Brad and Ozzie in a school setting. We could hang out, using our gambling skills and tricks against the white boys in the stairwells, and take off afternoons to go to the movies. For us school life was a piece of cake. We went when we wanted to and didn't go when we didn't want to. Things were different for our people in the South. Integration was coming to Southern schools amidst much national turmoil. Central High School in Little Rock, Arkansas was the first to blow up. Mobs of white segregationist prevented black children from entering the school under the threat of violence. The actions of the officials of the school and the officials of the city and the state governments encouraged the mobs. The threat of large-scale death loomed so alarmingly that President Eisenhower had to federalize the Arkansas National Guards and send units of the crack 101st Airborne Division armed with carbines and billie-clubs.

The Daily News always promoted itself as New York's picture news paper and it always tried to entice purchases of its newspaper with dramatic large front page pictures under provocative headlines. The picture in *The Daily News* on the morning of Wednesday September 25th, 1957 brought joy and pride to San Juan Hill. The picture was of a truckload of Paratroopers from the 101st Airborne Division unloading to go into action in Little Rock. The first guy climbing from the truck with his carbine at the ready was Benny Wright, a neighborhood guy whose family still lived at 40 Amsterdam, and whose brother, Eddie had been in my class at P. S. 141. The family bought a house in New Jersey shortly after that glorious picture came out. *The Daily News* sold out early that day at Al and Ben's Luncheonette and also at the other newspaper vendors in our neighborhood. People bought two and three copies. Some to send to relatives and one to hang on the wall. I took pride in the fact that someone from my neighborhood was helping to win the right for our people to attend school in the South. But I didn't see the irony that here in New York where I had the right to go to school with whites; I wasn't making the best of it.

The other occasion when *The Daily News* brought notoriety to our neighborhood happened on what must have been a slow news day. Some boys from our neighborhood went to Central Park and rented a rowboat for an hour. There were more boys than were allowed into the boat, so three of them went to get the boat. Then they rowed the boat to a spot where they couldn't be seen. The other three boys hid there. All the boys took turns sharing the boat. They alternated turns until their hour was nearly up. The second group of boys, on the third switch in the boat, came upon a group of three white boys in a rowboat. They hatched the idea to commandeer the white boy's boat so that they and their comrades could all be at sea together. They lay siege upon the boat carrying the white boys and nearly got it to shore to secure the appropriation, but the white boys put up a resistance that attracted onlookers. Then it appeared some of the onlookers might come to the aid of the besieged white boys. The attackers grabbed a radio, a lunch pail, and some other belongings of the white boys and abandoning their boat in shallow waters made off into the woods with their pillage. The headline on the front page of the next morning's *Daily News* read: **Piracy on the High Seas.** It hung over a picture of a vacant rowboat in the Central Park Lake. The inside article told a distorted story of all the riches; watches, rings and hard currency that had been plundered.

One rainy Saturday night, I didn't have any place to go and no money, so I took an early bath and went to bed. I was rereading an old Alfred Hitchcock novelette when someone knocked at the door. Sarah, Ed Lewis and my two sisters were watching television. I heard someone open the door.

"He's gone to bed," I heard Sarah say.

"I just want to talk to him for a minute," it was Brad's voice.

"Go on back."

There was a knock on my bedroom door.

"Come in."

"What you doing in bed this early man?"

"It's raining and I ain't got nothing to do"

"I come all the way down here to hang out with you and find you in bed. Get dressed, let's go hang out."

"Brad, where in the world are we going to hang out in all that rain?

"We gonna make some money."

"Make some money, what are you talking about. It's raining cats and dogs out there—you crazy?"

"Perfect weather to snatch a pocketbook."

"Oh yeah, now I know you crazy."

"Come on get dressed Grady, don't be a punk. I'll show you, we can make some quick bucks. Ain't much people out there in all this rain. Once we find our mark, we hit and get."

I knew it was way cross the line for me, but resisting Brad's charisma had become impossible to do and the next thing I know we're walking West End Avenue from 65th street to 72nd Street looking for a target. It's raining like crazy and we are soaking wet. On our first trip back down from 72nd Street, when we reached 67th Street, there was a white woman walking ahead of us alone. "This is it," Brad said. "You get the pocketbook." We walked faster and then when we were right behind the woman, Brad hollered "Get it" and started to run. I ran with him and in a couple of steps, we reached the startled woman. I grabbed the pocketbook, which fell easily from her hand. The woman let out a scream and we ran to the corner of 66th Street and turned west into the block. That this was the last block of Manhattan before the train yard and the Hudson River never dawned on us. The woman stayed at the corner screaming. A few doors down the block; there was a parking garage. The attendant heard the screams and came out into the streets with a large wrench in his hand. We ran right by him. He took off after us. We ran to the end of the block where there was a sign that read: DEAD END. There was a six-foot brick wall that separated the street from the drop to the train yard and the tracks that led to where the old slaughterhouses used to operate. Without any hesitation, Brad jumped up and straddled the wall; then dropped out of sight. I made a leap for the top of the wall, but I missed. The parking attendant was closing in on me. I threw the pocketbook over, I made a desperate leap, and my hands clutched the top of the wall. I pulled myself up to the top. Because of the darkness, I couldn't see how much of a drop there was. I hung from the top and then released my hands. The fall must have been twenty feet; I landed on my stomach. When I got up from the fall, I saw Brad on his hands and knees searching for his eyeglasses.

"Come on let's go," I said as I picked up the pocketbook.

"My glasses, my glasses," Brad babbled. His voice had a vulnerability I had never heard from him before. I grabbed him by his arm and pulled him away. We could hear the siren from a police car at the entrance to the train yard on 60th Street. We ran some more and came to an open boxcar. We climbed up into the boxcar and sat in a darkened corner. Through the holes in the walls of the boxcar, we saw the police car speed by. It was still raining hard. We sat in silence. In a few minutes the police car returned down the driveway between the tracks. It exited the yard and drove up West End Avenue to continue its search.

"Where's the pocketbook?"

"I got it"

"Take the money out and leave the pocketbook in here."

"Okay."

I emptied the pocketbook; there was a five dollar bill and two ones. We left the boxcar, climbed over the fence at 64th Street and ran across the street to the Phipps complex. We entered the last building and walked to the back hallway door that led to the courtyard. We crossed the yard, walked up the back steps of the first building on 63rd Street, and emerged from the front door. Now we felt safe. "How much?" Brad asked.

"Seven dollars."

"Damn, we could have gone to jail for seven dollars."

"That's right, 'I said, "here you keep it, I'm going home and go back to bed."

"I lost my glasses. We gotta go back for my glasses."

"Not me."

Brad looked at me like he wanted to fight. "We gotta go back for my glasses," he said clinching his teeth.

"I'll get your glasses tomorrow."

"You better."

"I'll call you if I find them. I'm feeling sick, I'm going home."

"Walk me to the subway station.

"Fuck you," I said and walked on home.

I read Sunday's newspaper looking for any report of the crime. Two days later, I went into the train yard from the 60th Street entrance. There would not be anything suspicious about my wandering around, because kids from our neighborhood had been doing that for a century. During the early twentieth century so many kids from San Juan Hill were killed by the West End Avenue Trolley and in the train yard, that West End Avenue was called "Death Avenue." I walked up to the spot where we had jumped over the wall. The eyeglasses were on the ground unbroken. Later I called Brad for him to come pick up his eyeglasses. He was calm when I saw him.

"No more shit like that for me," I said as I gave him his glasses. I was anxious and ashamed. I thought about the woman.

"Hey, you win some, you lose some," Brad said taking out a handkerchief to clean his eyeglasses. "Walk me to the subway."

"Fuck that," I said knowing at that moment that I would never again be influenced by Brad in the way I'd been for all the time we hung out. I felt a surge of independence well up inside me against Brad's charismatic pull. "Fuck you." I remembered some of the things Polly Wolly tried to teach me about growing up in our environment. "If you gonna make it, you can't feel sorry for nobody," Polly Wolly often told me. I didn't feel sorry for Brad, but I felt sorry for the woman and for myself. I had emotions that I couldn't deny.

They suggested that I wasn't gonna be a successful tough guy. This was the first time I seriously questioned my attachment to streetlife. I feared the consequences of getting busted—that's okay, but I also had feelings of remorse about the crime. This had definitely been a close call; had we been caught, we would have made *The Daily News* and been put into reform school—often the prelude to a life of crime.

San Juan Hill

CHAPTER FIVE
Like, Wow Man

<u>1</u>

When Brad moved back to Harlem, I didn't think that Ozzie would continue to hang around with me. And he didn't at first, because he was busy in the recording studio and then, for a period, he acted the part of a budding star. He recorded four more songs that were never released. By the time it became clear to him that his career was over, at least, with that group of people, he came around. I was really surprised. By then I had resumed hanging with my old friends down in the back when I wasn't working at the cleaners. I went to Evane Smith's house often and when I didn't go there, I went to Bill Chapman's house. Ozzie started knocking at my door or calling me from the window. We were a team of two now. We'd go to the movies. Sometimes we went to Joan's house on 53rd Street when Butchie was there. When we had money, we'd go to Harlem for a five-dollar bag. Once when Ozzie and I made some money in the playground playing cards, we went uptown and bought a ten-dollar bag of marijuana. Our intentions were to roll up the entire bag and sell loose joints. It was during the week and for some reason, we didn't divide the bag up that evening. Two days later when I saw Ozzie and asked for my share of the reefer, he told me that it was gone. His younger brother Chad found where he hid the bag and Chad took it and smoked it all with his crew. I fell for it right away and wanted to confront Chad about it.

"That shit ain't right," I said as we walked to the community center. "You gotta get my money from him."

"I know," Ozzie said, "but what you gonna do—kick his ass?"

"I don't want for it to get to that."

"Don't worry, I'm not gonna let him get away with this. I'm gonna get him back."

"How?"

"I don't know yet, but believe me, I ain't gonna let him get away with this."

"Ozzie, I know it's your brother, but this shit just ain't right,"

When we got to the community center, I left Ozzie downstairs playing ping pong. I went up to the gym to play basketball. In between games, I sat on a bench sorting out Ozzie's tale. Ozzie had a mind inspired by intrigue and duplicity. If I confronted Chad, he would deny taking the reefer. That would lead me back to Ozzie. I concluded that at the very least, the two of them conspired against me. My money had gone up in smoke I smiled. I was mad, but decided to let it go.

I started avoiding Ozzie, but the more I evaded him the more determined he became to hang out with me. He even went with me down the back. Ozzie hated going to Evane's house and he didn't care for the crowd there. He called them squares and said that they were not with it. He didn't like Evane at all and she didn't like him. Evane was a bright girl, street-wise and articulate. And she didn't mind telling Ozzie what she thought of him. Whenever we went to Evane's house, Ozzie had a smart-ass attitude.

"I hope you ain't planning to stay here long," is the first thing he would say to me loud enough for everyone to hear him.

"You didn't have to come," was Evane's usual retort.

"I wasn't talking to your nosey ass."

"But I'm talking to you—you little weasel. Ain't nobody here send for you."

"Grady, I'm going—I can't stand being around this funky bitch."

"Funky bitch? You called me a funky bitch. I bet you wish you could get some of this funky bitch—you little dick weasel."

"I wouldn't fuck you with a borrowed dick."

"That's the only way you would have a dick—borrow it."

All this would die down in a few minutes and Ozzie and I would stay there for hours after his encounter with Evane. The girls admired his good looks, but they couldn't stand his personality. He went there with me partly because he had nothing else to do and partly out of his sense of duty. We had been partners for four years now and he must have wanted to preserve what was left of the dynamic triad we had with Brad.

The teenagers from the back didn't go to the community center nightly. They were more secure at home and at each other's homes. This might have been because they felt that the community center was for street kids—teenagers without comfortable home settings and teenagers without homework from school. The teenagers in the back had their own hang out—and that was at Evane's house. We were always welcome at Evane's house. Evane's mother, who had been a dancer at some of the most popular Harlem clubs in the late forties, had two rules: no fighting and no cursing. "Sit your little ass down and behave or go home," she told anyone who got out of line. She joined in on all the conversations. She laughed and joked with us as equals. Many of the teenagers addressed her by her first name and she seemed to enjoy it. She was a dark-skinned, pretty woman with a high-pitched voice and a birthmark on her left cheek. I always called her Mrs. Smith.

"Now that Malcolm Tibbs is a good looking boy," she once told me.

"You think so?"

"Now Grady, you know it. And your friend, that what's his name, he's good looking too, but..."

"You mean Ozzie."

"Yeah him, with his arrogant self."

"And what about me?"

"Grady what you don't have in looks, you make up for in personality. You too sweet and I'm going to marry you one day."

I've always appreciated Mrs. Smith's keen insights.

Evane loved music. She had all the latest rock and roll records. Latin music was popular among black teenagers during this period of time. Evane had some Latin music and other kids would bring Latin records with them. Tito Puente, Eddie Palmieri, Ray Barretto and the Latin bands were now filling the dance halls that once catered to the calypso beat. Little Moe was the best Latin dancer in the neighborhood and everyone marveled as he swung two girls at once on the dance floor. Evane and her sister Patti had lovely voices and they would often sing along with the music that was playing. Their record player was always on, so it was like a marathon dance party at their house.

It was at Evane's house that I fell in love with Audrey Marble. She was a tall dark skinned girl with short hair, a heart-melting smile and sparkling brown eyes. She had a divine voice and sang in a group that included Patti Smith and Charlotte Monk. Whenever I danced close with Audrey, my legs would tremble uncontrollably and the more I tried to control the tremor the worst it became. I was embarrassed by it, but I constantly preferred to dance with Audrey. She always seemed pleased whenever I asked her to dance. While I clung close to her soft enchanting body, I imagined that she cherished being able to induce this affect on me. And, I could tell that she enjoyed dancing with me. I didn't know then that I loved her or, that she loved me—or that the tremors were set off by the genuine attraction we had for each other. It wasn't until years later when we were both in committed relationships with other people that we acknowledge our love. Many love affairs got started at these after school sessions at Evene's house, but I still feel melancholy about what did not develop between Audrey Marble and me. After school, during the week and on the weekends, the party went on. Building 242 was the most popular building in the back. Besides Evane and her family, Manny Black and Willie Clark lived there with their families.

Some of the more popular Puerto Ricans kids lived in the back and came to Evane's house. Julio Nun, a tall popular Puerto Rican boy lived in 242 with his family. Julio and all of his family were close to the Clark Family. Julio was once at Clark's house when I was there and the three of us were lauding Bobby Darren's version of the song "Mack the Knife." Clark's father, a dark-skinned West Indian man, from whom Clark surely got his work ethic, asked us if we wanted to hear the real version of that song. Then he played a Louis Armstrong recording of "Mack the Knife." We were floored with the authenticity of its arrangement and its superior musical quality. The Armstrong version of "Mack the Knife" had a realness that made the Bobby Darren version sound like tinsel. Roberto Santanna, who was spectacularly gay and for a time was Evane's best friend, also lived in the building. Roberto was a bohemian dresser who discovered the unorthodoxies of Greenwich Village far before I knew how to get there. Everyone was always welcome at Mrs. Smith's apartment except during school hours. No one ever hung out there when they should have been in school.

2

My attendance at school was so miserable that I failed my first year at high school. It had become easier for me to go to the movies than to go to school. I had gotten to the point where I didn't need the enticement of Brad or Ozzie to skip out on school. I'd go to the movies by myself. I spent the better part of my tenth grade school season in the movie houses on 42nd Street. The price was as little as a quarter if you got there before nine in the morning. I'd smoke a joint, hop on a train to forty-duce and buy a dozen-glazed donuts to eat in the theater. The theaters on the duce didn't play current pictures, so I got a chance to catch up on some old classics. While other teenagers were going to school to acquire skills and learn rudiments that would prepare them for college or jobs, I became a film critic. The combination of Orson Welles and Joseph Cotton intrigued me. I saw them in "Citizen Cane," but I've always felt that their finest picture was "The Third Man." The theme song in that picture, played on a guitar-zither by Viennese Anton Karas, has haunted me for life. That music exposed me to a new instrument and a new sound. Karas was a self-taught musician who was discovered playing in a tavern in Vienna and tapped to score the 1949 movie. It was the beginning of my acceptance of and interest in the music of other parts of the world—although I didn't know it at the time.

The espionage author Graham Greene, who also had a hard time in school, wrote "The Third Man." Graham dropped out of school at the age of fifteen and became a writer. The story takes place in post World War II Vienna and is really an old theme about war and corrupt profiteering. In this case, the villain, Harry Lime, an American expatriate, runs a multinational coterie that used the devastated aftermath of the war to run profiteering schemes. Post war Vienna had all kinds of swindles going on. Black marketing in food, gasoline, cigarettes, tires and fake passports were expected and, to some degree, acceptable, but Harry Lime and his associates were despised because they hustled diluted penicillin that was adding to the death toll in that section of war torn Europe. The plot revolves around the mystery of Lime's death as the authorities were closing in on him. And, his newly arrived down and out-writer friend Holly Martin's efforts to get to the bottom of the riddle and clear his name. To raise the suspense, Harry Lime, the central figure in the film, doesn't appear on screen until halfway through the movie. Plus, we learn that he and his co-conspirators have faked his death. But the soul of this film is in the starkness of unfamiliar Europeans faces, the black and white beauty of the scenery, even in a bombed out setting of eighteenth century buildings and cobblestone streets that echo foot steps at night. And those interludes of seductive zither strumming combine with that to make this movie a cinematic success.

I had given up school for the movies, but I hadn't given school up to cease learning—I was still learning. Learning is forever possible under almost any circumstances. To paraphrase the poet, Amiri Baraka, you will learn God knows what, from God knows who. I was getting an education at the movie houses of 42nd Street. "The Jackie Robinson Story" taught me about perseverance. That if you work hard and get to be the best at what you do no force can hold you down. Robinson proved that the best way to combat racism was to whack it out of the arena with a baseball bat and show it up for what it is—an inferior human failing.

"The Grapes of Wrath" gave me a lesson in Social Studies. The American oligarchy would use poor white people to make a profit with the same degree of malice they applied to Negroes. It didn't matter to the patrician if the victim was black or white; you just needed to be weak, defenseless and exploitable. A decade of drought and the dire farm conditions at the end of the Great Depression conspired to drive Oklahoma sharecroppers into the net of the exploiters. Thousands of families were driven from their homes because they couldn't produce enough crops to eat and pay their bills. They were kicked off the land they farmed. There were rumors of work in California, so the Okies headed west. The roads to California were littered with hardships and exploiters. This is a sympathetically written story of exploitation and calamity. I became interested in the writer who wrote this heart-rending portrait of the downtrodden, and then I learned the named John Steinbeck. But here's the rub. From my earlier experiences with some of the same kind of crackers as the Okies were, it was plain that they, in the pitiful state that they were in, still identified more with their white oppressors than with the analogies they shared with the Negro.

John Steinbeck, who must have analyzed and exposed all the traits of human behavior in his many novels, also wrote the screen play for the movie "Life Boat," staring the renowned Tallulah Bankhead and directed by none other than, my man, Alfred Hitchcock. The movie has an all star supporting cast including Canada Lee, whose black character is treated with dignity and portrayed with distinction. This movie went far beyond what I would have been taught in my tenth grade psychology class on the state of human behavior in a psychoneurotic situation. A German war ship sinks a luxury liner. Eight people are cast away in a lifeboat. They picked up a ninth passenger from the hostile waters and he happens to be the captain of the Nazi ship which itself has gone down. The passengers are from diverse backgrounds, which gives the author and the director a chance to experiment with the interactions of people who, under normal circumstances, would have had little contact with each other. Here, alone on the high seas they have to coalesce for the sake of their survival. They must include the enemy in on their coalition; his expertise is necessary to their staying alive. They even let the German take control of the boat, but he again betrayed humanity by hoarding water and hiding a compass which he secretly used to steer the boat towards Nazi-controlled waters. When the castaways discovered that a Nazi is always a Nazi, they do what the rest of the world must always do—they slay the demon.

From the movie "Inherit the Wind," I got a lesson in Religion and Science. I learned how the participation of zealot religious absolutists in the political polemic can poison the discussion and obscure reasonable thought. Those people, who claim that God talks to them daily, seek to impose tenets of their faith over scientific theory and believers of all stripes. The people who really talk with God daily and keep the conversation to themselves are the ones who struggle to find peace and a satisfactory accommodation for all people. God, I think, never plots against His creation. But God is often used by some, to polarize God's people here on earth. If William Jennings Bryan had prosecuted the Copes-Monkey case before his three failed attempts to become president of the United States, the popularity he would have gained from being on the dark side of that issue, would have propelled him into the White House. Every generation has its fanatics.

The movie "Advise and Consent" augmented my Political Science knowledge by giving me an understanding of the working of two of the three branches of government and demonstrated how the element of partiality often works against the common good. Politicians often lose sight of the main objective and confuse what is good for them personally or what is good for their party, with what is good for the people. Rulers mask their true motivation in pious prose about the uplifting of humankind while they line the pockets of their clique. The multitudes are fed encoded promises in empty chatter that are never realized. A sucker is truly born every day. I didn't know then that by the first decade of the twenty-first century the common good of the people would be a meaningless sentiment to nearly all politicians. Or, that the more blatant politicians became in their ill treatment of the people, the more popular their doctrine became to the people. This kind of anomaly, I believe, portends monumental reversals in the future or the end of the march towards a true democracy.

"12 Angry Men" put me in touch with the judicial system, at least at the point when the peers of those who are accused of going afoul of the law take over. And the lesson I learned from this movie is to stand up for what you believe in, even in the face of seemingly insurmountable odds. That, when all things are equal, the system could work. I know that it once worked in my favor. I wondered how Polly Wolly would feel about this assessment—does the system recognize often enough, the sometimes-arbitrary injustice of the circumstance that brings one before it. Should it?

International Studies: I received my first comprehensible lesson in geopolitics in the Movie "The Ugly American" way before I read the contemplative thinking on revolution by Karl Marx, Ernesto "Che" Guevara, Mao Tse-Tung, and Malcolm Shabazz. All of the elements that the competing powerful countries used to fight surrogate wars in under-developed countries to further their influence around the world came clear at me. The West is always pushing its way on the rest of the world in often violent and ugly struggles. America is always pushing this thing it calls democracy while a little black boy, who should have been in school, sits in a movie theater eating a glazed donut thinking "It ain't worked for me." If democracy is all they say it is, they wouldn't have to force it on countries at gunpoint. Just leave it on the front seat of a car parked in front of the United Nations building and countries would steal it. I learned this lesson even before the real lesson of Vietnam was taught on the nightly news telecasts. Apparently, a lesson the fathers and mothers of George Bush's Iraq war have not yet learned.

Psychology 101: The only movie, that I watched completely and still had six of my twelve donuts when I walked out of the theater was "A Face in the Crowd" staring Andy Griffith as the philosophical hillbilly singer Lonesome Rhodes. This movie took away my appetite for the sweet delights and kept my attention riveted to the screen. Lonesome Rhodes rose from a small town jailhouse drunk to become the most powerful and influential entertainer in the country. Rhodes patterned his image on that of the down-home good old boy—aw-shucks now.

He was first a sensation on the radio. His stardom attracts sponsors, endorsements, and fans. Rhodes is given a TV show and his popularity increases even more. People listen to his every word; they love his home-sprung wit, enjoy his singing, laugh at his jokes and buy what he endorses. Rhodes has forged a huge audience of conformists. People who are drawn to the enticement of cultural patterns that makes them feel safe in the illusion that robotic obedience is normal. He has a whole region of the country in his hip pocket, but Rhodes is a fraud with Machiavellian political aspirations. And, there did come a time when his powers of persuasion over the people would be put to the ultimate test. Would they vote for the person Rhodes endorses for president, a man who had secretly discussed Rhodes' bounty, of a special cabinet level position created especially for him? And then would Rhodes eventually ascend to higher heights and become master of the political universe?

We never find this out, because the woman, who discovered him in the jailhouse tank, exposed Lonesome Rhodes to his legions of fans as a fraud. At the end of one of his broadcasts, Rhodes is smiling into the camera while the credits are rolling down the screen and the sound is turned off. As he smiles into the camera, Rhodes is verbally deriding his audience as dupes and hicks. His smile disguised his words. The woman, a long time mentor who had been jilted by Rhodes for a buxom high school cheer leader, is in the sound room and disgusted by his deceit, she turns the sound back on so Rhodes' wide audience can hear him. And, as the credits continued to roll, he continued to smile and scorn his viewers as two-bit suckers. He smiles broadly into the camera and boast of having them all in his pocket like sheep under his command. Suckers, nincompoops, suckers he says into the camera smiling, not knowing that his viewers can hear his every word. Then the phones at the station start to ring; all hell erupted on Rhodes. All of the duped wants their pound of Rhodes' flesh. The picture ends with Rhodes raving about how he would rise again, "You'll see, you'll see," he says as the credits that end the movie roll down the screen. As I review the events of the years since I saw this picture, Rhodes has, indeed arisen, time and time again, disguised in other personalities. Currently, he is back on the radio. This picture taught me something about how the masses are controlled and herded in any direction those in power choose. Whenever I hear modern day political pitchmen speak I think of old Lonesome Rhodes, put on my safety helmet and call out the names of my father's three dogs, Bozo, Battlemazo, Kazam.

Now while I learned all the lessons these films taught, their immediate application lied dormant in me for some many years. But as incidents arose that provoked memory of this or that lesson gleaned from this or that movie, that education has proven to be very precious, although the school system and my tenth grade teachers would have thought it a poor substitute. And maybe I should have too. I can't trade my movie tutelage in for a diploma that attest to the fact that I have achieved a certain level of proficiency in this or that area of endeavor. Our society has to have some authenticated way to measure what it is we have learned and my way was surely too whimsical to be gauged by those standards.

3

On Saturdays, in the summers, the playground was crowded all day. In the morning, the sound of Thelonious Monk and Charlie Rouse, or one or the other of Monk's sidemen could be heard floating live out of his opened window on 63rd Street. Young mothers would be over at the small swings with their toddlers. Young boys and girls climbed the monkey bars by the fence. Dennis' mother would be setting on a bench by the sandpit as he played nearby. Old junkies would be nodding off or grooming each other like primates, on benches that bordered the big swings. The park attendant would be up at the bar having a beer and waiting until park closing time. In the center of the playground, a group of white and Spanish boys would be playing a game of hockey on roller skates. The area around the basketball court was the primary focal point for the main crowd. On the benches that bordered the basketball court, there would be a card game or two going on. There would be a group of old men in their fifties, drinking and talking loud. Another group of old men, also in their fifties, sat watching the games and shouting instructions to the players on the court. A group of boys waited for their turn to play the winners of the game in progress and talking shit to pass the time.

"You can't play no ball. You ain't shit," Kenny, a short annoying boy, said to a tall lanky boy named Ello.

"I'll run over your ass," Ello countered.

"Can't nobody in your family run over me, I'm ya boss man."

"Oh shit, that Negro playing the dozen with you Ello," another boy instigated to heighten the tension.

"My family ain't got nothing to do with this," Ello said, "I'll beat you doing anything."

"Of all the insects in the world, I'd rather be a mosquito, to climb up on your Momma's knee and exercise my peter." Kenny said falling for the instigation. The crowd roars with laughter. Ello put on a serious face that warned the other boy that he had gone too far. "That's a rhyme man,' Kenny says in retreat.

"I'm getting mad," Ello said, "I don't want to hear your shit, so you better put a egg in your shoe and beat it." The crowd roars again, as the basketball game ended and new players took to the court.

Duke Reeves was the best basketball player in our neighborhood. He was only 6 feet tall, but he was fast and cunning. He was a good outside shooter and a good ball handler. He was a skinny young man, but tough as nails—off and on the court. Duke was a few years older than I was, but we played during the same period—I was, for a brief period, his successor. I was the second best player in our neighborhood during that time, but behind us, about three years, were a group of boys who were to revolutionize playground basketball. The most prominent among them were the three Donovan brothers, Ivan, Chico and Vern. Ivan, dubbed Ivan the Terrible was 6 feet 5 inches tall. He was a rebounding machine and he could shoot from the outside. Chico was 6 feet 2 inches. He was tough and unmovable under the basket. Vern was 6 feet 1 inch. He was like a magician who flew through the air like Superman making the defense commit itself before he decided whether to shoot with the right hand or the left hand or to pass the ball. Chico and Vern had personality on the court as well as off the court. Ivan's personality was invested in the game and in scholarship. In the sixties, while he was still in college, Ivan tried out for the New York Knickerbockers basketball team. He didn't make the cut, so Ivan played for the South American league before becoming a New York City bureaucrat. They, along with two or three others from their age group, brought a spectacular rhythm of movement to the game that made it even more exciting to watch.

Saturday mornings in the playground would start off with half-court games and by noon, teams for a full-court game would have been chosen. There was always a conscious effort to choose sides that were balanced in talent because it made for a more interesting challenge. These games were long and argumentative because on most occasions they were played without a referee. The players called out whenever they believed they had been fouled. All but the most flagrant foul was contested. Often the dispute was decided by a set of the finger twosy. The mix of the teams constantly changed during the course of the day. Mr. France, who had once been coach of a team I played with, sat with George Kelly, Robbie Barnes and other old men shouting out directions to either team, they just wanted to see good basketball played.

There was a popular man known only as Pops. He didn't hang out so few people knew his real name. The only thing I had ever heard him called was Pops. That is the only way I know him. Pops would walk into the playground with a folded newspaper hanging out of his back pocket. He was always dressed in a rumpled suit, a plaid shirt and necktie. He always wore a hat and sometimes wore a thin tan raincoat. He had a presence that would be distinguished the moment he entered the playground. Sometimes a game would be in progress—but whenever Pops reached the half court line, someone would throw him the ball. Pops would place his hat gently on the ground. He would hold the ball for a moment as he eyed the basket. Then he would take his leaping two-hand shot from the half-court line, the tail of his coat flying behind him. If he made the shot on the first try, everybody roared their approval. If he missed, he asked only one other try. Then, as quickly as he arrived, Pops picked up his hat, waved bye to everyone and he was gone.

"Later Pops," we all cried out.

Pops' stats were recorded on the back of a bench that bordered the basketball court. An o cut into the bench indicated a missed shot; an x was a basket. Over the years, Pops shot an amazing 75 percent from the half-court line.

Duke and I seldom played on the same team. Whenever two guys were choosing sides they made sure to each pick one of us. But I remember how games usually turned out when we were on the same side. Once Duke and I were paired with his brother Truman. Truman was nearly as good a player as I was then and when he got to college, he became even better than I was. Our other team members were Ralph Lopez, a Puerto Rican boy with game and Little Moe whose game was as deliberate as his joint rolling. Little Moe had called to play the winners of the current game and choose us as teammates.

The winning team was a much taller and beefy set of guys. Rube and Rave France, the sons of Mr. France, the coach, were big strong boys. Rube would have made a formable center, but he always played a little man's game. He dribbled the ball too much and it was often taken from him. It was a case of Rube not recognizing where his true talents were because he wanted to do what everyone else did. Rave had a presence on the court, but he couldn't shoot and he played a lazy and disinterested game. Rave shot the ball as if he was waiting for a photographer to snap a picture before he released the ball. The third player was Sweetpea Monk, the nephew of the pianist. Sweetpea wasn't tall, but he was fast. His weakness was that he played around too much always seeking attention. He hogged the ball and played with poor judgement. He was one of those guys who played rough but was always calling foul, and when his team was down, he criticized his teammates during the game. Their fourth and fifth team members were solid players; boys who contributed the most to their previous winning game. One was a boy named George Hodgkin, who a few years later wrote a book about drug addiction. The other boy was Ernest Kahn, who would later become a musician.

The games usually lasted until a team reached sixty points. This game started fast, with our team scoring at will. We smoked them throughout our first thirty points. There was a time in the game when the score was forty-four to thirty. Sweetpea was disruptive and protested every play. At one point, Rube, who should have been in the backcourt, dribbled the ball down the court unguarded. When he crossed the half-court line, I picked him up. I reached my long arms out and touched the ball with my right arm as it was coming up to his dribbling hand. The ball came loose. I ran it down and started to dribble it towards the basket. Rube was slow in reacting but Sweetpea was able to make it down the court to guard against the fast break. Duke and I converged on him from different angles of the court. Sweetpea positioned himself in the center of the key to be able to both intercept a pass and guard whoever tried to shoot the ball. As I approached him dribbling the ball, I swung the ball behind my back with my right hand as if to pass it to Duke who was approaching from the opposite side of the court. Sweetpea thought that a behind the back pass was happening—he fell for the fake pass and ran off to guard Duke. I stopped the pass with my left hand making a loud smacking sound, took another step with the ball back in my right hand and made a leaping lay-up shot. Sweetpea was left with an incredulous look on his face, astonished that he was guarding the man who didn't have the ball. My teammates and the spectators roared with delight.

In those days, players who made spectacular plays were ridiculed if they showed sign of gloating. The proper etiquette was to show no emotion and to appear simply ready for the next play. I turned around and ran down the court expressionlessly. Then I displayed a disappointed frown, as if something even more spectacular should have occurred. Those days, to humiliate an opponent by showing no emotion was the most resounding way of saying this was how much better I am than you are. Like saying you're not surprised at your superior abilities. To celebrate was far too shallow and egotistical.

Sweetpea called "Walking." He even reenacted my movements making sure to make an extra step to illustrate that it was impossible to make such a play without taking too many steps. The game was disrupted with arguments for a long while. Then the old men on the bench intervened.

"The play looked legal to us," Mr. France said.

"Forty-six—thirty," George Kelly called out the score to suggest the game should be continued.

"Play ball," Mr. Barnes instructed.

Sweetpea took the ball and slammed it down on the court. He went to the bench, took up his towel, wiped his face and started walking out of the playground after cursing his team members. Through it all, I never showed my pleasure for having caused the controversy, but, of course, that was the ultimate celebration.

4

Some of the guys on the benches across the playground, high on dope, took notice of the upheaval and mocked Sweetpea as a sore-loser as he passed them on his way to the gate. Mo' The Mississippi Gambler, this is how Martin Rider referred to himself, waved a "Get lost" sign at Sweetpea. This is the kind of attention a display of emotion brought you in this New York City playground. Sitting with Mo' The Mississippi Gambler was Duke Jose, who had not noticed a thing. Duke was still engaged in what was known as sucking your own johnson. This is when a dope fiend got off on a nod that winds up with his face in his lap. Pedro Ruiz sat next to Duke Jose. Pedro had once been a boxer. Vance and Marsha sat on the same row of benches, a distance down from the other group with enough space between them to suggest that the two groups were not together. Vance played the trumpet and when he got high, he liked to talk of the days when he was the president of the St Louis Musician's Union. These were old junkies, in their thirties—about as old as junkies get to be, but many of them were very colorful characters.

Mo' The Mississippi Gambler was a tall light-skinned man. He was fond of saying that he would bet that the next day wouldn't be whatever the next was to be. On a Saturday he would say "I'll bet you that tomorrow ain't Sunday—U'm The Mississippi Gambler."

He also fancied himself a gangster. I once saw him sitting on a playground bench playing Tonk with some young boys. Mo' was high and nodding. His eyes appeared closed and a cigarette hung from his mouth. He had his money spread out on a newspaper in front of him. Every time it was his turn to pluck a card from the deck, they had to call out his name. Everyone was sure that he was out of it. One boy reached over to take a dollar off of the newspaper in front of Mo'. "Put that back motherfucker." Mo' said in a slow, dawdling voice without widening the slits in his eyes. In the sixties, Mo' fathered a child with Tommy Borden's sister a girl named Anna. The day after the baby was born, Mo' got high to celebrate the occasion, and then he went to the hospital to visit Anna and their new son. Mo' slowly bopped into Anna's room empty-handed. Anna was very disappointed and asked "Where's the flowers?" Mo' looked at her through tiny eye slits; brought both of his hands to the center of his chest and in a dry and distant voice he said, "Baby, real gangsters don't buy flowers."

Pedro Ruiz, the boxer, would get high in the evening and go to a section of the projects where the benches were placed in a square. To him, this might have resembled a boxing ring. There, he would attract a crowd of on-lookers as he went through his shadow boxing routine, grunts and all. He threw punches into the air, danced around, thumped his nose and ducked imaginary blows. His workouts lasted nearly an hour and at the end of his exhibitions, he wiped his face with a towel as he received a round of applause. Then he would sit down and nod off.

Vance Ford was a good musician. He moved to New York with his wife and children hoping to hit it big. In the fifties, a lot of jazz musicians were influenced by Charlie "Yardbird" Parker the great alto saxophonist. There was a myth built up around Bird and his use of heroin. Musicians thought that it was heroin that ignited Bird's creative genius. They all admired Bird and wanted to imitate him. Vance sensed a deeper connection to Bird. Bird grew up in Kansas City, Missouri and Vance grew up in St. Louis, Missouri. They were brother musicians from the Heartland, so it took little effort for Vance to fall into the drug myth about Bird. Vance carried his horn with him all the time as if to remind himself that he was a musician. He found some work in bands around the city, but never anything solid and lasting. He lived in a building in the rear of the projects with his wife and children, but his wife became weary of his ways and sent him packing.

Vance moved into a small apartment in the Phipps complex with Marsha Oxford. Marsha was a dark-skinned woman who knew the street life as well as any dude in the neighborhood. She had been to jail a few times for drug possession and the street crowd respected her. I was once up at their apartment drinking wine and smoking reefer with them. They seemed eager for me to leave, but I didn't respond to any of the signals at the time. We were all sitting at a table near the bathroom. They got up without a word, went into the bathroom, and closed the door. I poured another drink of wine and took a sip. Pretty soon, I heard Marsha crooning through the door. She sounded like she was having sex. I looked at the door and she groaned again. I couldn't believe my ears, that they would go into the bathroom with me sitting at the kitchen table to have sex. I should have gotten up and left, but this was all too incredulous, I had to see for myself. I opened the door. There was Vance, and Marsha fully dressed. She was setting on the side of the tub with a long round rubber band tied around her upper arm and a needle stuck into the vein in the lower part of her arm. Vance sat on the toilet cover leaning over her controlling the flow of the substance. When she signaled him, he'd push down on the needle's stem. Marsha moaned in euphoria. I closed the door and left.

5

The new Greenwich Village branch of Old Dutch Cleaners closed earlier then did the Amsterdam branch so sometimes on Saturday evenings, Clark stopped by the cleaners where I worked. For weeks, he had been telling me about the people, places and the bohemian life style in the Village. Many people there, at that time, referred to themselves as "Beatniks." One Saturday evening, Clark insisted that I accompany him to the Village. We got cleaned up and I met him at his house. We took the subway to West 4th Street. We emerged to the street right under the marquee of a movie theater. The smell of pizza, sausages, peppers and onions was everywhere. We walked across 8th Avenue by the basketball court and in a few steps passed a jazz club. We crossed a street, turned a corner and the crowd grew larger. There were hundreds of people walking the streets checking each other out. It seemed to me, from looking at the shop windows, that everybody in the Village was into making something. There were dozens of shops that displayed hand-made jewelry. There were many art galleries; clothing shops featuring avant-garde clothing and shoe shops that sold mostly sandals. There were also an inordinate number of bookstores, jazz clubs and coffeehouses.

That night Clark and I walked the streets taking in the scenery of this New World. Most of the people were from other parts of the city and there were many people from out of state, but somehow, it seemed we were all able to latch on to the mood of the place. Everybody acted the part of a member of the beat generation—open to anything, but questioning everything. Everybody in the village, visitors or not, were Beatniks and our favorite expression was "Like, wow man." Whenever Clark and I heard music or laughter coming from a café or club, we'd peep into the door. Almost all of the people in those places were white. We passed a small pizza shop that had a large hunk of meat, like a giant one hundred-pound meatball that revolved around in a vertical rotisserie. It was interesting and it smelled like it could taste delicious. We stopped and stared for a moment.

"What is that?" Clark asked the man behind the counter.

"That gyro. Gyro—is good" the man answered in a heavy voice and broken English.

"What's in it?" Clark asked

"Beef, lamb, pork. You try?"

Clark looked at me. I shook my head in approval.

"Two," Clark ordered.

The man placed a pan with a handle under the meat and he began to slice off pieces as the meat continued to revolve around. The places where he sliced from would reveal the meat's undercooked layer. When he had enough meat for two gyros, he stuffed the meat into two pita-breads and topped it with onions, tomatoes, spices and a white sauce. Clark paid for the gyros and we walked off eating.

"This is good," Clark said.

"Like, wow man," I agreed.

During the next week, I told everybody about what I saw in Greenwich Village. Bill Chapman had heard about the kind of place it was, but had never ventured down there. We started going down to the village on the weekends. At first we'd just walk around and get something to eat. Then on one visit Bill suggested we go into a café. We chose a small dark place with few patrons. The tables were small and looked homemade. We sat down and a guy in an apron came over to us. He gave us a list of five different styles and flavors of coffee and five different wines. We ordered two glasses of White Mountain wine. Just after our wine came, a bearded fat white guy walked up to a microphone that stood between the curved end of the bar and the telephone booth. He didn't introduce himself, he just took out some papers and began to read from them. Some people stared off from the reader as though they were in deep contemplation of his words. Others looked directly at him, patted their feet and nodded their heads to the cadence of his voice. He read a long poem that went on and on for pages. But he wasn't reading so much as recalling it seemed. He read in a cadence that was at one time hurried and other times slow and expressive. He was using words the way musicians used musical notes to create harmony of sound. The pitch of his voice characterized and gave flight to the words that came from his mouth and as the words welded together, they formed chaotic images of insanity, Negro streets, despair, drugs, Zen, jazz, homosexuality, suicide, capitalism, addictions, scholarship, protest, weeping, love, the abyss, innocence of the soul, socialism, bombs and destruction. When he had finished reading the poem, he said almost meekly "Howl."

In my ninth grade English class, I had to read some poems by Emily Dickinson, Robert Frost and Carl Sandburg, the names I remembered at the time, but those poems were about birds, trees, and paths not taken. This guy, whom I later found out, was named Allen Ginsberg, was talking turmoil. I was confused. Can a poem be chaotic and still be a thing of beauty? Poetry, I had come to believe, was supposed to be about beauty and laud the splendors of life. They didn't expose us to Ezra Pound in that ninth grade English class.

The next time Bill and I went to the Village we went back to that same coffeehouse and to my surprise, the poet that night was a short, brown-skinned bearded man. The poems he read were shorter than Ginsberg's "Howl," but they contained some of the same elements of anarchy and indignation. He was even more expressive and rhythmic than Ginsberg was—like he was dancing with his words. I was delighted to see a black bohemian commanding the respect and attention of a mostly white and intellectual audience. Now I was really overwhelmed with reverence for the written word. At the end of the reading, I went up to him and said, "Like, wow man, I really enjoyed hearing you," although I understood none of it. And, at that moment, I would have never believed that that poet would one day write a blurb for one of my own books. He later changed his named from LeRoi Jones to Amiri Baraka.

As word about the Village spread in my neighborhood and other groups of boys from the neighborhood discovered the place on their own, we started going to the Village in larger and varying groups. The ambience of the Village made a big impression on all of us. Many of the guys wholly adopted the guise of the Beatnik. Their dress got more impromptus and they carried books with esoteric titles. In their speech, they used "Like" as a prefix and expressed agreement or amazement by saying "Like, wow man." They joined the "Mingus Cult" and jammed club appearances of bassist Charlie Mingus. I was among those who tried to combine the laid-back demeanor of the Village Beatniks with our uptown black hipness. We came to it with one thing in common with the Village crowd— our affinity for marijuana. The essence of Greenwich Village was embodied and expressed in its acceptance of avant-garde art and unorthodox behavior.

I was seventeen and attending the tenth grade again. I wasn't interested in anything other then writing, but nothing I did in school connected to that. I didn't know how much I wanted to learn to write—no plan had been articulated in my own mind. I hadn't yet had the experience that would reveal my desire clearly to me. Brad dropped out of school early in the year and Ozzie followed after Christmas. One school day I went uptown to hang out with Brad. He wasn't home and couldn't be found in the neighborhood. I ran into Zip Jackson who was on his way to 130th Street to see a friend. Zip said that he hadn't seen Brad in a few days. I told him I'd walk with him and maybe by the time we were back, Brad would be around. We walked down 125th Street to 7th Avenue then began to walk uptown. Across the street, I noticed a storefront that had a large globe of the world painted up top. I had seen this store on many other occasions, but because of its cluttered appearance I never took in all it tried to convey. It advertised itself as "The House of Common Sense/ Home of Proper Propaganda." Below that sign was another that read "World History Book Outlet On" and below that, "2,000,000,000 Africans and Non-White People." And, below that were painted pictures of African Heads of States. This place also had a sign to the right of the door that listed it as the Repatriation Headquarters and recruiting center for the Back to Africa Movement. A sign hung over the door that read "Harlem Square." At the top of the window were pictures of black dignitaries from around the world and finally in the lower part of the window, there was a display of the stores main commodity—books.

I can't say why, but this time this place really caught my interest. I told Zip I'd see him later and I crossed 7th Avenue at the middle of the block to where the store was. Two old men sat at a table on the sidewalk with two large pickle jar collecting donations for different causes. I browsed around the front of the shop.

"Go on in," one of the men at the table urged me. "Go on in brother."

I went in and discovered that the clutter on the outside was mild compared to that on the inside. There were books, posters and pictures everywhere. All the shelves were stuffed with books. Framed pictures of great black leaders leaned up against the wall. All the wall space that didn't hold books was used as a world bulletin board for political slogans and the announcement of different political causes. The bombardment of information tried my patience and I had to struggle to remain focused. Over in a corner of the store a little old man sat at a desk. He wore a brown suit, a multi-colored shirt and a colorful tie with a big knot. His hair was cropped short. He was light-skinned. He wore black framed glasses above his broad flat nose. He never looked up from the clutter of papers on his desk. He looked so natural in this setting, as though he was a companion to the books, posters and pictures. He looked like he was formed from the millions of words in the thousands of books on those shelves. This place felt strange to me, not in a scary way, but in a way that made me feel I was unprepared. I got nervous and walked to the door.

"Can I help you?" The man asked.

"I was just looking," I said.

"My name is Brother Lewis Michaux, do come again."

Years later, I was to have many, more meaningful, encounters with Mr. Michaux after his National Memorial African Bookstore was forced to move to 125th Street near Lenox Avenue. I went there to seek advice on reading material and his assessment of the world Nationalist Movement. It was Mr. Michaux who later introduced me to the works of Langston Hughes, Arna Bontemps and Gwendolyn Brooks. Lewis Michaux was a Black Nationalist in the Marcus

Garvey mode. He believed that integration would never come to America and, I think, he may have also believed that integration would not be a good thing for Americans of African descent.

Lewis Michaux was also an intellectual. His National Memorial African Bookstore was a hub for intellectuals from all over the world, but a major hub for national black intellectuals. Mr. Michaux associated with the major black leaders of the period and he was their equal in influencing the direction of the racial discussion. His views were far more extreme than the popular civil rights leader's views. He was even more extreme than Malcolm X, whom he mentored and gave advice to. Mr. Michaux came up during the age of Marcus Garvey and believed exclusively in the Back to Africa Movement as the solution to the Negro problem. He was often at odds with the conventional black leadership, but they understood and respected his scholarship.

My first visit to Mr. Michaux's bookstore was short, but it had a profound and a lasting affect on me. I liked everything about the look and the feel of the place. It had the same feeling the Museum of Natural History produced in me. It told an indisputable story and the evidence was on the wall. The museum told many stories; the story of mankind, and the story of all animals, the story of insects, the story of inventions and many other stories. And, through its exhibits, it illustrated that it was the authenticated authority on each of the stories it told. The National Memorial African bookstore told one story, the history of Africa and its expatriated people around the world. And, it could equally claim to be the ultimate source on the subject. I wanted to know that story and to become a part of it. Later that day I bought a hot dog with my carfare and hopped over the turnstile to get back downtown. That night I wrote my first poem.

I attended school more often my second year in the tenth grade. Machine and Metals Trade School had two main buildings. One building was for academic studies and the other was the trade component where they taught welding, machine shop work, and tool and dye making. I took welding and found the shop work interesting because the time went by fast. I had a geography class that held my attention and a class on the Middle Ages that kept me alert. I even participated in these classes, but in all the others I took a seat in the back and daydreamed the time away. It must have been my improved attendance that got them to pass me on to the eleventh grade.

<u>6</u>

In the winter of 1958, moving trucks became a common sight in the neighborhood across Amsterdam Avenue. Lincoln Center for the Performing Arts was coming. All of the structures from 60th Street to 65th Street, Amsterdam Avenue to Columbus Avenue were to be demolished to make way for the new Arts complex. The tenement housing from 60th Street to 62nd Street was occupied largely by white families, 63rd Street to 65th Street housed mostly Puerto Rican families. All of it, every building except Power Memorial High School on 61st Street, was slated for demolition. The neighborhood lost two major institutions, the NBC studio on 62nd Street where the Steve Allen show was broadcast. It was outside of this studio, one block from my apartment building, that Steve Martin and Louie Nye did their funny "Man in the Street" routine. And, across the street from the NBC studio was the Roller Derby Rink. Roller Derby races were broadcast from the rink and competed with Professional Wrestling for the same audience. The Roller Derby Rink was replaced with the Lincoln Center campus of Fordham University's law School and the Lincoln Square campus of Fordham's Undergraduate University. A decade later I would be a student at that campus.

The neighborhood also lost many old and beloved haunts. Al and Ben's Luncheonette, Rocco's Delicatessen, the Green Gabriel Bar, the building that housed the drug store with the bank of telephone booths, and to which Sal Pasquale's shoeshine hut was attached. The Italian vegetable store that fronted for a numbers operation, a couple of store front churches, two cucifritos and Old Dutch Cleaners, which put me out of a job were also lost. The work site was boarded up for a year as they drilled, laid the foundation and poured cement. The neighborhood's character was changed forever. This change also laid the groundwork for the grand gentrification that the future would bring. The neighborhood went through a shock while it anticipated the change the new structures would bring. This was a fast changing time. It had put so many local people out of work. Bartenders from three bars were out of work. Crunch Collier who had worked at Al and Ben's full time for ten years was now unemployed. Cooks and waiters from two greasy spoons were now looking for work. The people who worked at the Spanish language movie theater on Columbus Avenue were out of work. We were a neighborhood in transition. My generation was growing up and forming real interest.

Some of the neighborhood guys who were going to the Village regularly became interested in learning to play instruments. They were given a room at the community center to practice their instruments. Five nights a week a melange of sounds came from that room. Rave France and Eddie Bishop practiced the saxophone. Paul Neuman practiced the trumpet and the other white boy in the room, Benny Moreah, practiced the vibraphone. Tommy Borden played the drums. Charma Cosmos played the conga drum and timbales. Thomas Bedding played the bass and Ernest Khan played the piano and later switched to the vibes. Most of this group learned their instruments. Charma was probably the guy with the most natural talent and played on a professional level a decade later. Ernest Khan formed a group in the seventies and played local clubs. Thomas Bedding switched altogether to painting and became a well-known artist. Eddie Bishop died in a tragic automobile accident. Tommy Borden became a draftsman and did some studio work on the side. Paul Neuman became a city cop and turned against his black heritage.

When these guys first took up instruments, I wanted badly to join them. I loved the sound of the flute and wanted to learn to play one, but I was broke and out of work. Bill Chapman had a Cal Tjader recording with Paul Horn playing on the flute that I loved listening to. Herbie Mann was the best known flutist of the period, but Yusef Lateef, the saxophonist, also played a notable flute. I knew it would be senseless to ask Sarah to help me buy a flute. She had her hands full trying to feed and clothe us all. I went to Aunt Dorothy.

"A flute? Boy where in the world did you get that idea?"

"I want to learn to play the flute and join a band Aunt Dot."

"You should be paying more attention to your school work. You know I tell you all the time that if you graduate from high school, me and your Uncle Bertram would pay for you to go to college."

"I know Aunt Dot, and I'm gonna try harder. I'm not doing so bad this year."

"Sarah tells me you hardly attend school, she get so many truancy notices for you."

"That was last year, Aunt Dot, I'll go to school every day and I'll try hard to do my school work. Please."

"How much this flute cost?"

"I saw a used one in Manny's instrument store for about fifty dollars."

"Fifty dollars? Now I really don't know about that—fifty dollars is a lot of money.

"I know it is Aunt Dot, but if I learn to play it well and get into a band and..."

"Gone home and take this package to your Momma. I'll have a answer for you next week. Get another piece of fruit before you go."

"Yes ma'am. I love you."

"I know you do, now get."

"I love you," Aunt Dot yells out of the window as she watched me walk up the block to the bus stop.

The next Saturday Aunt Dot gave me fifty dollars and a stern speech about school. I went directly to the diamond district where Manny's instrument store was located. The used flute I saw in the window was fifty-nine dollars. The salesman saw me *coming* and let me have it for fifty dollars—no taxes. He even threw in the carrying case. I walked home proud and determined. But I didn't have a plan or someone to teach me music and how to play the flute. I felt that the ability to play the flute would simply come to me in much the way my ability to play basketball did—from raw natural talent. I got the thing home and couldn't even make a sound come from it. There were no instructions. The only thing in the case was an old booklet on the cleaning and care of the instrument. In a few days, I learned that a young man who lived in building 40 named Earnie Deberry played the flute. When I approached him, he agreed to help me get started on the instrument. From Earnie, I learned placement of the mouthpiece, how to control the air I put into it, and how to hold the instrument and my shoulders. I practiced those aspects for a few months. Now I needed someone to teach me to read music and to play my horn.

7

One day, near the end of July 1959, Butchie called to tell me that she was at Joan's house. She wanted me to come down there and bring Ozzie with me. I said I would, but I didn't even look for Ozzie or call his house. As I was walking, I heard lots of sirens and saw a big crowd of people gathered near Saint Paul's Church on Columbus Avenue. I decided to walk Columbus Avenue down to Joan's house so I could see what I thought might have been a fire at the church. When I reached the church, people stood orderly behind police barriers. There were policemen and empty police cars everywhere, but no fire or fire trucks. Two policemen stood in the street directing traffic around the horde of double parked cars and limousines. Then I notice the long black hearse. I got into the crowd and decided to hang around to find out what was going on. I saw a woman from the projects that I knew.

"What happened here?" I asked her.

"Billie Holiday died. They're having her funeral here.

"Billie Holiday?"

"Billie Holiday the singer. 'Lady Day?'"

"Oh, Billie Holiday. What happened to her?"

"Everything happened to her. She was born into a bad situation and she grew up on the wrong side of the world. When she was born, her Momma went crazy and her Daddy got drunk. She knew the wrong men and enjoyed the forbidden pleasures. She was fifteen million colored women in America who couldn't find the protective arms of a strong and trustworthy colored man. She loved and lost. She had a great voice, but her eyes and her face told her stories. She was only 44 years old, but she packed some living into those years. Everything, that's what happened to her—everything. And now, every black soul who is somebody is in that church to pay tribute to her. I been here from before they started and I've seen them all."

I ran the name through my memory bank, but came up blank. I had heard the name before and I knew that she was connected to jazz, but I had never heard any of her music.

"Why are they having her funeral here?"

"She was a Catholic and this is a Catholic Church," the women said. "I saw Dizzy Gillespie and Sarah Vaughan and Duke Ellington and…" she went on and on.

I milled around until the funeral was over and the people began to file out of the church. There were reporters and photographers there from the newspapers and magazines. When they brought the casket out to return it to the hearse, I saw a black photographer approach Mrs. Denver, who was a school crossing guard and lived in the projects. She was wearing her uniform and badge. She was standing with her six-year-old son. The photographer spoke with her, and then he began to arrange her son into a pose. He coached the boy to put his hands to his eyes in a display of grief. When he was satisfied with the pose, he took his pictures. Whenever certain famous jazz musicians or singers emerged from the church people pushed forward and called out names. Finally I remembered my mission and continued on to Joan's house to meet with Butchie.

When I arrived, they were having cake and milk and listening to John Coltrane's "My Funny Valentine." I knew they had been smoking reefer, but they didn't offer me any and I didn't ask for any.

"Where is Ozzie?" Joan asked

"I couldn't find him."

"You called his house?"

"Nobody answered, and he wasn't in the playground.

"What about at Evane's house?"

"He don't go there without me."

"Why?"

"Nobody there likes him much."

"My poor baby."

"I just passed Saint Paul's Church on 60th street. They had Billie Holiday's funeral there."

"Yeah," Butchie said, "everybody in Harlem is talking about the death of Lady Day."

"Oh, you're hipped to her?"

"My mother and my Aunt are always playing her records."

"Never heard of her," Joan said as she replayed the Coltrane record.

"They say they saw her singing in the clubs. They say she was real down and all—and that she got high."

"Maybe that's what killed her," Joan said, smiling at the oxymoron.

"Huh?" I said.

"Being 'down' and 'high', maybe that's what killed her."

"I think you'll are high and I'd be down to get high if you'd offer."

"All gone," Butchie said."

I stayed talking with them, avoiding Joan's questions about Ozzie and listening to "My Funny Valentine" until near dark. When I was ready to leave, they decided to walk with me back uptown. We walked up 10th Avenue past the bus depot and the police station where Brad had had the argument with Jack Rudland about the cigarettes. The girls were in a playful mood. I walked in the middle and occasionally they'd each grab an arm and pull in different directions as if to tear me apart. 57th Street is a major cross street with a fast light. Just as we reached the corner, the light changed to green.

"I must be fine," Joan said. "Even the street lights blink at me."

"You are fine," I said.

"Everybody in our family's fine," Butchie said. "Ain't I fine, Grady?"

"You're the finest."

"I am?"

"Really."

"Does Ozzie think I'm fine?" Joan moaned.

"Joan, I'm sure he can see that you are."

"Then why does he act like he couldn't care less?"

They walked me to my building. We talked some more for a brief period and they left to walk back downtown to Joan's house. A week later, I went to Mr. Wiggs barbershop across the Avenue from Joan's house to get a haircut. Mr. Wiggs' shop used to be on 60th Street near Columbus Circle, but he moved the shop to 53rd Street early in the fifties when the block was demolished to make way for the Coliseum. Mr. Wiggs died a few years after the move and a younger man name John Farley took over the business. Everyone had been going to Mr. Wiggs for so long that although he had been dead for years, we still called the shop by his name. It was always a long wait to get into the barber's chair, because John never hired any help. I grabbed the latest Jet magazine to browse through as I waited. I always started reading Jet at the centerfold. The centerfold always had a picture of a pretty girl in a bathing suit. Then I read the pages back to the front cover. I turned the page back from the centerfold and got quite a surprise. There was the picture of Mrs. Denver, the school crossing guard's son, at the Billy Holiday's funeral with his hands to his eye and a mournful grimace on his face. The caption read: Youth Mourns at Billie's Funeral. Underneath the picture there was a sentence that read: Six year old Gregory Denver mourns the death of jazz great Billie Holiday who died in a New York City hospital on July 17, 1959.

"I was there when this picture was taken," I told John, and the three people who were ahead of me waiting for a haircut. I showed them the picture in the magazine. "It didn't happen like this pictures shows. Why, I don't think that boy even knew who Billy Holiday was. The photographer placed him into this pose."

"You went to Billie Holiday's funeral?" An old man, whom I had never seen at the barbershop before asked. It was obvious that he didn't know that the funeral was held at Saint Paul Church just seven blocks away from the barbershop.

"The funeral was at Saint Paul's Church. I was walking by; I saw the crowd of people and found out what was going on. That's how I saw the photographer posing the boy and taking the picture. Man this is a phony news picture. I can't believe that this is how the news is made up."

"Don't feel hurt," another fellow said, "it happens all the time. What you saw is mild shit compared to what is really going on. When it's a black versus white situation, do you think we get the truth from the news people—why hell no. They tell you what they want you to know to keep your black ass in the dark. Newspapers in New York will tell you all you want to know about segregation in the South, but they won't tell you shit about why there ain't no black firemen and far too few black policemen, right here in New York City."

"Goes to show, you can't believe everything you see on television and read in newspapers and magazines, John said.

"I still can't believe it," I said, "it's the news. They can't make shit up.

" You see the size of them titties on the girl in the centerfold," John said, "you think they're real?"

A week later I turned eighteen. I had gotten nowhere. This was promising to be the worse period of my life. I had no potential to succeed in school, I wasn't employable in any meaningful way, and I had grown to fear going to jail, so lucrative criminality was out of the picture for me. Though it took years to reach this point, happening in daily increments, the realization came to me all at once. And although I had watched this process as it happened to the older groups of boys when they reached this age, I was still shocked and surprised. A funk was setting in on my disposition, I was developing a mild clinical depression—this is a personal diagnostic that comes decades after the fact, and entering into the zone where...shit happens.

In the eleventh grade, I went back to my old ways. I missed classes and often skipped entire days. There were some women in their twenties in the neighborhood, who had apartments of their own. They would let me, and others, spend the school day with them watching television, getting high and trying to do them in. These women were almost exclusively single mothers without any clear direction in their lives. No matter what age you were, in this community, there were lots of pits to fall into. I hardly missed any of them growing up. I was thinking about dropping out of school and trying to find a full time job. My family could use the extra money and I would not continue to be a financial drag on the family's budget. I was afraid to broach the subject with Sarah, but I knew that the time would come.

After the cleaners closed down, I was unable to find another after school job and I was continually broke. At home, I was moody, uncooperative and sullen. I'd pawn my flute, then had to hustle to get enough money to get it out in two weeks time before I lost it. This habit became a vicious circle. My brother and sisters had grown bigger and their needs demanded larger portions of the family's meager budget, so Sarah didn't have money to buy me shoes. All of my clothes had grown tattered. Many of the guys my age had graduated high school, although few of them had found work, so I felt self-conscious about still going to school. The high school drop out rate for boys in my neighborhood was so high that there was no stigma about being a dropout—it was rated right next to going to jail. Everyday was the same. Ozzie and I hung out in the playground playing quarter Tonk, going to the movies, walking the streets aimlessly.

Brad came downtown occasionally. He always looked swell. He'd be dressed in the latest styles. He always had a pocket full of money that he shared none of and lots of smoke, with which he was quite generous. Brad's hair always appeared freshly cut. He always had a cheerful smile and exciting stories about how he was making a successful hustle in Harlem. Brad was becoming what I'd describe as an underground entrepreneur. He accomplished for the underground movers of goods and services, what lobbyist in Washington, DC does for the United States Congress and American businesses—get shady shit done. He had moved out of his mother's apartment and was living on his own in a rooming house on 154th Street off of Broadway. He had never owned up to being the father of the baby the older girl gave birth to, but he was still sneaking to her apartment while her boyfriend was at work. During these episodes, he told us, he didn't have time to look us up to hang out a bit. His uptown hustle really kept him busy—it sounded so exciting to me. It was clear that Brad was having a good life.

One evening, late in the fall, I was standing by the mailbox on my block talking to Butchie who had stopped by on her way down to Joan's house. She was dressed real nice in a black coat; a cute knit hat and boots. Butchie had a great sense of style and a body that sculpted her clothing well. I wore an old pea coat, a tattered cap, brown corduroy pants and shoes that actually had holes in the soles. Butchie was in an exuberant mood. She was bursting with the excitement of the many discoveries of young adult independence. I faked steadiness. A car pulled up to the curb with several guys in it. The driver door opened and the driver got out. It was Brad Buffert.

"Hey Grady, I was driving back uptown and I saw you. What's happening my man?" Brad said looking at Butchie as he shook my hand. I was aware that he was talking to me and looking at Butchie, but I couldn't take my eyes away from the car.

The car was a red and blue fin-tail 1959 Chevrolet—the very latest model. Brad was dressed in a unbuttoned black raglan sleeve coat that revealed a Burberry wind-breaker underneath it that had the collar zipped up to his neck. He wore an olive green blocked style hat with the front pulled down gangster style.

"Hey Brad. Ain't nothing-happening here man. Same old, same old. Nice ride."

"Yeah, thank you. I had to get a little something to get around in the city with. That old Iron Horse just ain't getting it anymore.

"A little something? Man that's a boss ride."

"How's my man Ozzie?"

"Ozzie's cool."

"Oh, he knows Ozzie?" Butchie said, creating an opening into the conversation and smiling broadly at Brad.

"Brad, this is Butchie. Butchie, Brad."

"Hi, love your hat."

"Yeah, I know Ozzie. Grady didn't tell you that we all used to be partners. Him, Ozzie and me. You look like you from Harlem."

"He never mentioned you Brad. You know, I'm from Harlem."

"Ha hum, so where you coming from Brad?" I asked.

"Had some business in Brooklyn man. See that's why I need the ride. I could've used you with us. Maybe the next time, I'll stop by and take you with me—let you make a little chum-change.

"Yo Brad," the guy in the front seat yelled out after he lowered the front window "you forget our other stop uptown—we late man."

I looked over towards the car; the only face I recognized was Lem Shuttleton the guy who had once counted out all that money for him and Brad to spend. From what I could see, they were dressed identically. I had never before seen the two guys in the back seat.

"I would give you a ride uptown, but I've got a load already."

"Maybe some other time. I happened to be going downtown anyway," Butchie said teasingly.

Then both of them said goodbye and walked off from me at the same time, Brad to his car and Butchie towards Joan's house. I had just had the dubious honor of being in the presence of my good friend and the girl I liked and having them hit up on each other in front of me. I just stood there alone for a while. I was really disappointed with myself. That's just how life was going for me. I was living a true Beatnik existence absent the intellectual rudiments and the esoteric interest. I was in a corner and saw nothing but hopelessness. I wanted to learn what Brad was doing that brought him such success—maybe he would let me in on it for old time's sake.

San Juan Hill

CHAPTER SIX
Going Nowhere Fast
1

I went to see Brad at the rooming house on 154th Street several times, but he was never home. Even times when I called ahead to tell him I was coming, when I got there he would be gone. When I asked him about that, he'd just say something came up. He explained that he was in a position where he had to move at a moment's notice. "That's how I make my money," he said. I thought he was trying to avoid me, but I kept trying to catch up with him.

One day I went to see Brad and again he wasn't at home. I thought I'd check out his hangouts in the projects on 125th Street. I only had enough money for carfare home, so I walked from 154th Street down to the projects. I went to the basketball court behind the building where Brad's family lived and to a few other places in the neighborhood without finding Brad. Finally, I went to the bar across the street from Brad's old building. There were a few people in there, mostly older men. I walked back out of the bar and saw one of Brad's cousins, a guy named Teddy Buffert, who also went to high school with us. As soon as we met up, the door from the bar was kicked open and one of the older men inside emerged with a sawed-off shotgun in his hands. "I told you I was gonna catch you—you no good son-of-a-bitch," he said. As soon as Teddy recognized the man, he ran to reach a parked car for cover. I stood there as if in a dream. Before Teddy could reach a car to protect himself, the shotgun went off and he yelled out in pain. Teddy was hit in the shoulder, but he was able to duck behind a van as the man walked right by me trying to take aim for another shot. "Don't kill me, don't kill me," Teddy was screaming in agony as he ducked around the van.

Two older men came from the bar and quickly convinced the shooter that the cops were coming and that he should get rid of the gun. They all disappeared back into the bar as Teddy ran down the street through traffic towards an approaching police car. When Teddy reached the police car, it stopped and two cops got out of the car. Teddy was holding his shoulder and talking furiously. A crowd had formed around the spot where the police car stopped and was beginning to stall traffic. A smaller crowd formed around the entrance of the bar trying to see the shooter. I snapped out of it and decided it would be wise for me to leave and avoid being questioned—afterall, I was an eyewitness to the shooting. A witness oblivious to any of the facts that to led up to the shooting. The 8th Avenue subway was three blocks east. I headed towards it shaken but feeling lucky that I had not been shot in the commotion.

On my way to the subway station, I ran into Lem Stuttleton. We stopped to say hello. I told him that I was looking for Brad. He said that Brad was in Brooklyn. Then I told him what had just happened.

"No shit," oh man, I knew that shit was gonna happened."

"And I was standing right there."

"I told Teddy not to fuck with that man."

"I was gonna ask Teddy if he knew where Brad was, but before I..."

"He ran?"

"If he hadn't taken a few steps away from me trying to get to cover, I would have been hit too."

"He ran?"

"Yeah, Teddy ran around a parked van and then he ran down the block towards Amsterdam when the cops came. People from the bar took the dude back inside. They were yelling for him to get rid of the gun."

"Damn, that's fucked up."

I wanted to ask Lem what the shooting was about, but I knew it was not cool to be too inquisitive. I didn't respond to him for a moment to give him a chance to volunteer any information on what was going on between Teddy and the man who shot him.

"Look Grady, Brad's taking care of some business in Brooklyn, you want to come upstairs and hang for a while, he may be back before you leave. I got some smoke and a bottle of Duff."

When we got to the apartment where Lem lived with his mother, he put on some jazz records and poured two drinks of Nina Sherry into paper cups. He rolled two joints and we each smoked one. Lem Shuttleton was a stocky dark-skinned guy with a face that carried a permanent sneer—like he could chew you up and spit you out.

"Brad's got his own place uptown, you know."

"Yeah, that's real cool."

"I'm looking for a place myself, but I want to move to Brooklyn. That's where shit is happening in the future—Brooklyn."

"I don't know much about Brooklyn."

"What you doing for yourself, Grady?"

"Ain't nothing happening man, that's why I want to talk to Brad."

"Oh you looking for a hustle."

"Sort of."

"Brad ain't gonna do nothing for you. Brad's a solo act. He dibs and dabs, here and there, you know what I mean? But I'm looking to add a down motherfucker to my crew. You get to be a member of my crew and it's all over—you living it up."

Lem went to a back room and returned with pistols in each hand. I immediately showed signs of fear.

"They ain't loaded right now," Lem said. "You ever fired a gun?" he asked handing me a gun. "Hold it in your hands."

"No," I took the gun and held it in my opened hand. It was heavier than I expected.

"Hold it like you're gonna use it. Put your finger on the trigger," Lem coached me. "Point it. Hold it right there—while I tell you something. When you point what you got in your hand in the face of any motherfucker, he gonna know you the boss right off, But his mind gonna be fixed on resisting you—he gonna be searching for ways to check the upper hand your gun gives you. So he ain't ready to do anything you say just yet. Oh, he'll keep still and keep his eyes on you 'cause you got a gun in his face. But, you know what will make him obey you?"

"No."

"The look in your eyes that will tell that motherfucker that you will shoot him. It's not the gun that's gonna put fear in a motherfucker, it's your willingness to use it that will make him shit in his pants—and he gotta see that in your eyes and on your face. You gotta be able to scare a motherfucker with your eyes and you know how you get to be able to do that?"

"No."

"By telling yourself that you will shoot a motherfucker. You gotta convince yourself for real that you would shoot a motherfucker. The quickest way to get that look in your eyes is to go out there and shoot somebody—that way you know that you'll do it and your eyes will tell a motherfucker that you'll do it. And when you point a gun in a motherfucker's face, he will fear you, and he will do whatever you ask, because he will see his death on your face. Grady, the key to creating fear in people is not only the gun; it's your intentions. You dig?"

"Yeah, I dig."

"There was a motherfucker in a bar we hit once playing like he couldn't get his diamond ring off his finger. This motherfucker made me furious, you hear me. Here I am sticking up this joint with two more people, all of us with guns and this motherfucker is trying to play me—he can't get the ring off his finger. I went behind the bar and found the knife that they used to cut shit up with. I told this dude to put his ring hand on the bar. When he saw the knife in my hand and the look in my eyes, that motherfucker hurried up, took that ring off his finger, and offered it up with apologies," Lem said with a satisfying grin.

"I see what you're saying."

"So, you want in? You want to be one of my boys?"

"What kind of shit will I be doing to need a gun?"

"You ain't a member of my crew yet," Lem said, irritation sounding in his voice, "you can't get into my business. When you're in, you'll know what you need to know."

"I'm sorry, I really didn't mean to ask that. Lem, I really need to do something, so lemme think on it and get back to you. Is that cool?"

"That's cool with me—don't take long though."

"I'm gonna make it on back downtown. Tell Brad I was looking for him."

"Fuck Brad, you look for me from now on. Lem reached into his pocket and pulled out some bills. He took a twenty-dollar bill from the roll and handed it to me. "Members of my crew don't want for nothing," he said.

I handed the gun back to Lem. He took a bullet clip from his pocket, placed it into the handle of the gun, and cocked it. He raised the gun a foot away from my face. I dropped the empty cup. All of a sudden, his face turned stone cold and ashy.

"Pick the cup up," he yelled; his voice had finality to it.

I bent down to pick the cup up. When I straightened up, the gun was back in my face.

"You see the look on my face—you see my eyes?"

"Yeah," I wanted to tell him that this demonstration was unnecessary, but by now, I had figured him out. Those would have been too many of the wrong words. He would have had to make his point by shooting me...somewhere. "Yeah, I got to do that for you, you'll see."

Lem slowly pointed the gun to the floor. He removed the clip and discharged the chambered round. I could actually see the tension being released from his face and body.

"Call me in three days, I got work for you."

My hands shook as I wrote his phone number on a piece of paper and went out of the door. My legs were so shaky I almost fell walking down the stairs.

On the train ride downtown, I tried to think clearly about what I would do, but my mind was agitated by the close call of the shooting and by having Lem stick a loaded pistol in my face. I was concerned about becoming associated with Lem Shuttleton; he seemed deranged and dangerous. But because he wasn't locked up, he must be having success at whatever he's doing, I thought over the clamor of the subway noise. In my mind, the overriding point was that I needed to make a move. My life was stagnated; I was reaching adulthood and going nowhere fast. All of my thinking was funneled through the limited experiences of my existence—I couldn't imagine what my adult life would be like, or me having a life outside of my experiences. So, this choice I was about to make would be coming from within the realm of my reality. I took a deep breath and upon its release, I decided not to join up with Lem Shuttleton. I had blown in the wind for most of my life. I was without bearings, unprepared for life and I'd done some pretty detestable things, but I was no hardcore gangster. And now that the question was right up against me, I had to reject it.

That night in my dream, my dog Spot met me at the 135th Street subway station. We waited for the train to come into the station. When it did, we entered through the open doors. The train, as always, was crowded; I held on to a center pole, Spot at my side. Then the next time I looked at Spot, he's wasn't a dog any longer, but a pretty girl that lurked somewhere from a time to come. For the first time, the girl in the dream had a face that I could remember even after the dream. The features of the face made the dream more striking and more puzzling. How can I remember a face I had only seen in a dream? She had smooth brown skin, lips that broke into a wonderful smile, a nose that was perfectly molded and innocent brown eyes. She was my soul mate. It was a face from the future— my future.

<u>2</u>

A couple of days later, to my utter surprise, Brad came to my house to see me. He asked if I wanted to take a ride and I jumped at the chance. As soon as we got into the car, Brad lit a joint and he drove off. The car had red and black interior that matched it's outside color.

"How's your cousin doing man, you know I was there talking to him when he got shot."

"Yeah, I heard. He's doing okay—comes home tomorrow."

"This old cat just comes out of the bar and bang."

"Yeah, I know."

"Why'd he shoot Teddy?"

"It was over some money Teddy owed him. I don't mess with those people, so I don't know much about it."

I took that to mean that that was all Brad was going to say on the subject. Brad had always made it his business to know everything that was going on in and around his orbit—nothing escaped his field of knowledge. He drove up Riverside Drive. We could see the sun go down over New Jersey on our left side and the quiet charm of white stone townhouses on tree lined streets on our right side. Brad drove up to Grant's Tomb. He parked the car and we got out. We walked across the street and sat on a bench next to the Tomb.

"Lem told me that you was gonna do a stick up for him."

"What?"

"He's just waiting to hear from you."

"What?"

"Didn't you tell him that you wanted to join his crew?"

"Stick up, what?"

"Look, Grady, take it from me man, don't fuck with that guy. He's too slick for you. That cat's got dudes going to jail for him and if you get involved with him, you'll be one of them. I just feel I owe you this warning not to get involved with his crew. All them cats are crazy, but they're slick and they'll hang you out to dry."

"I just told him I would think about it."

"You ready to do stick ups with guns? It ain't the same as sneaking a bag of quarters from off of a cash register or stealing a box of change from a cab driver—this is the real shit where you could die or go to jail. You ready for that?"

"Man, I ain't made no deal to do nothing like that. I just need to make some money."

"What this cat does is put you in a situation where if anything happens, its you who's gonna take the weight or—the bullet. He puts the gun in your hand in the last minute; he has another cat to watch you and he walks away to be the look out man. Behind that shit, after you get the money, he wants to be the paymaster. He tried that shit on me, I told him I wasn't going for it. On the one thing I did with them, I was the look out. But even that ain't for me."

"Oh man," I said standing up from the bench and throwing my arms up in despair. "I don't want none of that. I've got to call that dude and let him know."

"Good, I'll take care of it. Don't call him. I'll talk to him about it—just stay away from him."

We got back in the car and Brad drove up to his rooming house. He lived in a three-story building that was once a one family house. It was now rented out in one and two room apartments. Brad lived in a room on the second floor. It was a large room in the front of the building with a twelve-foot ceiling. There was a tiny enclave for a kitchen with a sink, a small stove and a tiny refrigerator. The room was divided into a sleeping area and a sitting room. In the sitting area, Brad had large, cushioned wooden-backed chairs near the windows, a coffee table and a short sofa. He had three paintings on the wall. The painting that caught my eye was of a common tenement building in what might be any part of the ghetto. It was a six-story red brick building. The lower half of the building was lit from the street light. The building had a large doorway that must have led to the basement. Lurking from that doorway, was the figure of a sinister looking dude, with a mean stare and a dark cap pulled down over his face. Brad was in the kitchen getting some ice cubes for our drinks.

"Hey Brad, I dig this picture," I said as Brad returned with two glasses of scotch.

"Yeah, it's called 'The Stick-up Man.' You see the dude peeping down the block; he's looking for someone to rip-off. He's waiting for his victim to show up. He's on the hardest part of his job— waiting for opportunity. There are dudes like him in every ghetto neighborhood in New York City. This picture reminds me of who to look out for and what I don't want to be. Grady, you got to be slick to survive in this world. You talk about how you need to make some money, what you need to do is get a job—I know you, this shit out here ain't for you."

"You gonna take me back downtown?" I appreciated Brad's looking out for me, but now he was giving a lecture I didn't want to hear.

"I'm gonna drop you off at the subway station. I got a run to make."

"I need carfare."

"You got it."

My emotions were mixed when I left Brad. I was relieved that I had decided not make the mistake of joining up with Lem Shuttleton and I was happy that Brad schooled me on the dude. Then I began to question Brad's motive. What he did was uncharacteristic of him. He had never before showed any real reverence for our relationship. I wondered if he had done this to hold me back, but I quickly dismissed the thought. It was better to think that Brad did appreciate the years we spent together with Ozzie, growing up and learning to survive. And, I got the feeling that Brad saw something in me that I hadn't myself become conscious of—a basic anchor to an orthodox existence. The other part of my feelings was that now I would have to go back to the drawing board and figure out what to do with my life.

3

"I want to get a job and quit school," I said to Sarah, finishing my grits and eggs before school one morning. She looked at me, frustration showing on her face. Sarah was raising four children all by herself. She got some financial help from her sister, but giving her children direction and guidance was solely on her. She had received a limited education in South Carolina and had hoped for more for her children. But she didn't know what the true possibilities were for her children or how to guide them in that direction. She was a disciplinarian who kept us out of serious trouble and in my case, that took some luck, but she didn't have any experience with the powers of education. She didn't know the importance of getting us to be enthusiastic about education. I had become a problem. I wasn't going to school, so what was she to do?

"Are you sure that's what you want to do?"

"I am."

"What will you do?"

"I'll get a job. I'm eighteen now; I should be able to find some kind of work. I'll look in the papers for a job as a shipping clerk. I hear that's the easiest job to find. That way I can give you some money to help out with the bills."

"I think you should try to finish high school. You know your Aunt Dorothy and Uncle Bertram will help you go to college. Why don't you think about it for a little while," she said out of an instinctive sense of duty.

"I have, really, but I'm eighteen and in the eleventh grade, I should be out of high school by now. The way I'm going, I won't be out of high school until I'm twenty or twenty-one."

'Still I want you to think about it for a bit—okay?"

"Okay."

Two days later, I told Sarah that companies in the garment center were doing a lot of hiring. I asked her to come with me to school to sign the papers for me to drop out. She agreed and we went through the short procedure that freed me from the education system. Momma Dolly always had a homily that says: You can lead a mule to water, but you can't make it drink, "Lessing ya sweeten' da water." The education system hadn't sweetened my water. On our way back home that day, I bought the newspaper to read through the Help Wanted section. A few years earlier there had been a popular novelty song called "Get A Job" and now I would hum that tune as I looked through the job ads. The unemployment sections of the newspapers were fill with lots of jobs. I had never looked in the unemployment section before, so I was surprised to find that it was categorized by the types of work in alphabetical order. I started at the beginning of the listing and found that there were lots of positions opened for accountants. I didn't qualify for that. Architects. Nothing there for me—go to the "B's." Baker's, banker's, boiler repairmen. No I can't do any of that. Clerks, what they do? Dietitian—What's a dietitian? Engineers, electricians—this short reading brought home to me the vast array of employment possibilities and how wholly inept I was for any of them.

All the time that I was consciously telling myself that what I wanted was a job, what I meant, subconsciously, was a good job. Reading the want ads made my subconscious aspirations surface. But I knew that I didn't qualify for any good job. I hadn't learned any skill in any area of endeavor. Now I had quit school where I was learning to become a welder. I had picked up on some of that. I knew the safety rules. I knew how to handle the welding tank. I could strike an arc, weld a beam and cut through steel. I started skimming through the listings to see if there were any welding jobs opened. There were some welding jobs listed, but the applicant needed experience and something called a resume. I didn't need to read an entire ad to know that I didn't qualify. After a few days of reading the want ads, I circled a few general labor openings that said "No Experience Necessary" and went out to try my luck.

At all of these places, I never got any further then filling out an application. But in my second week of job hunting, Segal & Sons, a company that made coats out of imitation fur hired me. I was hired at thirty-five dollars for a forty-hour week. My duties were vaguely specified, I would work around the cutting floors as directed and make deliveries. It was the delivery part of my job that had me concerned. I wondered if I would have to push one of those hand trucks or rolling racks we called Cadillac's. Manufacturer's in the garment center had goods delivered to show rooms, finishers and retailers by a variety of wheeled wagons that were pushed or pulled. The streets of the garment center can resemble a street in Peking, China with hundreds of coolies pulling rickshaws of merchandise from place to place. In the ghetto, these wagons were labeled the uneducated black's Cadillac. The worse thing that could be said about a dude was that he had been seen in the garment center pushing a Cadillac. This was the ultimate sign of failure and the surest implication of a dissolute future. These were jobs at the very bottom of the work spectrum with wages and duties that were shameful. Many of the people who preformed these jobs, dulled the humiliation of being seen by someone they knew by taking regular wine breaks. But the most dreadful stigma about these jobs was that they were dead-end jobs from which one could never move up.

Segal & Sons operated from a four-story building on 37th Street between Eighth and Ninth Avenue. On the first floor was a showroom and offices. There was a door in the showroom that led to a hall with the punch clock and a locker room where the laborers housed their belongings and stored their lunch. The skilled workers had their own locker room on the second floor. For the first few weeks, I worked in the building. I did whatever I was told to do. I swept the cutting table and the floors clean of scrap materials. I took dolly loads of cut fabric from the cutting table to the sewing floor where sleeves were sewed to shoulders and collars sewed to the garment's back. This company contracted another company to sew the liners into the coats. These unfinished coats were delivered to the contractor on rolling coat racks that were pulled, in the streets, two at a time. One coolie would push and another would pull the racks. There was even a hierarchy among the coolies. The position of pusher was preferred to that of the front position because it was easier to push than to pull, but more importantly, it was a less visible position. The rear position usually went to the senior guy or to the toughest guy.

I wasn't happy with the job, but it enabled me to donate to the household and to begin to refurbish my wardrobe. Almost every payday, after work, I would walk down to Klein's on 14th Street and buy a pair of pants or a shirt or sometimes, both. And, I would have a little change in my pocket to hang out with. On the weekends, I had money to go to a dance or to the movies. At this age, it became cool to travel alone. Everyone would meet up at the same places, but there was an alluring mystique about what showing up alone said about growing up and independence. Friends no longer prearranged going to a club in the Village, to the movies, or to a dance hall in large groups. It was both chic and more fun to meet there in mock surprise.

One Saturday I went to a very late movie with a group of neighborhood boys. We had been drinking and got bored so we decided to make the ten o'clock show. Movie houses on 42nd Street were noisy places late at night filled with drunks and perverts. We sat upstairs in the smoking section. We were noisy and joking about whatever happened on the screen. During a lull in our merry making, I heard my name called from the seats behind us.

"Grady."

I looked back and saw that there was a group of five girls sitting four rows behind us and as my eyes focused, I saw Butchie.

"You know them girls?" one of my companions asked.

"Yeah, I know one of them."

"Grady..."

I climbed over the rows of empty seats that separated us to reach Butchie and her friends.

"Hey what's happening?" I asked as two of the girls moved over a seat so I could sit in the seat next to Butchie.

"Ain't nothing—you left your friends?"

"Yeah, what you doing here?"

"The same thing you're doing here—watching the movie."

"I see Joan's not with you," I said. Butchie and I sat with two of her friends on each side of us.

"No, she's couldn't come. Theses are my friends, Rita and Mary, Terry and Jean."

They all waved. Most of them sat with their feet on the upper back of the chairs in front of them. Their evening prior to the movie was probably similar to ours. Even in Harlem, there are weekends that were so dull that it sends you to a late show on Forty-Second Street.

"Is Ozzie down there?"

"No, that's Bill Chapman and some other guys you don't know."

"So what you been doing lately?"

"Oh, I'm working now."

"Yeah, what are you doing?"

I have long had this awful habit of offering more information than was necessary and it always made me have to tell a lie, or sometimes get caught in a lie.

"I'm a shipping clerk."

"You quit school?"

"No, I'm working and going to night school."

Mercifully, something happened on the screen that turned Butchie's attention to it. We were watching one of those Troy Donahue; "Boy meets Girl" stories and it had reached a scene where the essence of the main conflict was being introduced. It was a scene that captured the attention of everyone and brought quiet to the theater. We paid attention to the movie without speaking for a long while. Later, one of the girls said that they had reached the section of the movie that they came in on and she was ready to leave.

"Call me next Friday evening at Joan's house," Butchie said as they rose to leave. I walked down the stairs with them, said good night and went to the men's room as they left.

4

Many of the neighborhood guys in my circle stopped going to the community center every weeknight. We felt we were too old for that kind of juvenile diversion. Our view of the community center changed at the same time we started to feel too independent to have moonlighting teachers baby-sit us. We started hanging out at the only neighborhood bar that was left after the blocks across Amsterdam Avenue were demolished. One evening I was in the bar waiting for Ozzie, Tommy Borden, and some of the other guys to show up. Hyman Nesbit was sitting at the corner of the bar by the window. He had a glass of warm beer that had been sitting in front of him for a half-hour. Hyman was high and nodding off. The owner didn't like for guys to come in his place high on drugs, but if they bought something to drink, they were sometimes nudged, but basically left alone. Ted Meeks entered the bar in high spirits. Ted

Meeks was a construction worker and compared to the other men in the neighborhood, he made good money. Ted Meeks was a muscular rugged looking man whose aura exuded strength. Mr. Meeks was a good-natured man who always wore a smile. He stood on the corner across the street from the bar most evenings laughing and making jokes with everyone passing by, his pint showing from a brown bag in his back pocket. Each evening, after work, Ted Meeks bought his liquor at the liquor store and when he reached a certain level of drunkenness he'd go to the bar for one or two more drinks.

"Everybody," Ted Meeks yelled out. He had a thick voice that seemed to hover in the air. "Everybody," he repeated with a big smile on his face; the doors of the bar still held open with his powerful hands. He looked over at where Hyman sat still nodding and the smile left his face. Ted Meeks adopted the serious consoling expression of a physiotherapist. He staggered to where Hyman sat and put his arm around Hyman's shoulder.

"Slick'um," he said, "Slick'um you ought to stop this shit. Ain't no good for you. Slick'um, you need to straighten up and fly right."

Hyman looked up at him and tried to speak, but all he could say was "Yeah."

"Harry, bring me a drink and bring Slick'um here a cold beer," Ted Meeks said to the bartender as the smile returned to his face. "This beer here ain't fit to drink no more," he said as he moved the warm glass of beer to the edge of the bar and he sat on the stool next to Hyman.

"Thank you," Hyman finally said, "but why you got to let everybody peek my hold-card."

"Peek your hold-card? Hell, Slick'um I ain't the only one in here who kin see you nodding in your beer. You ain't got no hold-card boy, your cards is all right-side up, it's just that the rest of them in here don't want to say nothing, but I likes you."

A job like Ted Meeks worked wasn't even a far off possibility. Even a laborer for a construction company belonged to a union and made good money, but the real attraction was that there was an opportunity to move up. But the chances of my landing such a job was as remote as being struck by lighting. Where I worked now, there was nothing to gain. I wanted to quit my job on several occasions when I was made to go out on a delivery, but the holidays were coming and I knew that I could use the little money I made working. I started thinking more seriously about applying to night school as the reality started setting in that this was all I would be able to do for the rest of my life.

Business really picked up at Segal & Sons as Christmas came near. They were sending racks and racks of coats to the finishers for linings and were using the entire labor crew for deliveries and pick-ups. They were so busy one day that they sent a cutter from the floor with a laborer to make an urgent delivery to a retailer. Every time we went out on a delivery, they insisted that we returned right away. They knew that during regular times, the guys would linger back, killing time with a jug of wine or sitting on a stoop in some out of the way block and they didn't mind that much. From their perspective, for what they paid us, they were getting their money's worth. But the holidays were different; this was when they made the larger percentage of their yearly sales—so during this period they really cracked the whip.

I made it through Christmas. I was able to get presents for Aunt Dot and Uncle Bertram. I bought a set of plates and a plain dress for Sarah. And I bought a Christmas tree a whole week before Christmas. When I was younger, Sarah used to send me across the street to the fruit and vegetable stand next to Old Dutch Cleaners on Christmas Eve with a dollar. "Tell that man he better sell you a tree for that dollar, he ain't gonna have no use for them trees in a few hours, but he'll always have a use for that dollar." After explaining this kind of logic to the fruit man, I would come home with a five dollar Christmas tree and we would hurriedly decorate it while we sang Christmas carols. Christmas dinner was always at our house. Aunt Dot and Uncle Bertram were always there and Aunt Lacy and Uncle Henry came down, though less frequently.

On New Years Eve, everybody I knew was planning to go to the dance at the Renaissance Casino in Harlem. Clark asked me to go to a house party at his cousin's house in Corona Queens. I thought that would be something new and maybe even fun so I decided to go with Clark. The party was free and I had never been to Corona. That night Clark and I drank a pint of scotch. An hour before midnight, we started out for the subway station. Earlier that morning, the leaders of the Transport Workers Union had met with thousands of their members in a hotel in mid-town Manhattan and took a vote to authorize a work stoppage if a new contract had not been agreed on by midnight. It was all over the newscasts on television. The front-page headline in the evening *Post* told of the pending strike. Like all New Yorkers who used the subway to get to their New Year's gatherings, we held faith that the negotiators would reach a pact, but we weren't going to let the threat of a strike ruin our plans. We went through this charade every other New Years Eve. The trains ran slow and there were longer than usual intervals between trains. We had to make three transfers to get to the number 7 train to Corona and at each change of trains, we had to wait a long time for the next train. The New Year arrived while we were waiting on the platform for the number 7. The number 7 train arrived a little behind the arrival of 1960.

After two station stops in Manhattan, the train entered the tunnel under the East River. The only difference in the ride was that the sound the train wheels made on the track echoed in the tunnel. When the number 7 train emerged from the ground and climbed the elevated portion of the route in Queens, I was able to see Manhattan in the distance. I stood up from my seat and looked out of the door glass. At night, Manhattan is a city of lights. I could distinguish certain buildings by their height, shape and location. To see all of Manhattan is a marvelous sight, but it is also a sight that highlights the division of the city. The beauty of the lights from midtown to the city's south distracts attention from the blight to the city's north. I had only seen this luminous view of the city, on postcards and on television. This real life look gave me another way to see the economic disparity of the city.

The house was a few blocks from the elevated subway station. Clark's uncle's house was the first house on the block. This was a large tree-lined street with a tree-lined median. Few cars were parked in the streets. Most houses had a car parked in the driveway. The house was a huge wooden building and with the street light shining on it, I could see that it was painted light blue and white. This neighborhood, I later learned, was home to Louis Armstrong and many other black celebrities.

Clark had led me to believe this was going to be a party for young people but it appeared to be more of a family gathering. The people there were mostly older and all members of Clark's family. They were courteous to me, but I sensed that they had reservations about me. This was a middle-class black household, people who probably came from the world I presently inhabited, so they recognized me. Not only were they familiar with my physical surroundings, but they also knew my heart. The charm of the setting had an instant affect on me—I masked myself as one of them. But they knew who I was.

The family offered the traditional black New Year dinner of pork, collard greens and peas and rice. Clark and I ate a piece of cake. The grown ups were drinking, but in a way I was unfamiliar with. They drank in a refined and dignified manner—I hardly knew that liquor was present. Being in this house and seeing with my own eyes that there was another possibility impressed me. The change in my behavior at the moment was superficial, but the deeper change was to come. Clark's cousin's name was Kathy. She was a tall skinny girl. She was a very pretty girl who spoke with sophisticated confidence. The three of us sat in a little enclave off from the living room where the gathering was taking place. She was seventeen and as she spoke, I imagined that she was interested in me.

"Would you believe it's 1960 already?" Kathy said.

"Yeah," Clark said, "time is moving on."

"1960," I said.

"Why don't you come to the city some time?" Clark asked.

"I don't care much for Manhattan."

"But everybody comes into the city sometime."

"Oh, I do. I go to shop on 34th Street once in a while. Two weeks ago we went to Radio City Music Hall for the Christmas show."

"Why don't you come to visit us sometime?"

"In the projects?"

Clark felt the bourgeois sting and dropped the subject. I had lived in worst places than the projects. I took up the challenge.

"What wrong with the projects?" I asked.

"If you live in the projects and don't know what's wrong there—you've really got a problem."

"Everybody can't live in a nice big house like this one."

"How true."

"Don't you at least go to school in the city?"

"No, I go to Roosevelt High here in Queens. I'm graduating this June."

"Then what are you gonna do?" Clark asked.

"I've been accepted at Columbia University. I'll be studying Journalism. What college are you two attending?"

Clark rose to go to the bathroom.

"College," I said, "I'm going into the army." I don't know where the words came from because I had never had this thought before. I knew that I needed to say something and this may very well have been one of those times when my mouth acted on its own. When Clark returned, we joined the party in the living room. It was nearly daybreak when we left. We spent the first morning in the year 1960 riding the subway into a deserted and partied out Manhattan—the threatened subway strike had been averted.

5

After the New Year, business got slow for Segal & Sons. They laid a few of the laborers off, but I was kept on. With a smaller delivery force, I was assigned more often to make deliveries and to pick up rolls of fabric. It snowed lots that January. It was very difficult to maneuver the four-wheel carts in the snow and slush while dodging cars and trucks. Normally, they sent two of us with a cart to pick up a load of fabric and even for two people this was a tiring task in the snow. One Monday morning, they sent me out alone. The company where I was to make the pick up was eight blocks away and I was exhausted getting there with an empty cart. Coming back with a cartload of rolled fabric was even more complicated—almost impossible. In certain spots, I had to try to pull the cart through snow that had turned into slush. In one section, it took me an hour to move a block. The front wheels on the carts were freewheeling and when I pushed, the snow would take the wheels to the side. It was extremely difficult to control the direction of the cart. At one point, I decided to leave the cart of goods on the street and go home. I started to call up Sol, the boss who dispatched me on this mission, to tell him where they could find the cart of fabric, but they owed me for last week's work and I was sure that they would withhold it if I left in this manner. So, I decided to take the entire day to get back from this one delivery and to quit that evening. I got back near closing time.

"Where in the hell you been all day?" Sol yelled out. "I called Polk Fur and found out that you left there since eleven o'clock—don't tell me it took you six hours to come eight blocks." I only knew Sol by that name. He was about fifty years old. He seemed to be an all around man at Segal & Sons. He worked in the cutting room when he was needed there. He was in charge of assigning chores to the laborers. He attended the loud meetings of the department heads in the cluttered back office. He was always lying and yelling to buyers and contractors on the phone. He may have owned a piece of the company, but I had nothing to lose, so I started to embellish my claim.

"I didn't have no lunch," I said, "I want to get paid for not taking lunch."

"You didn't have lunch, for-Gods-sake kid, you were gone long enough to have lunch on a sunny beach in the Caribbean."

"There is too much snow on the ground for one person to control the cart and I kept getting stuck."

"You know the phone number here, kid?"

"Yeah."

"What do we tell you—if you have a problem call us. I'd send someone to help you kid."

"Yeah, but you didn't give me a dime to make the call with."

"Look kid, I was told to let you go, but I'm an understanding guy so if you can promise me that this won't happen again you can keep your job."

"I quit."

"You what?"

"I quit. I'll be here Friday for my last paycheck."

"Why ain't you the ungrateful one. Here I am going out on the limb for you and this is how you act."

I knew that Sol wanted to keep me solely because it would be difficult to find people willing to do this kind of work in this kind of weather.

"Make sure I get paid for today with an extra hour for not having lunch," I said as I walked out of the door.

"Get outta here," Sol said throwing both of his arms into the air.

I was back on the streets hanging out with Ozzie and Tommy Borden. They were both out of work. Tommy Borden had graduated from high school the previous June, but the only job he was able to find was as an attendant in the restroom of an upscale midtown restaurant. Since he quit school more than a year earlier, Ozzie had worked in several machine shops that made or repaired things. But, now, he hadn't worked in several months. We spent most of the cold winter mornings at Ozzie's house watching the 10 o'clock morning movie on television. We'd spent the day loitering in a hallway in one of the Phipps buildings on 64th Street in a crowd of other out of work young men. Some mornings we went to the employment office and filled out applications for jobs, then we went to the movies. I never stayed home. I left the house early as if I had an appointment.

My frustration with my predicament was showing at home. I spoke angrily to my brother and sisters. I was moody and downcast. I felt unjustly disparaged when Sarah spoke to me about finding a job or going back to school. I was in denial when it came to realizing the rut I was in and the misery I was causing my family and myself. Sarah got on me all the time "A job or school," were my options at first. By the end of the month, she added "Or leave this house." I left the house at 7 o'clock in the morning and returned at ten to go to bed. There was a week when I hardly spoke to anyone in the household. My relationship with my family had really gotten tense and to a boiling point. I was definitely not making an optimistic entry into adulthood.

One Sunday evening, Tommy Borden, Ozzie and I chipped in together to buy a loaf of bread, a pound of spice ham, and a large soda each. We went to Ozzie's house to make sandwiches and watch television. In our conversation, we found out that we were all having similar problems at home. "I gotta stop this shit and really find a job," I said.

"Me too," Tommy said, "my moms okay, but my pops is giving me hell. He gets on me so much about not contributing to the household that I don't eat anything around him."

"I just want to get out of this house and out of this neighborhood," Ozzie said.

"I'm gonna join the army," I said just as I did on New Years morning, without thinking about it. It was as though something in my subconscious was guiding the statement from my vocal cords without first clearing it with the cognitive section of my brain.

"For real?" Tommy asked.

"Yeah," I said, "I'm gonna join the army."

"When?" Ozzie asked.

"I don't know."

"I'll go with you." Tommy said.

"I'll go too," Ozzie chimed in.

"Then lets do it tomorrow."

"There is a army recruiting office in the building next to the Apollo Theater," I said, turning a mist of a thought that came from some unknown place into a call for solid action. "Lets meet in the morning."

We all agreed and we finished eating our sandwiches while we watched the late night show. The next morning we met in front of Ozzie's building. We talked it over again and still agreed that we were going to join the army. Walking out of the neighborhood, we ran onto Willie Clark, who was on his way to work. We told him where we were going and why. He decided to go with us. Just like that, Clark made up his mind not to go to work, but to join us. We had seen movies about friends who joined the army together and were allowed to stay together as a group. This is what we hoped would happen with us. We arrived at the recruiting office on the second floor of what was then known as the New York State Office building. The recruiters interviewed us and took us to different little testing rooms where we were each given a folder of test questions.

Clark and Tommy had both finished high schools. Ozzie and I had quit high school without graduating. Yet, Ozzie and I passed the test while Clark and Tommy failed. We were disappointed because we felt that the larger a group we were in, the better off we'd be. Ozzie and I were given information packages and told we would receive reporting dates in the mail. The information package detailed the few things we needed to bring with us and described what would take place during the first week. Clark went to work late. Tommy and Ozzie went to the movies afterward. I went home to tell Sarah what I had done.

"You done what?" Sarah was genuinely surprised; she never gave a thought that this might be one solution to my problem. My joining the army surprised her as much as it had surprised me.

"I joined the army."

"You sure that's what you want to do?"

"I'm sure."

"I don't want you to say I run you into the army."

"I know, but I really want to do this. Ozzie is going too. We gonna get a notice in the mail when to report to Whitehall Street."

Over the next few days, the word spread through the neighborhood that we were going into the army. It seemed people viewed me differently. Maggie Clark came on to me sweetly now.

Some of the older guys in the community who had been in the army offered advice. Bill Chapman treated every day he saw me like it was my last day as a civilian. He took me to clubs in the Village, gave me reefer and bought me lunches at neighborhood eateries. When Sarah made fried chicken, she offered me the leg. Ed Lewis was proud of me and he anticipated having the bed to himself. The notice came in the mail on February 12th. My reporting date was February 23rd 1960. Later that day, I checked with Ozzie to see if he received his notice and if the reporting dates were the same. We had both been ordered to report to the army enlistment center at Whitehall Street at 7 o'clock on that morning. Now it all seemed real with just eleven days to go. Everything I did, it seemed, was for the last time.

Two days before we were to report, I told Ozzie that Joan called me to invite us to spend our last evening as civilians with her and Butchie at her house. He didn't seem aggravated about it. In fact, he seemed pleased, even eager. That evening when we arrived, the girls were in the apartment alone. Joan had somehow arranged for her parents to make a visit to relatives in Harlem.

"How does it feel to be going into the army?" Joan asked.

"What do you mean?" Ozzie replied. "It feels like anything else—it's no big deal."

"I feel great about it," I said. "For me it feels like a new beginning."

"How long will you'll be gone?"

"I don't know," Ozzie said.

"Eight weeks," I said. "We've going to take basic training then we come home on leave."

The conversation went on like this for a while. Joan seemed interested while Butchie stayed silent for the most part. Joan played the role of the concerned sweetheart lamenting the imminent loss of her man about to march off to defend the home front. Butchie's behavior was more like a woman fulfilling an obligation by her mere presence. Joan was adept at using Butchie to lure me knowing that this was how she would get to see Ozzie. We were acting out the roles young men and young women have performed since the beginning of time. Didn't Ogg go to the cave of Papola the night before he went off to hunt for dinosaur meat? Didn't Princess Gwenadaire meet Sir Lancelot under the bridge over the moat the night before he rode off to slay the green dragon? Didn't Fatima spend a last night under a cola-nut tree with Jomo before he set off to the Boar Wars? Didn't Sally Sue make passionate love with Billy Bob just hours before he joined his unit for the battle at Bull Run? We went out for pizza. When we returned, Joan put the music on and we separated into different rooms.

The next morning, Sarah woke me up early. She made me some grits and eggs. I washed and got dressed.

"You are sure you want to go?" she said.

"I'm sure." I said goodbye to Ed Lewis and my sisters as they slept. Sarah gave me five dollars and we kissed goodbye.

6

Ozzie met me on Amsterdam Avenue in front of my building and we walked to the subway station. We arrived at the induction center on time and after we were sworn in, it was like we gave up all sovereign rights to our own actions. There were forty or so new inductees. We were shuffled from room to room like something being manufactured on a production line. We filled out dozens of forms and were seen by all kinds of doctors. We got to know each other as we passed in the hallways or waited outside this or that office door. There was one fellow who got noticed by us all. He was a loud pompous black guy about eighteen. He talked incessantly and had an opinion on every subject that arose. What rubbed many of the guys wrong about this guy wasn't the fact that he was opinionated but rather, the fact that he expressed his opinions as *the opinion*. Soon everybody got to know him. Some of the white boys started referring to him as "The Professor." We had a light lunch and were loaded onto buses for the trip to Fort Dix in New Jersey. The Professor was on the same bus as Ozzie and me. He talked constantly the entire trip. That evening, at Fort Dix, we were fed, assigned barrack beds and given bedding.

The next morning, they woke us up early for what would be a whirlwind day. We were fed breakfast, then given what they called "A flying twenty." Then they marched us from location to location to spend the twenty dollars on a haircut, toiletries and other personal items. For the next three days there was nothing for us to do while we awaited orders to be shipped to our training bases for boot camp. But, the army doesn't waste talent and manpower, so each morning they assigned some of us to "Butt Patrol" picking up cigarette butts from around the barracks and other buildings. Some of us were assigned to the hospital to run errands and do small cleaning chores. I was assigned to a guy in uniform at the hospital. The first few chores he had for me to do were either to pick things up or to take something somewhere. But mostly I just sat around until he ordered me to do something. After lunch, he called me over to his desk and sat me down. He looked me in my eyes and spoke earnestly. "I've got a very important mission for you," he said, "very important. Are you ready for your very first crucial military assignment?"

I hesitated for a moment not knowing what to think or say. I was a soldier in the United States Army, what else was there to say, but..."Yes sir."

"What's your name private?"

"Grady Murrow, sir."

"Private Murrow, this office has been running out of headspace for months now. I want you to go to every department in this hospital and collect all of the extra headspace you can find and return it here. It is now 13:30 hours; you are on your own until 16:30 hours when you should return here before chow time. Private Murrow, I am depending on you to find me some headspace—do-you-think-that-you-can-handle-it?"

He made it sound so crucial my heart sunk. "I hope so sir," I said doubtfully.

"Sure you can Private Murrow. I'll call around to some of the departments to let them know that you're coming for the headspace."

I liked the sound of that. "Private Murrow," I had just joined the army, I didn't even have a uniform yet and already I had rank. I was dismissed and told to get on with my mission. I went to the first station I saw. A group of nurses and a man who might have been a doctor stood talking. I interrupted and told them that I was sent to collect any extra headspace they might have. They looked at me puzzled for a moment. Then, almost simultaneously, their eyes lit up.

"We don't have any extra headspace at the moment," one nurse said.

"I saw some on the third floor in room 334," another nurse said, "try there."

"Thank you," I said feeling I had made a good start. I didn't take the elevator; I hurried up the stairs to the third floor and searched out room 334. The door was closed. I hesitated for a moment, wondering whether to knock before I entered. I knocked at the door and waited, but no one answered in what I considered a reasonable amount of time, so I turned the doorknob and walked in. There was a guy sitting at a desk reading the newspaper. From the equipment in the room, I surmised that this was a x-ray lab and this guy must be a technician. He looked up from the newspaper as he heard the door open.

"Can I help you?" he asked.

"I was sent to collect any extra headspace you have."

"Who sent you?"

"I don't know his name. I was assigned to this guy in an office downstairs and he told me to go around the hospital to collect any extra headspace that was out there."

"Do you think that I would give you headspace without knowing where it's going? Or, who sent for it? Go back and get me an authorization letter, then you can have all the headspace I have."

I walked back downstairs thinking that what the technician said made sense. My boss should have explained who he was and given me something that would have authorized me to collect this precious headspace. When I got back to his office, the door was shut. I tried turning the doorknob, but the door was locked. I stood outside bewildered. I wondered where I would find this guy to explain the situation and get on with the job he assigned me. I must have looked frightened. A black Sergeant who was passing took notice of me and asked if I was lost.

"No, I don't think so. I'm new. The guy in this office sent me to collect all the extra headspace that people have."

"Oh he did, huh. Let me put you wise Youngblood. That was a gag he pulled on you. The only place you'll find headspace is on a 50-caliber machine gun. Headspace is the gap behind rounds that allows the bullets to chamber one at a time and prevents the gun from blowing up in the shooter's face. You'll find out about headspace later in your training. There is bed space, but there isn't any headspace in a hospital. Whoever that person was that sent you on this wild goose chase probably didn't have anything for you to do. So, this was his way of getting rid of you so he could go goof off himself."

"So what should I do?"

"I can't tell you that, but if I were you I would get lost until chow time then report back to my barracks."

That evening we received orders that we were going to Fort Gordon in Augusta, Georgia after lunch the next day. The army finds it more efficient to organize its personnel in alphabetical order, so Ozzie Donaldson was called in the first busload. I was called in the third busload along with the boy they called "The Professor" who's name turned out to be Charlie Nash. We left Fort Dix right after lunch. It was a long grueling bus ride made worst by having to listen to all of The Professor's bullshit. No matter what topic the group conversation centered on, he knew something about it and portrayed himself as the final authority on it.

"The New York Yankees is always going to be the best team in baseball because it will always attract the best players. Everybody who plays baseball really wants to be a Yankee," he said when someone lauded the Boston Red Sox. Someone mentioned house plants and he offered this "This woman in The Bronx was found dead in her apartment. The police were puzzled about her death because there were no signs of foul play. Her apartment was filled with plants and all of the windows were sealed shut. She had more than three hundred plants of all kinds and sizes. The forensic expert connected the amount of plants and the lack of oxygen in the apartment to the woman's death." On religion: "The American Indian believes that Nature is God." On the birth of the galaxy he said: "The stars are made from molecular hydrogen that cools into solids to form spheres." On the mythology of the American West: "Tonto found the Lone Ranger in the plains after he had been ambushed and left for dead, and he nursed him back to life."

We arrived at Fort Gordon around five in the morning to a loud cadre of shouting non-commissioned officers, after spending 17 hours on the bus. We were half-awake, tired and disorientated and all of the shouting only served to further confuse us. We thought that we would be given a bunk and some time to sleep after the long trip. New inductees from other parts of the country were arriving at the same time. They lined us up in front of the buses, took a roll call to account for everyone and assigned us to our drill instructors by company, platoon and squad. Ozzie and I wound up in different platoons of the same company. There were forty-four people in each platoon. We had a platoon sergeant, an assistant platoon sergeant, and four squad leaders. The guys in my platoon were from all over the country and had last names that began with L, M, N, and O; of course, Charlie Nash was assigned to the same platoon. We spent the morning of our first day collecting bedding, boots and uniforms. That afternoon we went to an orientation session. We were back in the barracks after dinner in the mess hall. We were all so tired that the late occurrences of the day seemed surreal. We were instructed, needlessly, to go to bed early because we would have roll call at 5 am.

During the next few days, we were fully equipped with field packs, entrenching tools, and assigned a rifle number from the arms room. We quickly settled into a routine of getting up at five in the morning to run two miles in the chilly Georgia morning air in only our pants and tee shirts. Then we were herded into the mess hall, where we did pull-ups on a chin bar before entering for a quick breakfast. At six o'clock, there was an inspection of the barracks. At 7 o'clock we assembled for roll call followed by physical fitness exercises. In the first few weeks, training to march as a unit followed the morning exercise. The army breaks down everything it teaches to its smallest parts—even marching. Each movement in making an about face, a turn in marching directions, standing at attention or standing at ease is taught and rehearsed over and over and over and over. The army believes repetition is an effective teaching tool and it employed that tool in teaching marching, hand to hand combat, marksmanship, bayonet training, map reading, assembling and disassembling of weaponry, and even the intangible components of loyalty, duty, and honor.

One morning, during our second week of training, as we were marching back to our barracks, Charlie Nash, 'The Professor," who marched directly behind me, continually stepped on the heel of my right boot. I asked him in a smothered tone to stop stepping on me. He said out loud that my timing was off and that I was out of step. And, he continued to step into my heel as we marched. It seemed to me that he was making an extra long stride to catch my heel with each right step he took. "Stop stepping on me." I said not intending to arouse the attention of the drill sergeant.

"Get in step Murrow," The Professor said.

"Settle down in rank," the drill sergeant said. "I don't want to hear another word."

We were near our barracks, so I stayed silent and tolerated the abuse for the final few yards, but I knew that I would have to fight this guy. When we were dismissed from formation, I rushed up to our squad room on the second floor and waited by the double doors for Nash who wasn't far behind. He entered through the door talking a mile a minute, as usual. I stepped out from behind the door and without saying a word I whacked him in his face. He seemed surprised and tried to get away from me, but I was all over him, hitting him in the face and chest. He fell to the floor and I got on top of him still beating his face. The shouting from the other platoon members brought the drill instructors running into our bay area. When the men saw that the sergeants were running in, they started to pull us apart to separate us. All of our drill instructors were white Southerners and the army had only been integrated for a decade, so I knew they must have found it amusing to see two Negro soldiers fighting each other with all of those white boys around. By the time they reached us, we were both on our feet. "Attention," one of the drill instructors called out in command, but I was so mad that I was still trying to swing on Nash. In my mind, this was not just a lesson for "The Professor," I remembered Lem Stuttleton's lesson about intentions so I wanted to send out a message to everyone in the platoon that I was not to be messed with. My squad leader, a staff sergeant with ruddy skin grabbed my arm and said sternly "You're at attention soldier." I dropped my arms to my side and assumed the position. Everyone was silent. The platoon sergeant walked in slowly. He looked around as if to assess the situation. We were all standing at attention in a scattered formation. The platoon leader walked through the different groups looking us each in the eyes.

"This time, this time I repeat, I don't want to know what happened here. This time, I'm gonna overlook this disturbance, this time. But, ooh boy you let this happen again and every man in here will be sorry for the day he was born."

The platoon leader walked over to Charlie Nash, took a good look at his swollen right eye, "You'll be all right," he said to Nash. Get'um ready for the riffle range," he ordered the squad leaders.

The Professor marched behind me for another six weeks without ever again stepping on my heel. He went on babbling as before and that was fine with me. I never won him over as a buddy, but I did win his respect. Besides Charlie Nash and myself, there were two other guys in our platoon from New York City. One was a Jewish boy named Joel Kornberg and the other was an Italian boy named Tony Nelleta. All the others were from the South or the Northwest. Joel slept in the bunk above my bed. We became friends and looked out for each other. Joel Kornberg was a secular Jew who used Judaism to get out of participating in our Saturday schedules. I was jealous because it was a scam I couldn't pull off and I was mystified that the army permitted it.

During our fifth week of training, we were having bayonet practice each morning after breakfast. They divided us into two lines facing each other, but with enough room between us to prevent contact with each other in our movements. We were instructed to mount our bayonets in place on the tips of our M1 rifles. Then they would give us the command to get into the "On Guard" position. They taught us two different attack movements and each morning we practiced them on command. The attack movements were the long thrust and the short trust. Each movement was intended to make us efficient in using the stock of our rifles to thrust a 10-inch bayonet blade into the chest of the enemy. From the "On Guard" position we were commanded to "Long thrust and hold," upon which, we would growl wildly as we made thrusting motions while extending our arms and right legs out. We were taught to twist the blade to make a big incision that would make the blade's withdrawal from the bones surrounding the enemy's chest cavity easier. Then we would bring up our left leg for balance. Then pull the arms and right leg back as if withdrawing the blade from the enemy's chest. Bringing the left leg back to resume the "On Guard" position was the final move in the series. A hundred men face another hundred men with fixed bayonets growling and repeating these movements over and over for hours.

"Long thrust and hold—move. Short thrust and hold—move."

One morning, we were served oranges along with our breakfast. Joel decided to save his orange for later in the day. He put it in his pocket intending to leave it in his locker when we went up to our barracks to prepare for our assemblage for bayonet practice. In basic training, Everything is done in such a rush that Joel forgot to remove the orange from his pocket before we were rushed outside. While we were on the drilling field in the "On Guard" position, drill instructors came by each of us to check the correctness of our stances. When a drill instructor got to Joel, he noticed the orange bulging from his pants pocket.

"What's that you got in your pocket soldier," he asked Joel.

"Nothing sir," Joel said momentarily forgetting the orange in his pocket.

"Reach into your pocket and hand me that nothing soldier."

Joel remembered the orange. He broke his position to reach for the orange. Then he handed the orange to the instructor and he resumed the "On Guard" position without being told to. The drill instructor took the orange and held it up.

"This is what this soldier goes to battle with. He brought an orange for an enemy of the United State of America. He doesn't want to kill the enemy, he wants to feed him." Then he took the orange and stuck it down on Joel's bayonet squeezing the juice down the barrel of his M1.Then we resumed our bayonet practice. One hundred men face another hundred men with menacing growls, glistening steel bayonets and an orange stuck to one of them.

"Long thrust and hold," the instructor said.

Joel went through the rest of the morning with the orange on his bayonet as he growled and thrust his bayonet, with the orange stuck to it, into the chest of his imaginary opponent. This was one funny sight. The only thing I could do to keep from laughing out loud at this absurdity was not to look at him.

"Short thrust and hold, move."

After each bayonet practice, in the evenings, we always disassemble our weapon to clean them. That evening, after I finished cleaning my rifle, I had to help Joel clean the dried orange juice from his. The juice of the orange had dried hard and couldn't be wiped away, we had to wash the barrel with soap and hot water. We dried the metal parts of the riffle and applied an extra coating of linseed oil to prevent rusting, before Joel reassembled his riffle.

7

Ozzie had grown tight with some black boys in his platoon from Brooklyn, so I saw very little of him in our spare time on Sundays. I spent Sundays playing ping-pong in the dayroom and on my bunk reading the Alfred Hitchcock magazines, Sarah sent me.

I received letters from Maggie, Evane, Joan, and even Brad wrote once, but nothing from Butchie. In the evenings when training was over, we were all so tired that most people showered and went to bed. We were rushed through a variety of activities from five in the morning until five in the evening, six days a week. There was time for nothing more than reflection. For me, this was eight weeks without a drink of wine or a joint, but Ozzie and his friends from Brooklyn went to the canteen some nights and drank beer.

The eight-weeks in boot camp had snapped me from my routine of the last few years. Plus associating with other young men from different parts of the country was laying the foundation for my reformation. I was being exposed to the attitudes and cultural differences these young men brought from their environments. I went into the army thinking that all that I had experienced growing up in New York City was superior to what I would have learned in any other part of the country. I also believed that my experience growing up in the Amsterdam projects was referred over any other part of New York City. Now I was meeting guys, black and white, whom I considered substantial and they were from places like Detroit, Atlanta, Mobile and Rocky Mount. I even met white boys from rural areas of the South who were impressive to me—in a foreign kind of way. I was discovering how narrow minded I had been—a recognition that would allow me to begin to grow and grow up.

Near the end of the eight weeks of basic infantry training, we were given generalized placement tests to see who would fit best where. The result of these tests, in most cases, would determine what military occupation we would each be trained for in the next eight weeks of training. Some recruits had been promised certain occupations based on how well they did on these series of tests, before they signed up. I was completely oblivious to the concept that I could partly determine my military destiny by performing well on these tests. I muddled through them, but had I known at the start, what I later learned, I would have tried to score well enough for a position with the *Stars And Stripes*, the military newspaper.

A few days before the end of basic training we all received orders for our next assignments. What we did next was closely tied to how well we did on the tests we took. I got orders to take a two-week leave of absence and an airline ticket to report to Fort Hood Texas for advance infantry training—I was going to be a foot soldier. Joel Kornberg received orders to report to Fort Mammoth, New Jersey, for pictorial training—he was going be a photographer. Joel didn't get any leave time; he didn't need it since he was being stationed back home, nearly. The Professor was going to train to become a medic. I found out that Ozzie and two of his friends from Brooklyn had signed up for Special Forces training and were being shipped, without leave time, to an undisclosed location. Ozzie was the type of person who was over zealous about things in the beginning but his enthusiasm always diminished before long. These guys from Brooklyn had convinced Ozzie that they should join the army's elite cadre of assassin warriors. These next few days would be the last times I would see Ozzie for the next four years.

When I got home, Sarah planned a big dinner. Aunt Dot and Uncle Bertram came downtown for the family gathering. I had gifts for everyone that I bought from the PX. It was the happiest time my family had with me in years.

"How's the Army treating you," Uncle Bertram asked.

"Doesn't he look healthy," Aunt Dot said smiling approvingly.

"Do you think you're going to stick it out?" Sarah asked.

"It's not bad," I said. "I don't think I'll make a career of it, but I'll do my three years."

"As long as there ain't no war, you'll be alright, Uncle Bertram said.

"Hush, there ain't gonna be any war," Aunt Dot said.

"There's gonna be a war?" Ed Lewis asked.

"Nobody's talking to you," Ann Ruth said, there ain't gonna be no war while my brother is in the army."

I was surprised at how much my little sister Beatrice had grown. Ed Lewis and Ann Ruth were as thin as ever. Eight weeks hadn't changed them much, but Beatrice's growth was very noticeable. She was taller and plump. Everyone wanted to see me in my uniform, but I couldn't wait to put on civilian clothes. When I went into the streets and met old friends, they all wanted to know where my uniform was. No one wanted to see me in the same clothes I wore before I left. Besides, I had gained a few pounds and had firmed up some, so my old clothes were a bit tight on me.

Sarah told me that Brad had been by our house the week before asking if I was home yet. Bill Chapman wanted to know about everything I had gone through. Clark was always busy working, but I did see him once went I when to their house to see his sister Maggie. I went looking for Brad in Harlem, but his sister told me that he had moved to Brooklyn. I found out that Butchie was hanging out with the Rudland brothers and that they had graduated up from marijuana. The Rudland brothers were get high freaks early on. It was Jack Rudland who, when they first moved to the Amsterdam projects, started the craze of sniffing the clothes cleaner cobona to get high. Although it was a short-lived fad, it lasted long enough to cause the death of a boy from down the back. The Rudland family had moved back to Harlem and Butchie met Jack and Leroy up there. They found out about the connection they had to San Juan Hill and started hanging out and getting high together. I never saw Butchie while I was home on leave. In fact, I never saw Butchie again while she was alive. Even after I got out of the army in 1963, I searched Butchie out, but I could never find her. A few years after that I heard that she died from cancer.

On the third day of my last week home, Maggie Clark wanted me to go with her to her cousin Kathy's house. When I got to Maggie's house to pick her up, she was highly disappointed.

"Where is your uniform?" she asked.

"Home."

"Aren't you gonna wear it?"

"Do you want me to?

"Yes."

I went back home to change into my army dress greens. Sarah looked at me and smiled a knowing smile. Sarah didn't know Maggie well, but she liked her and was amused to see Maggie putting me through the hoops. Maggie was dressed up real pretty. On the train, she looped her arm through my arm and we sat talking and looking like an engaged couple. Maggie beamed to be sitting with a soldier. I think it made her feel grown up at seventeen.

My two weeks leave went by fast. The day it ended, I found myself on an airplane for the very first time, flying to Houston, Texas. In Houston, I boarded a smaller plane to Temple, Texas. Summer was beginning in a week. I had no idea how hot it got in Texas, but I was about to find out. Advanced Infantry training was some-what more relaxed than boot camp. Here, in addition to Sundays, we had most Saturday's off also. We were granted passes to go downtown to Temple on the weekends. Our workdays weren't nearly as tiring as they were in Boot Camp. Some nights I went to the recreation center where we played pool and ping-pong. The recreation center also had a book and record library. It was there that I discovered a book called "The Hemingway Reader," a collection of short stories and excerpts from the novels of Earnest Hemingway. I had heard of Earnest Hemingway before and I saw a few movies that were based on his works. Whenever I heard anyone speak about Hemingway, I could discern reverence and adulation in their voice and words, so although I had never read any of his works, I knew he was someone rather consequential. Signing the book out of the library made me feel smart, like I had done something important for my future. I wasn't going to read this book just to enjoy the read. I was going to read it to learn what I could about the craft of writing.

It was in Fort Hood that I ran into the term headspace again. We had three days of training on the 50-caliber machine gun. High up on a hill looking down into the valley that was our firing range an instructor explained to us the importance of proper headspace between rounds. There was a gauge to adjust the headspace, which set the timing between rounds that allowed the rounds to be chambered one at a time. This gauge is called the headspace gauge. Those days, I thought about the intern who had me going around the hospital looking for "Headspace." Advanced Infantry training was about improving our marksmanship and learning to fire larger weaponry. We were also taught how to direct artillery fire and how to use a map and compass. We learned platoon and squad level attack and defense strategies. We spent nights on field maneuvers and it was then that I first saw the Texas sky in July. The moon and the stars were so bright that we were able to write letters. My letters were inspired by the mood the bright moon set. "It's so hot here during the day, I saw a dog tracking a rabbit and they had both agreed to walk," I wrote to Joan. "I will love you even after the end of time," my letter to Maggie concluded. "Hemingway is a hell of a writer," I told Evane in a letter, "and I'm going to write well myself."

A few Saturdays I explored the streets of Temple. One Saturday I found a small bookstore and went in to browse. It was nothing like Mr. Michaux's bookstore in Harlem with volumes of books on the black experience. But I did find a copy of the Hemingway Reader, a book entitled "Improve Your Vocabulary in Ninety Days and another little book called "The Prophet" with a drawing on the cover of a white headed man, that seemed to pull at my attention. I bought all three books. Now I owned my very own copy of the Hemingway Reader. Later I added to my collection a book called "The Fundamentals of Good Writing" and these books formed the foundation of my early library.

I didn't get to know many of the guys in my unit very well. I read a lot and listened to jazz at the recreation center. There was a white boy in my platoon from Galveston, Texas who went home some weekends. He usually came back with a few joints that he shared with all his friends. I was once invited to take a few puffs with them. They wanted to have a laugh on the square black boy who was always into a book. They were surprised to learn that I was as familiar with marijuana as they were. It was from one of this group of boys that I learned there were reefer dealers on the streets of Temple near the black USO club. In the South, they had segregated USO clubs. I had been to the black USO club a few times. On the weekends, they held dances attended by local girls.

"There is a bar a block down from the street from the USO club," he told me, "where you can buy a matchbox of reefer for five dollars. "Just walk down by the bar and someone will approach you."

The next week, I took the bus from camp to the city of Temple, Texas. I was going to get me a five-dollar box of reefer and spend the rest of the weekend reading. The ride to Temple takes an hour and a half. I took the Hemingway Reader with me. When I arrived in the town, I stopped in at the USO club first. It wasn't fully dark yet, I was in uniform, and I wanted to make my buy under the cover of night. The USO building was an old three-story house. It had been remodeled to make the rooms larger. It was cozy inside, but I heard that the white USO was a large institutional type building with an auditorium, a stage and a dance hall. As far as racial integration was concerned, the army was more advanced than its civilian support systems and the southern localities where its forces were stationed. It was still early in the evening and the place was nearly empty. I shot a game of pool and read an old copy of Jet magazine. When it was dark and more people began to flow into the USO club, I decided to walk to the bar.

The bar was dark, loud and crowded. A blues band played music in the back of the room on a small make shift platform with a banister draped in purple crepe paper. This was a soldier's bar—almost every man in the bar in uniform had stripes. These were experienced veterans out for a good time. I squeezed in at the bar and ordered a whiskey with a beer chaser. I looked around the place. The women held on tight to the men they were with. They were, for the most part, older women in their late thirties and forties with big breast, big butts, big hair and lots of make up. I saw a young sergeant I recognized. He was in his early twenties and he sat in a booth with a woman who looked old enough to be his mother. He looked like he might have been there all day drinking, but she looked alert and occasionally played with his face. There was also a young guy there, who sat at a small table by the door with what appeared to be an empty beer bottle. He was dressed in civilian clothes and the fact that he looked out of place didn't register in my mind at the time—but I had seen this set-up many times in civilian life.

I drank my shot and finished my beer. And as I walked past the guy by the door, he made eye contact with me. I nodded. After I got a few steps out of the bar, he followed. "What you need, my man?" he asked as he caught up to me.

"A five."

He reached into his pocket and handed me a small-stick matchbox. In the South, a packet of matches didn't come with the price of a pack of cigarettes; they sell you a small box of matches for a penny. It's not unusual for people to purchase these matchboxes in packs of ten. This is the type of matchbox this guy used to sell his marijuana in. I gave him five dollars. Then I started to open the box to examine my purchase.

"Don't do that here," he cautioned me as he looked around in all directions with fear on his face. "It's too hot around here—the man is all about. And you in uniform—man you better be cool."

His voice had a believable urgency that put a fright in me. I put the matchbox into my pocket and walked to the bus depot. I looked at the bus schedule and saw that the next bus to Fort Hood would leave in twenty minutes. While I waited at the depot for the bus back to Fort Hood, I thought about the chance I was taking. Being caught with marijuana was a serious offense in civilian life and even more serious in the military. I would be court marshaled and given an undesirable discharge. I'd be disgraced. I felt disappointed with myself and decided right then not to do this again. The bus prepared to depart for Fort Hood. I remembered to get a seat in the back to avoid the embarrassment of being told to do so. I sat near an opened window two seats up from the very last seat in the back of the bus. The bus was nearly empty. It was still early and most people and indeed most soldiers were traveling in the other direction. The bus made its scheduled stops, but no one got off and it only picked up an elderly white woman, who sat in the seat behind the white driver. If it were any time after twelve midnight, this bus would be packed with drunken soldiers, the loud and the weary.

After we had driven for half an hour, I reached into my pocket making sure no one could see what I was doing and I pulled the matchbox out. I slid the box cover back to open the box. What I saw was crude—absolutely devastating to my image of myself as a slick, street-wise New Yorker. This hick hadn't even bothered to chop the grass in the matchbox to make it resemble marijuana. The box was filled with long stemmed grass, perhaps from a cow pasture, and maybe from under a pile of cow dung. I was enduring moments of cerebral trauma and cultural discovery—*there are slick motherfuckers everywhere.* He relied solely on his line about it being hot and my fear of being busted to rip me off. At first I couldn't believe that a country hick scammed me so easily, so I brought some of the grass to my nose to smell, although it wasn't shaped like marijuana. It was plain old grass and I could almost smell the cow dung. It took a while but later when I was certain that the content of the matchbox was useless, I eased it out of the window in my hand and let it fly. I started to laugh. The irony struck my funny bone and I laughed out loud. Then I opened my book and read Hemingway's story "The Fable of the Good Lion."

<u>8</u>

I had never before paid any attention to politics but in July of 1960 when John F. Kennedy won the Democratic nomination for president, there was so much excitement that it was hard to escape the melodrama. The excitement about Kennedy's upcoming campaign against Richard M. Nixon was everywhere. The pace of training was so eased that I even had time to follow some of the issues in the campaign. I hadn't thought of Catholics as a maligned minority before. All the Catholics I knew, except the Spanish speaking ones, did well where I came from. All the talk about the country not being ready to elect a man, who was a Catholic, president, was new to me. Well, that Catholic did win the election and I got to march in his inauguration parade. Before that campaign, I saw the issue confronting the country as black versus white. I had no understanding of the demographic of the white element of that equation. I didn't know that there was a sizable non-Catholic, Anglo

Saxon population, or that whites were divided into conservatives, Democrats, Dixiecrates, Republicans, Moderate Republicans, liberals, and kooks. Nor did I know that by the beginning of the 21-st Century, the kooks would be running the country. The John Kennedy/Richard Nixon presidential campaign got me hooked on politics, so I was able to follow the downward spiral of politics from that point to where it is today.

The last week of advanced Infantry training, recruiters from the 82nd Airborne Division came to show us a film and entice us to enlist to become paratroopers. At the same time, a rumor went out that everyone in my company was being shipped to Hawaii for the remainder of their enlistment, which, in my case, was thirty-one months of a three-year enlistment. And, there was talk about how expensive everything was there. There were also tales about how black soldiers were treated even worst in Hawaii than we in the South. I wanted to avoid going overseas even before I heard these rumors. The letters I was receiving from Maggie Clark were encouraging. She sounded like she had made her mind up and was choosing me over Malcolm Tibbs. It would be easier for me to nurture that feeling in her if I remained reasonably nearby. The film they showed us exalted the history of the 82nd Airborne Division and its role as an elite unit of the army. It promoted the fact that fifty-five dollars a month in jump pay was added to the pay of paratroopers. It challenged me with a line that asked: "Do you have the courage to be the best America has to offer?" I agonized over what to do—go to Hawaii, or jump out of airplanes to stay in the States?

On the deadline day to sign up, I got a telegram from my Uncle James in South Carolina that told me that my grandfather, Robert Murrow had died. Uncle James wanted to drive to Texas to bring me back with him to South Carolina for the funeral. Robert Murrow was my father's father, but I hadn't heard a word from him. I telegramed Uncle James back that I was joining the airborne and that I would soon be in Fayetteville, North Carolina. I loved my grandfather. When I used to spend the summers with Momma Dolly, I always spent at least a night with Pa Bob, as we called him.

Pa Bob had a large house with a porch that ran around the entire house. A married daughter lived in one potion of the house with her family and the two teenaged granddaughters of a deceased daughter lived on another side of the house. I would get my cousins Bannie and Tuffy and we'd arrive early to play in the yard until it was time to eat dinner. That night Pa Bob would tell us scary stories and we'd all fall asleep in the same bed. After I sent the telegram to Uncle James I went to sign up to join the 82nd Airborne Division.

San Juan Hill

CHAPTER SEVEN
The Angel of Death
1

I was paid for the month of July in Fort Hood. I arrived in Fort Bragg, North Carolina, August 1st, four days before my nineteenth birthday. I was assigned to an already formed unit of experienced paratroopers. All of the men in my new platoon had finished "Jump School," except another newly arrived boy, also from New York City, named Murray Cohen. This would be our assigned outfit once we finished jump school. This was an airborne infantry battalion. These guys were sharp. Their work uniforms were starched with a distinctive crease. They wore silver jump wings on their hats and on the chest of their uniforms. Their jump boots were like black glass. Their attitudes were lively and swift. Their voices were clear and sharp-witted—these guys were on the ball. In six weeks, I would be one of them.

The next day all the new recruits, over four hundred of us, were given an all day-orientation class. We learned that our training wouldn't start for ten days. There was a class graduating that weekend, then the instructors got a break and time to prepare for the next class. This time the talk wasn't so much on the glory of the airborne but rather, about the hard physical ordeal we had before us. We were warned that ten percent of us wouldn't make it through the six weeks but those that did would be better human beings in all ways. Most of us were given K.P. duty during the week that we waited for our class to start. Some of us were given make-work projects to keep us busy. There were two weekends in the ten-day period before our class began and those who wanted could have three-day passes for one of those weekends. The next day we took a fitness test that we all had to pass in order to get into jump school.

That morning all the new recruits were marched to the quarter-mile track near the gymnasium where the fitness test was held. We all ran two miles and had our heart rate checked before we entered the gym. There were mats on the floor, chin-up bars, and knotted ropes hanging from the ceiling. The instructors were set up at different locations in the gym. They had stopwatches and whistles. Everyone was dressed in white tee shirts, green fatigue pants and boots. We filed into the gym and went from station to station doing chin-ups, pull-ups, rush-ups, sit-ups, knee squats and so on. I did well in everything except the sit-ups. They wanted 50 sit-ups in 90 seconds. I think I may have been a little lackadaisical in my performance because I underestimated the sit-up to second ratio. I finished 50 sit-ups in115 seconds. I had failed an exercise, but I was allowed to complete the tests I had left to do. I was told that I would be dropped if I failed to do the required amount of sit-ups in the required time on the next day. We all went back to our barracks bone tired.

It didn't take me long to get into the spirit that was all around Fort Bragg. There were airborne wings everywhere I went. I could feel the gung-ho, can do spirit everyone here exuded. In the narrow streets, columns of paratroopers ran in formation repeating the sergeant's song in cadence.

I don't know, but I think I might.
I don't know, but I think I might.
Jump from an iron bird, while in flight.
Jump from an iron bird while in flight.
Am I right or wrong?
You're right.
Am I right or wrong?
You're right.
Sound off.
One, two
Sound off.

Three, four
Break it on down.
One, two, three, four
Airborne.

Here was something I could be proud to be a part of. That night, I never wanted anything more than to me able to wear airborne wings legally. I have always said prayers before I went to bed, but in a rather apathetic meaningless manner. This night I prayed to be heard and I prayed for 50 sit-ups in 90 seconds. I prayed a mindful prayer. I could feel myself communicating to The All Mighty—I knew that I had reached God, but I didn't know if he would grant my wish. I'd find that out in the morning when I returned to the gym. That morning, there must have been thirty of us who had failed one or two exercises. I sat on the mat with my legs stretched out and my hands folded behind my head as I waited for the instructor to say go. He set his stopwatch and kneeled down beside me. "Go," he said. My mind went blank as I furiously started to bend my back so my face touched my knees and laid back down to the mat. I was in a black hole where nothing registered in my mind. The only thing I was aware of was my movement. I felt the instructor's hand on my shoulder. "That's it, he said. He had put his hand on my shoulders to stop me. I had done the 50 sit-ups in far under 90 seconds and for a moment it appeared to him that I had lost control and he wouldn't be able to stop me. God had answered my prayer. I was in, now the rest was up to me.

I hadn't gotten chummy with any of the guys in my platoon yet, so on my nineteenth birthday I decided to go into town by myself to celebrate with a few drinks. August 5th fell on a Saturday. I still had most of my pay from the previous month and it was clear to me that there would not be any time to spend money once jump school started. I took an early bus to Fayetteville. The ride downtown took 35 minutes and ended in the black section of town near the train station. I arrived in town around twelve-thirty. I walked down the block across from the train station where the bus emptied. The block had a barbershop, a soul-food restaurant, two bars and a blues club. This was the heart of the black entertainment district, but I would find out later that there were other black restaurants, clubs and jook joints scattered in other sections of the black communities of Fayetteville. When I reached Main Street, I turned down it. Main Street is a six-block long area of small shops, department stores, and general business district. There was also a movie theater on Main Street. This area gave the town some semblance of urban life. I walked back up to the restaurant and had a lunch of fried chicken, rice and lima beans. Then I went to the bar.

The bar was named "May West," which I thought was a bad choice of imagery. Even though we hadn't even yet started jump school, we had learned some of the language and phrases involved with the airborne, from just listening and being attentive. One of the things I learned was that a May West is when a parachute doesn't completely open up, it has a valley in between two round air filled sections that, to some, resembles giant women's breasts. May West was an actress with big breasts, so this kind of parachute malfunction was named after her. Because the center of the parachute is deflated, the speed of descent is greatly increased. Paratroopers had been known to survive a May West, but only with serious injury. Why would anyone want to name a bar that I wondered? Women's breasts can, at times, cause some fuzzy decisions.

The barroom was small and well lit from the daylight, but it reeked of cigarette smoke and beer. It had seven or eight round wooden tables scattered about in no particular arrangement. There was no one at the bar. Three men sat at the table nearest the bar. One was an old man in his fifties. He was thin and though the weather was warm, he wore a gray sweater and a cap. When he talked, I could see two gold teeth in his mouth. The man in the center of the three wore an apron. He was, maybe, thirty. He was big and muscular. He was dark skinned and his hair was conked. The third man was just a little older than I was. He must have been in his early twenties. He wore a black, thin-lapeled suit that appeared to be too tight for him, a pink shirt and a skinny black leather necktie. As soon as I got into the door good, the man wearing the apron spoke.

"What you know soldier?"

"Good afternoon. You open?"

"Yeah, we open. This place slow for the next few hours—then the whole Fort will be in here."

"So it seems," The older man said.

"What can I get for you?" The bartender asked as he rose from his chair.

I sat at the bar. "Gimme a scotch and soda."

"Scotch and soda," the bartender repeated as he walked behind the bar to make the drink. He put the drink before me, I paid him and he went back to the table. I felt strange sitting there at the bar drinking all alone, but everything I was going through these last months was new and strange.

"Don't sit there by your lonesome," The old man said. "Come join us at the table. I hate to see a man drink alone, 'specially a young man."

I picked up my drink and went to the table. "My name is Grady Murrow," I said as I sat down.

"I'm Jesse Hopper," the old man said, "and this here is Hezekiah Brooks, the best bartender in Fayetteville. And that there," the old man said shaking his finger with mock contempt, "is Elroy Jones—better known around town as pussy galore—Dapper Dan, the lady's man. When you looking for some poontang, Elroy know where to take you."

Elroy grinned widely as we shook hands, "You look like you ain't been here a week yet," he said.

"That's right. I got here from Fort Hood, Texas just Tuesday."

"Then you must've come to town for a little action."

"Action? I don't gamble."

"Naw, you know what I'm talking about—a little trim. A nice soft young thang."

"Actually I came to have a few drinks for my birthday. I don't know any girls here yet."

"You don't know any girls here yet? Damn you sound square. You ain't got to know a gal to get a gal—shit you a lucky man. You ran into the right cat today. Little early yet, but later on I'm gonna take you someplace to get you some leg for your birthday. Old Elroy here gonna' show you the ropes"

'Happy Birthday," the old man said, and then Hezekiah said the same.

"Can I buy you guys a drink?"

"Thought you was never gonna ask," Mr. Hopper said.

After they had finished the first round of drinks, I was feeling a nice little glow. I offered to buy another round.

"Ain't no need spending your money on these expensive shots when you can spend five dollars and get a whole bottle."

"But where will we drink it?"

"Hezekiah sell Red-Dot liquor for little more than they do at the Red Dot store and you can drink it right here."

"Is that legal?"

"Shit boy, ain't you ever done nothing that the white man say ain't legal?"

"Yeah, plenty."

"If you only did what the white man say is legal, a nigger couldn't do shit," Elroy said.

"You want the bottle?" Hezekiah asked.

"Bring it," the buzz in my head said.

While we were drinking, Elroy talked about the girls he was going to take me to see. "Anyone you want is yours," he said. "I'll arrange it, and it ain't gonna cost you much. You'll get some leg, but it won't cost you a arm and a leg, " he laughed. Mr. Hopper talked about all the soldiers he knew from the base. "Some them boys been stationed here for so many years, Fayetteville like their home now. I been here all my life—I done seen them come and go, but there some I been drinking with for as long as ten years. And you know some them boys when they get out of the army settled right here in Fayetteville. Most 'cause some woman they done settled in with or married." Hezekiah didn't say much. There was something different about him, but I couldn't figure what it was. Every time he went behind the bar to serve a customer, his graceful movements seemed to hint at it. He was built like a prizefighter, but moved like a ballet dancer. He always came back to our table, although he had stopped drinking after the first drink. None of the people he served at the bar stayed, they'd drink a beer and leave. In little over two hour, we had drunk that bottle and was half done with another when I noticed that I was intoxicated. My ears were ringing with a rush of air; it seemed my hands moved in jerky movements, my stomach began to feel foul and I had to blink my eyes to focus. My drunkenness was reflected physically. Mentally I was straight and I knew that it was time to go.

"Gentlemen," I said, struggling to get to my feet, "I gotta go."

"Man it's too early to turn in. The fun ain't started yet," Mr. Hopper said.

"Wait another hour," Elroy said, "And I'll take you to the girls where you can have some fun. Shit this your birthday remember."

"Can't you'll see he's drunk," Hezekiah said, "This soldier can't hold his liquor."

"You want some coffee?" Mr. Hopper asked

I walked to the door without responding. I looked around to get my bearings. I remembered that the bus station was one block down and across the street from the train station. When I reached the bus station, I tried to check the schedule, but my eyes wouldn't focus. I felt like I would fall if I didn't sit down so I sat on the curb, my head in my lap and my feet in the street. I had never been drunk before in my life and now here I was on my nineteenth birthday alone in a strange town drunk as a skunk. The bus arrived some time later, I managed to crawl on board to a seat in the rear—even drunk a Negro remembers that he is in the South when addressing a white woman, when looking for a water fountain and when using public transportation. I dozed on the way to Fort Bragg. When I arrived, I exited the bus, found my barrack and my bunk.

2

That Monday I put in for a three-day pass for the coming weekend before jump school started. I wanted to go to South Carolina to visit my grandmother. We had a lot of leisure time that week, so I got to read the book "The Prophet." The book's author is the Lebanese, mystic visionary poet Kahlil Gibran. The book tells an enigmatic story in beautifully written prose. It's a book that I had to read over and over again, always meeting new understandings and making new discoveries. Every morning I got the word of the day from the vocabulary book. I'd put it in a sentence and practice its spelling. I was improving my vocabulary one-day at a time and it was working. That week I also looked into the Fundamentals of Good Writing" book, but I decided I wasn't ready for it yet. I needed to be able to give it a more sustainable amount of concentration.

Friday evening I took the bus to the train station. I bought a train ticket to Charleston, South Carolina. I had a four-hour wait for the next train to Charleston and the trip would take five hours, which would get me there at four in the morning. As it happened though, the train was running two hours behind schedule. I spent six hours in the "Colored Only" waiting room and then the train lost more time during my segment of the trip, so I arrived in Charleston at seven-thirty Saturday morning. Momma Dolly lived twenty-five miles outside of the city and I didn't want to pay a cab to take me that far. I asked some of the cab drivers outside the train station if they knew where George's Shoe Shop was. They all knew it. My Uncle Leroy owned the shoe repair shop in Charleston and I figured that if I made it there he might be able to arrange for me to get out to the country.

Uncle Leroy was surprised and pleased to see me.

"Boy you look like new money, how you doing?"

"I'm fine Uncle. You look well yourself. How's business?"

"I can't complain—the Lord been good to me. How long you home for"

"Just until tomorrow. I got to be back Monday morning to start training."

"Well I know you want to get out to the country to see your grandma and everybody. I tell you what, there's a fellow coming to pick up some shoes this morning; he's going back that way. I'll get him to take you to the country."

Uncle Leroy was a smart businessman. His main strategy for success seemed to have been to treat all his customers as if they were white. He said yes sir and yes ma'am and was extremely courteous to everyone. He smiled, shuffled and minimized his own personal merit as he put his customer's money in his cash register. Besides making his customers feel superior, it didn't hurt that Uncle Leroy was an exceptional shoemaker. He ran a profitable and successful business for nearly fifty years.

It wasn't long before the man came into the shop to pick up his shoes. "This is my nephew Grady Lee," Uncle Leroy said, introducing the man to me, while he gathered the bag with his shoes. "This here Albert Givens," he said to me. "I don't think you know any of his folks, you been gone so long."

"Grady Lee—who his daddy?" Albert asked Uncle Leroy while looking at me.

"That Big Joe boy. You kin see in his face he a Murrow, huh?"

"Big Joe boy, oh yeah. He a Murrow alright and I can see it. So what, Jack," Albert mimicked my father as so many of them did.

"Kin you drop him off at the Old Lady's house for me."

"Sho', I glad to do it."

Albert Givens drove a red pick-up truck. I had a small overnight bag that I placed on the seat between us. It was an old truck and it ran loudly. He had some empty baskets in the bed of the truck. He had just delivered a load of collard greens to vendors at the Charleston market, he told me. The Charleston Market is where slaves were once paraded, scrutinized and sold. Now their descendants sell fruits and vegetables from the site. Albert Givens was about my father's age, in his early forties.

"How long you been in the army?" he asked as he drove.

"Almost six months."

"How you like it?"

"It's alright. I'm gonna start airborne training Monday."

"What's that?"

"Training to become a paratrooper."

"What they do?"

"Jump out of airplanes."

"Why?"

I wasn't sure how to answer that, so I said, "To surprise the enemy."

"You gonna jump out a airoplane—shit you crazy. So what Jack. I been knowing your old man all my life and he crazy too. So what Jack"

I started to recognize things as we drove through the town of Hollywood. I saw the old icehouse and knew that Mamma Dolly's house was just a mile away. I hadn't been down South since my early teens. The last time I saw Momma Dolly was two years earlier when she spent a month in New York shuffling between Aunt Dot's house and our own.

"Well, there it is," Albert said as he pulled up near the house where I was born. When we left here in 1947, this house didn't have electricity or running water, but since then my two uncles had modernized the house for Momma Dolly.

"Thank you for the ride," I said handing Albert two dollars.

"Keep your money," he said. "I glad to help. Say hello to Aunt Dolly for me," he said addressing my grandmother as aunt even though they were not related. Then he couldn't resist one more "So what Jack." I grabbed my bag and thanked him again.

This small hamlet is where my ancestors on both sides of my family lived since the end of slavery. There are twenty or so houses that lined the highway. Behind the houses on the highway, there is a village of homes with crude dirt roads that gave access to them. Almost everyone is related on one side or both. The front and back doors to Momma Dolly's house were opened to let the air flow through. I knocked at the door as I walked into the living room. "Anybody home?" I cheerfully shouted.

"Back here," Momma Dolly yelled back.

I walked back to the living room where I could see her in her bedroom slipping on a robe.

"Who dat?" she asked just catching a glimpse of me.

"It's me, Grady Lee, ma'am."

"Grady Lee, boy just to look at ya. How you da do?" she said as she joined me in the living room.

"I'm fine Momma, how are you?" I asked as I embraced her and she kissed me

"Oh, I ain't da do so well, but the Good Lord da hold me right in He sight."

"I am surprised to see you in bed this time of morning."

"I ain't long come home. Been on da hill all night to Cos'n Hattie's house. We been holdin' da v'gil fer she."

"Oh, is she sick?"

"Taint nuthing da doctor ca' do fer she. It all in God's hands now. We been in v'gil since Tuesday. She near done but God ain't sent He angel fer she yet."

"I'm sorry to hear that."

"You mus'ta be hungry. Lemme fix you sumthing ta eat."

"No, you get your rest. I ate something in town," I lied.

"Put your things in da front bedroom."

"I will Momma. You go back to bed."

"I better 'cause I be back on da hill this evening, but I gwen make you supper 'fore I go."

"Momma don't you worry about me. Now you go back to bed and get some rest."

"I'll rest, but I won't sleep none I bet ya." With that said, she went back to her bedroom. I looked at Great Uncle Johnny's old sword and rifle leaning in the corner of the living room as they had been doing for decades, relics of a hidden and mysterious past. I put my bag in the front bedroom, and then I went to the kitchen to put some coffee on. I returned to the bedroom and hung my summer dress uniform over a chair. I took a bath and dressed into my field clothes and boots. I took a seat in the kitchen and I sipped on my coffee.

Mrs. Hattie was Momma's older first cousin. When Momma used to take me crabbing, Mrs. Hattie and a granddaughter named Gertrude sometimes accompanied us. Momma didn't have many older family members still alive. Of her three brothers and two sisters, only the youngest brother and an older sister still survived. Mrs. Gally, her cousin from the gully had died several years past. Momma was sixty-five years old and there was still a small group of people her age that still practiced the old rituals, traditions and sacraments of their mothers and fathers. Old people here, in 1960, had not yet begun to die in stolid, sterilized hospital rooms. That time was yet to come.

I looked in on Momma and saw that she was asleep. I decided to go next door to say hello to Aunt Wilemena, Uncle Leroy's wife and my cousins. Then I planned to look up my cousins Bannie and Tuffy. Aunt Wilemena made me a big breakfast of grits, slab bacon and crab cakes. I talked with my younger cousins for a while. Then I went to Bannie's house and found out that he was in Florida working. I talked there for a while with Aunt Ola who reminded me that she used to breast-feed Bannie and me both at the same time. Finally I went to my cousin Tuffy's house and found him at home. After I said hello to everyone there, we went next door to Tuffy's older brother's house. His name is Richard Murrow and he had been a soldier during the Korean War. "You see Big Joe yet?" Richard asked.

"No."

"He stay down the bottom in a trailer where Pa Bob's old house used to be."

"What happened to Pa Bob's house?"

"That house was so old, after the old man died, they tore it down."

The three of us loaded into Richard's car and drove off for the bottom. It was a six-minute ride. At this point in my life, I didn't have any animosity towards my father. Over the years, I hadn't thought of him much. Only at times when friends asked where my father was and for a while I'd lie, saying he was a long distance truck driver who spent near all of his time on the road. I had forgotten his violent rage and the terror his stare could bring. It wasn't until I had become a father and was able to fully analyze and comprehend the responsibility of fatherhood that I formed malice towards my father for his neglect of that duty. It took years for me to run the full range of emotions growing up in a one-parent household generated.

"Big Joe," Richard yelled, as he emerged from the car. "Big Joe, look who I got here."

A door to the trailer opened. Grady S. Murrow stood in the half-opened door, shirtless and a partially eaten pork chop in his hand. He was forty-one and balding. His skin was reddened and his hands had begun to wrinkle like Pa Bob's. I have the same reddened skin and the same hands that would some day also wrinkle. He came down the tiny wooden steps from the opened door. "Looky here, Looky here," he said as he reached me. He reached out his arms and grasped my shoulders with his hands, the pork chop still in his right hand. "Grady Lee, Grady Lee. Boy you all grown up and a soldier to boot." He kissed me and that created an awkward moment. "How are you?"

"I'm doing fine, and yourself?"

"I'm doing good son. Bubba," he said to Richard, "how you and Tuffy doing this glorious morning?"

"I'm good to go," Richard said.

"Morning," Tuffy said nodding.

"Anybody have some breakfast," my father offered as he stretched out his hand with the partially eaten pork chop in it."

We all declined.

"I got a pot of grits, plenty still left if you fellows want some breakfast."

"No thanks," Richard said for us all.

"Then let me put on a shirt and we can go up to Duffy's for a drink. I know it's early, but I'd say that the occasion calls for a beer. Huh?"

My father's diction was in sharp contrast to most of the other people in the area. I never knew how far he went in school, but he was clearly an articulate man and judging from the quality of the two poems he wrote during the war, this fluency came to him fairly early on.

"Now ya talkin'," Tuffy said.

Duffy's is an old jook joint on the edge of the community. I remembered my father taking me there one evening when a traveling black motion picture promoter was showing a Louie Jordan movie. In the forties, black movie producers didn't have theater outlets to screen their works, so they traveled from town to town using whatever black owned venue they could to show their movies. All over the country, places like Duffy's added to their earnings by becoming movie theaters for a night. I may have been just four years old, but I still remember the antics and the song "Open the Door Richard," all unfolding on a white sheet Duffy had put up on the wall. During the summers, I spent with Momma Dolly on many Saturday evenings my cousins and I would peek through the side door of Duffy's.

The place had a front door, a back door and a door to the side. All of them were opened. There was no one there when we arrived. Duffy's joint had a pool table, a jukebox, built to the wall wooden booths, and rough wood flooring. Except for a crudely built wooden bar, the place hadn't changed as I remembered it. Any man except preachers and deacons, could hang out there without tarnishing his reputation, but all the women who went there was said to be loose. We sat in a booth and waited. Duffy's house was behind the joint, so he heard us when we pulled up in the car. Soon I heard heavy footsteps coming up the stairs in the back of the joint. My father and I were sitting facing the rear so we saw Duffy first. He was short and extremely over weight. He wore pants, a sleeveless undershirt and he was bare foot. His feet were so fat they appeared swollen.

"Duffy looky what I got here," My father said as Duffy rumbled towards us.

"Who dat is, Big Joe?"

"That's my son, Grady Lee Murrow."

"Big Joe I forget you da had chillun. Who he Mama?"

"Aunt Dolly's gal' Sarah was my wife. We had three children—two boys and a girl. She took them to New York back in the forties—you know how that is Duff."

"Yeah Big Joe, I knows all 'bout it—so what, Jack. Well I sho is glad to meet you Grady Lee."

"Thank you sir."

"Duffy, I tell you what, how about letting us have a half pint of that old shine you got back there—then bring us a bottle of Mountain Dew and two quarts of beer.

"Big Joe you paying with cash money?"

"Jesus Christ, Duffy, you know I'm paying with cash money— so what, Jack," Big Joe said to Duffy. Then he turned his attention to me. "What they got you doing in the army?"

"I start airborne training in two days."

"Airborne. Airborne training, you must think you white."

I didn't know what to make of that comment. I remembered that my father was in the segregated army of World War II when only white soldiers were allowed to become paratroopers and I attributed the origin of his statement to that fact. I also considered the possibility that he was so absorbed by traditional racial stereotypes, that he may have thought I was stepping outside of my role unjustifiably. Duffy brought the corn liquor, the mountain Dew and one glass.

"Be right back with ya beer d'rectly," he said, "'frigerdar' in here broke—got to keep the beer in the house one."

"How's Ed Lewis and Ann Ruth doing?"

"They're doing good. Ed Lewis will be in high school next month and Ann Ruth is right behind him."

"That's good. How's your Momma? And, don't she have another child now?"

"She's doing good, I talked with her when I arrived in North Carolina. My little sister's name is Beatrice, she's gonna be six in November."

My father opened the bottle of corn liquor, which was in a recycled Seagram 7 half-pint bottle and he poured a drink into the glass. "Here's to the paratrooper," he said and drank the liquor down. Then he poured another drink and handed it to me. I drank it down. "You fellows can go for yourself," he said to Richard and

Tuffy. Duffy brought the beers and with them, he brought four glasses. My father took out his wallet and paid the jook joint owner two dollars and fifty cents. Our aimless conversation intertwined with my father recollections about his years in the war.

3

I arrived back at Momma Dolly's house around three in the afternoon. She was in the kitchen and had begun to prepare supper. "You da get some sleep now Grady Lee," she said. I hadn't been in a bed since Thursday night and the train ride, corn liquor and beer were now having an effect on me. I laid on the bed and immediately fell asleep. When I awoke it was dark outside. I went to the bathroom to wash my face and freshen up. Momma Dolly heard me. "I ga fix ya plate 'fore I gone," she said. When I reached the kitchen, a plate of stewed chicken and rice was on the table with a glass of sweet tea.

"Dat ya supper on da table," Momma Dolly said as she walked to her bedroom to get a sweater to fight off the night chill.

"I'll be up there after I eat," I said.

"I gone," she said walking out of the back door in the kitchen. I ate my dinner and washed my glass, plate and folk.

Mrs. Hattie lived in a house a short walk up the next dirt road over from Momma's road. It was a dark and chilly night. This section of the hamlet was called the Hill. Approaching the house, I could see a faint light coming from one window in the house. I smelled the smoke from the pinewood fire that was burning behind the house where a large crowd was talking, laughing, singing and crying. When I arrived, I went up the steps to the porch where two deaconesses from the church sat as if on sentry duty.

"I'm Grady Lee. I just want to let Momma Dolly know that I'm here."

"Good evening," one of the women said pointedly enough to remind me that I hadn't greeted them properly.

"Good Evening."

"We da tell she," the women said coldly, she seemed annoyed and remained seated.

"Thank you ma'am," I said embarrassed about my lack of manners. I walked around to the rear of the house where I heard the lively sign of life. The area was lined with pine trees. The section in the middle of the trees was clear and this is where the fire burned. People stood and sat in small groups. The light from the fire cast the shadow of those standing close to it beyond the trees where the upper half of their shadows blended in with the darkness of the earthen dirt road. There were people of all ages in this gathering. Children ran around playing some kind of game. Over in one dark area, by a cluster of trees, a group of men and a woman passed a bottle. A group of teenage girls stood silent and teary eyed. Near the house a woman I recognized from New York sat on an old car's rear seat that must have been used there in happier times. She was one of Mrs. Hattie's daughters who moved to New York even before my family went there. She sat shaking her head, a bottle of liquor near her side. Finally, I saw Tuffy and some other family members I knew. Also in that group was Sam Dyle, Mrs. Hattie's grandson. Sam was a tall lanky boy who played with us during my summer visits. We played an improvised kind of basketball game with an empty can, and a hoop nailed to a tree. I remembered him as being a prideful independent spirit. I went over to where they stood. We all greeted solemnly. "How long you been home?" someone asked. "You in the army?" someone else asked. "Big Joe's boy, So what Jack," somebody said. The conversation was intermittent and occurred in pulsating spurts. The mood was dire.

One of the women from the porch called out my name. I went over to her.

"Cos'n Dolly say fer me da bring ya dare."

I followed her back on the porch and into the house. We stood in a small dark room illuminated only by the faint light that came through the door of the tiny bedroom. Momma Dolly came, she took my arm and led me back to the room without saying anything. The room had the strong smell of liniments, ointments and futility. Mrs. Hattie lie on a single size bed surrounded by the senior women from the hamlet. Two women sat in chairs near the bed. One held Mrs.

Hattie's hand. The other woman occasionally patted her forehead with a damp cloth. Some of the women softly hummed and sung spirituals. Momma Dolly stood with me over Mrs. Hattie.

She was tiny and wrinkled. She had wasted away to nothing. It looked like the skin on her arm could be pulled away from the bone. She had no flesh under her skin. Her eyes were closed and her face was sunken. She breathed in short uneven heaving intervals. Sometimes it appeared the next breath was not coming and made her abnormally still. When that happened the woman holding her hands rubbed it gently and the other women wiped her forehead with the damp cloth. While I stood with Momma Dolly holding my hand, one of the deaconess started to pray in a mournful pleading tone.

> *Father, we come to you at this hour*
> *Seeking Your mercy Lord Jesus,*
> *Knowing that there is no sorrow*
> *That heaven can't heal.*
> *Lord, God we know that You can do all things*
> *And we ask that Your will be done*
> *Your will be done*
> *Your Will Lord.*
> *Father, if it is Your will*
> *Raise Sister Hattie from this bed of affliction*
> *Father, please ease her pain and suffering*
> *And lay out a smooth path for her*
> *Father, touch as only Your touch can*
> *If it is Your will Lord.*
> *And if it is Your will*
> *We beseech You to give Sister Hattie a seat in Your Kingdom*
> *That You put heavenly wings on her feet*
> *That you remove all burdens from her journey*
> *We ask only that Your will Lord be done Lord.*
> *All this we ask in Jesus name*
> *Amen.*

"Amen," I said and turned to leave as I felt my emotions building. Momma Dolly released my hand and patted my back. The women started singing "I'm Going Home on the Morning Train." I took a deep breath and walked back to the porch. "Going home to meet my Jesus," they sang. Although the night air had grown chillier, I walked over to the fire and held my hand over it more out of instinct than real necessity. The sight of Mrs. Hattie, the poignancy and beauty of the moment stirred a sweet melancholy in me. I wanted to shout for joy and cry for mercy all at the same time.

More people had joined the vigil. It was if everyone felt the duty to be a witness when death came to hover over this tiny hamlet. I got the feeling that the mourners knew that Mrs. Hattie could feel their presence and that their presence gave her solace and courage. This was why they were there. And although this was my first time experiencing this kind of death vigil, I could discern that this was tradition—almost everybody in this hamlet died a similar death witnessed by the entire community. These were people who lived together through disputes, bickering and all types of quarreling, but when the angel of death hovered, none of that mattered anymore.

"Grady Lee, come here boy," a man's voice called out from the cluster of trees where the drinkers stood. I focused my eyes and saw that it was a cousin who everyone called "Boat" because of the size of his feet. I walked over to the cluster of trees.

"This here Big Joe's boy," Boat told those around the trees. "You look like you need a drink," Boat said during the greetings. "We got some scrap iron," he said using another popular name for corn liquor. Boat handed me the bottle and I took a big drink.

"Thanks, I think I needed that."

"I see you in the army," Boat said looking over what he could see of my uniform in the dark.

"Yeah, I been in the military for a half year now," I said when a man behind me near the fire started singing. I turned to look at him. He was tall and dark. His face was squared and his eyes were hollowed. He stood alone by the fire.

I was sitting by the bedside of a neighbor
Who was heading to the other side-
He sang.
I asked, neighbor if you happen by
My old mother when you get there
Would you tell I'll see her
Bye and bye-

Before we heard another line from the singer a great wail arose from the house and in waves flowed through the crowd in the back of the house. Not only could I feel the grief, I could literally see the sorrow. People sobbed and wept.

"Death done com fer get she," one of the women from the house walked to the back repeating.

"Death done com fer get she."

"How swift travels God's angels of death," the man by the fire who had been singing said. "They come under the cover of darkness and tarry only long enough to carry out God's plan—then they haste away so of their appearance no tongue can tell."

Momma Dolly came to the back to get me. "Gone home now boy," she instructed, "I'll be dey direckly."

"Momma, who is that man?" I asked.

"That Deacon Black, da church lay preacher. Now gone home."

Sunday morning I arose early. I put on some coffee and went to the hen house to feed the chickens and collect the eggs just as I did when I as a boy on my many summer visits. I made breakfast for Momma and me. My train was scheduled to leave at twelve-noon. Uncle James, who worked nights at the main post office in Charleston, came by to take me to the train station after only a few hours of sleep. I told Momma that I wasn't stationed that far away, but I wouldn't be able to come back until I completed my training in six weeks. "Be sho ya da com back when ya da finish wha' ya da do. 'Til den God go wit ya."

During the ride to the train station, Uncle James counseled me to do the right thing while I was in the army. He had seen a lot of guys kicked out of the army and that ruined the rest of their lives, he said. I assured him that I was going to make the best of it. He offered me a twenty-dollar bill as we approached the train station. "I know you can always use a little cash."

"I don't need any money," I said, "I'm doing fine."

"Don't be hard headed. Go on take it," he insisted rigidly.

My train left the station on time and if there were no problems on the way, I'd be back at Fort Bragg by six o'clock. I would miss chow, but I would be able to get a full night's sleep before the first day of airborne training. On the train, I thought about the meeting with my father, it was strange that we were able to behave as if our relationship was the normal father/son relationship. It had been nine years since we saw each other and the best we could do was to drink corn liquor and beer. There was no discussion of our separation, no regrets, no remorse, no future plans. Some situations are difficult to talk about and we avoided them seeking resolution in the absence of discord. My mind went to Saturday night and the vigil for Mrs. Hattie and a feeling of pride swept over me. I didn't think I would even be able to convey the beauty my people had assimilated into such a sad event. I felt a bond to these spiritually intuitive people. Through them, I had discovered a link to my own identity. This wasn't how I'd envisioned spending my time home but I was satisfied, even pleased with the experience. This sense of satisfaction and the rhythmic clicky-clack of the train wheels upon the tracks lulled me to sleep.

San Juan Hill

CHAPTER EIGHT
Airborne

1

S o you want to jump from an airplane while in flight?" The Sergeant Major yelled out to four hundred men sitting in the bleachers on the grounds of the 82nd Airborne Division Training Academy. He was an impressive man in his early-forties. His fatigues were impeccably starched and creased. His cap was squared on his head and the beak lay inline with his nose so that his eyes were hardly noticeable. Master-jumper's wings with a star encircled by a cluster glistened from his cap. His rank was designated on his sleeve by three-humped stripes over three inverted stripes with a star in the middle. Another set of Master-Parachutist wings was pinned to his chest. His boots were blacker then any black I had even seen; the toe sections gleamed. I had been in the army for six months, but never had I seen a soldier as sharp as this one.

Early Monday morning Murray Cohen and I walked from our barracks to the location where we joined all the other jump students standing in formation by the trucks that took us all to the jump academy. Cohen was a large-lipped Jewish kid with light kinky hair. He had blue eyes and a broad smile. I had stumbled into the airborne by unplanned events, but Cohen joined the army intending to become a paratrooper. We were both from Manhattan and while there had never been any problems between us, we just never hit it off. Cohen offered his friendship to me in so many ways, but he reminded me of the people I worked for in the garment center. After a roll call we were loaded into the trucks and hauled off to jump school. For the next six weeks, this was our routine.

"You want to wear Parachute badges," The Sergeant Major continued. "You want to be among the proudest warriors the world has ever seen. What's holding you back? Five tiny jumps from a mighty C130, that's all. Well, we are going to help make this dream come true for some of you. Right now you've all got your heads in your asses, the ones of you who can take your heads out of your asses are the ones who will make it. The staff of non-commissioned officers you see behind me are going to train you to become paratroopers. Then we are gonna let you jump out of our airplanes—five times. This course will end with five jumps in five days. Those of you who finish this training and learn everything we teach you will get to jump out of our airplanes. And those of you who successfully make five jumps from our airplanes will get to wear the Airborne Parachute badge. Then, and only then, will you be paratroopers.

"This training ain't easy and it ain't easy for a couple of reasons. Number one, you can die jumping from an airplane if you don't know what you're doing. Number two, the Secretary of the Army and your parents expect us to keep you alive. The only way we know to do that is to take your heads out of your asses so that we can drill our instructions into you.

"How do we go about that? We first have to erase from your minds everything you think you know about learning. Here, at this place, there is but one method to learning and that is the airborne way. That is the most important lesson you will learn. Once it is clear in your heads that there is only one way to learn, then you will be ready to learn, the airborne way. Why is this important to you? Because what you learn over this next six weeks *will save your life.*"

There were other speeches. The academy Commandant spoke about the proud history of the 82nd Airborne Division and the distinguished record the academy made for itself in the training of all those fine men before us. He assured us that we would receive the best training from the most competent jump instructors on earth and that we would continue the gallant tradition of the airborne. Another officer spoke about the mission of the airborne. "Our primary mission," he said, "is rapid deployment. To be ready to go into operation anywhere on earth in eighteen hours, to seize airports and seaways, and to secure terrain to facilitate the arrival of our main fighting body."

Another sharp non-commissioned officer gave an interesting talk about the history of the parachute. "The Chinese used something similar to a parachute a thousand years ago. But the first known picture of a parachute was drawn by Leonardo da Vinci in the fifteenth century. The idea was that the parachute was intended to be used to jump from burning buildings and towers." This Master Sergeant held me spellbound with a host of amazing facts about the development of the parachute, from its inception to its evolution into a modern-day tool in the implementation of warfare. We had lunch and after that, we were broken down into small groups of twenty to twenty-five and assigned to the instructors who would be with us for the next six weeks. We were numbered from 1 to 400. Then we were given white tape to make our designated number on our helmets. My number was 333. From this moment on, the numbers on our helmets would identify us.

That evening, by the time our convoy returned to the base, we had missed mail call. Cohen and I went to our company's mess hall to eat chow. When I got to our bay in the barracks there was a letter on my bunk. The letter was from Brad. He wrote that he was doing well and was in the process of buying a brownstone in Brooklyn. The building cost thirty thousand dollars. I was impressed that at nineteen Brad was involved in a big money transaction. I couldn't imagine what it was Brad did to become so successful but I knew he was a hustler's hustler. He also wrote that Ozzie had been shipped to Korea. He had flunked out of the Special Forces training course he took at Fort Campbell, Kentucky. One part of the course was an accelerated airborne training program, which Ozzie completed, but on his first jump, he refused to jump from the airplane. He went up with the plane and came back down with it. I sunk to my bunk. I had heard many stories of the vilification that went on in such cases. I couldn't imagine the pressure Ozzie must have come under. I had heard a story of a guy who killed himself because the derision was so acrimonious.

"You come back down in that airplane and they treat you like shit from the moment the plane lands and the door opens until two weeks later when they ship your ass out to Korea," one of the guys in my platoon had warned me in a general conversation. "In the two weeks that they have you before your orders come through, they treat you like something stink. They put you in an old wooden barrack all to yourself. You eat at a table by yourself. Everybody looks at you like you're something nasty. Only certain people are allowed to talk to you and when they do, it's in a bad tempered way. You are a pariah and ostracized in all ways. They won't even let you pull KP or put you to work. Hey, in wartime they put prisoners to work. They treat you worst than they treat a prisoner of war. They make you feel worthless. Man, it's easier to jump out of that airplane than it is to take that shit."

But I knew Ozzie. He could make himself believe that what he did was a courageous act of defiance. I knew that Ozzie would have thought out the consequences beforehand then armored himself in some twisted logic to survive it. I knew that Ozzie would be able to turn himself inwards to draw on a power that rejected all the criticism of his cowardliness. He was capable of convincing himself that it took more cunning and courage to go against the grain than to go with it. And, if what they said about the treatment of people who returned to the ground with the airplane is true, he could be right. I just lay there on my bunk thinking about Ozzie and my own fortitude. I couldn't manipulate my mind the way Ozzie could his. I will have to jump. The fighting in Korea had ended less than five years earlier and there were still high tensions between the United States forces facing the North Korean forces on the border between North and South Korea. These cats were so close they could see each other with their naked eyes. Another conflict could easily break out and if it did, many of the American soldiers there would be killed while a main force was being mobilized. I will definitely have to jump.

The next day it rained. That morning I asked my squad leader if he thought training would be cancelled because of the rain. He laughed. "It don't rain in the army, it rains on the army." Something that was demonstrated to me many times over during my three-year enlistment. That morning, when we arrived at the jump academy, we fell into formation before our assigned instructors. We began our training by running two miles in the rain. We watched a film that explained airborne terminology and body positions in the plane, during the jump and during landing. All of the body positions were important, but the one they stressed most was the parachute landing fall—what they called the PLF. The PLF involves a relaxed body with the toes pointed towards the ground and collapsing the legs at the knees as soon as the toes touched the ground and flipping the body over in the direction of the fall. This prevented the lower leg bones, which are connected to the knees, from breaking or dislocating at the knee. The easiest way to prevent the body from stiffening up was not to look down. If you looked down it would appear that the ground was coming up to you and the body automatically tensed up. They put us in a markup of a C130 and had us jump off a two-foot platform performing the PLF.

We were not allowed to walk on the academy's ground. We had to repeat the word "airborne" every time our left foot touched the ground as we trotted from station to station. Wherever we went, if it involved moving, it involved running and the word airborne. All day, all that could be heard was the word airborne, airborne, airborne. The standard punishment for any infraction was twenty push-ups. So the next most common phrase was "Gimme twenty." The third most common sound was that of soldiers counting off twenty push-ups. And, the fourth was, "Get your head out of your ass soldier."

I was surprised that the elementary things they taught us in the first two weeks turned out to be the most indispensable. Something as basic as making a quarter turn on the leg harness prevented the strap from digging into the testicles when the parachute opened and jerked the body upwards. Or packing the M1 rifle in the weapon pack with the cocking rod away from the body so that it would not stab the leg if you landed on it. These were things that could prevent injury, but learning how and when to deploy the emergency parachute was a lesson that could save lives. During the early weeks of the course, we practiced things that would prevent us from getting injured or killed, then we moved on to the things that were more physically exhausting.

In the evening after training and on the weekend, I got to know a few of the paratroopers in my platoon. I fell in with a group of three black guys who were from different parts of the country. One was Tad Jones who had been in the army for a year and in the airborne for six months. Jones was from Queens, New York and he was twenty years old. Another was Charles Taylor, who was from Washington, DC. Taylor was a few months older than I was and he had been in the army eight months and graduated in the jump class right before my own. The third guy was a career soldier named Herbert Pinkney, who had the rank of corporal. He was months into his second three-year enlistment and was kind of a mentor to Jones and Taylor. Pinkney was twenty-four years old and from Arkansas. He spoke with a black Southern drawl and reminded me of some of the backwoods people I knew in South Carolina. These guys gave me advice and encouragement. What they told me about the jumping experience made me excited and eager to make those five jumps. On a few Saturdays, I went to town with any combination of these guys.

Another guy I hung out with was a white guy named Gary Harbinger from Indiana. Harbinger was a cool white boy whose character was in the Elvis Presley mode. He wore his hair as long as our platoon leader would allow him to and spoke with a deep voice. When he was off duty he wore dress civilian pants and two-tone shirts like Elvis. He had been in the army for fifteen months and had a car he brought from home with him. One weekend a month he'd get a three-day pass and drive home. Harbinger also read a lot. He borrowed my Earnest Hemingway book and read it in a weekend. I had owned it for nearly three months and I hadn't read it all yet, although I did read "The Old Man and the Sea" twice and Sordo's Stand, from "For Whom the Bell Tolls" three times.

I wasn't reading the book from front to back, but rather by how the story titles appealed to me. Gary Harbinger and I sometimes discussed the stories from the Hemingway Reader and this helped me to better appreciate Hemingway's ability to create imagery that stimulated his readers.

One Saturday afternoon I went to town with Harbinger. He drove to the train station and parked his car. We walked to the soul-food restaurant in the black district and ate fried chicken, red rice and collard greens. People looked at us in a surprised way but there wasn't the kind of incident we would cause later that evening in a white only establishment. We walked down Main Street and looked in the shop windows. Then we went back to the car and we drove to the Red Dot store and bought a fifth of Canadian Club. We got some cups and a bottle of Mountain Dew, then we drove around the countryside drinking and discussing stories from the Hemingway book. "Your book is the first time I read any of Hemingway's writings," Harbinger said lighting a cigarette with his right hand as he held on to his cup and the steering wheel with his left hand.

"Me too."

"I've read some Fitzgerald, some Faulkner and some John Cheever. How do you like them?"

"I don't know, I've never read any of them."

"What about James Baldwin?"

The name rang a bell, but I couldn't say when or where I had heard it before. "I don't know," I said.

Harbinger had spent a year and a half in college before he volunteered to be drafted for a two-year enlistment in the army. In one of our conversations, he told me he volunteered to qualify for the GI bill once he got out. The army would give him the money to finish college. "James Baldwin," he said, "is the best Negro writer in America."

I felt proud that there was a *best Negro writer* in America and ashamed that I didn't know about him. That would all change in the years to come when I would meet Baldwin and his family. I met the Baldwin family through Ross Blake whom I first met when

Brad moved back to Harlem. Ross married one of Baldwin's sisters and they lived in Baldwin's townhouse on 71st Street in Manhattan. Ross and I became close friends and I became a frequent guest at the Baldwin family townhouse. It was a good thing that I first read Hemingway to develop my own writing style. Hemingway had a precise but simplex writing style. Reading Hemingway made me feel I could do it. Had I been exposed to the writing style of James Baldwin and used it to derive my own writing style, I probably would have been discouraged—Baldwin wrote in such eloquent precision. I thought about Mr. Michaux and his bookstore in Harlem. Then I remembered a copy of *Ebony Magazine,* I saw in John Farley's barbershop with James Baldwin on the cover. "I know who he is," I said.

"Good, pour me a drink," Harbinger said handing me his cup.

We wound up back on the main highway out of Fayetteville. It had turned dark. We were headed back to Fort Bragg when we passed a drive-in movie theater. "You want to go to the movies?" Harbinger asked.

I had never been to a drive-in movie theater before and had wondered how you heard what was said on the screen. "Yeah," I replied. Harbinger turned into the entrance of the movie ground and paid for two. The booth was on the driver side of the car, so the clerk only saw my legs. We found a spot and Harbinger told me to take the speaker from the pole and hang it in my window. I hooked the speaker to my window and pushed the button to turn it on. We sat drinking and talking more than watching the movie. The novelty of an outdoor movie wore off quickly for me.

"I got to take a piss," Harbinger said half an hour later.

"Me too."

We got out of the car and walked to the refreshment building where the restrooms were. We got to the restroom unnoticed. When we were finished, we went to the refreshment counter to get some chips. A white man came from a room behind the counter. He took one look at me and turned red. "What in the hell are you doing in here?" he asked in a surprised voice. I didn't know what to say. It never crossed my mind that even the drive-in theaters were segregated. We were drinking and had forgotten that we were in the South.

"He's with me," Harbinger said.

"Son, you can't bring that boy in here."

"We're soldiers in the airborne."

"That don't matter none here."

"Give us two bags of potato chips."

"Look son, I don't make the laws. You got to get that boy outta here."

"He's a soldier just like me."

"It's the law of the land, now go before I call the law."

We went back to the car and Harbinger sped off the theater grounds. "I'm sorry," he said driving fast and recklessly. He was embarrassed for me and mad at the South, after-all Elvis was singing all those Negro blues tunes and changing the face of music—when was the South going to get with it? "You're a soldier in the United States Army, you got as much right to be in that movie theater as any them crackers sitting in their cars with their fingers in their girlfriend's cunt."

"Yeah, I know."

Harbinger was driving fast. We had another drink. The bottle was half finished and the Mountain Dew was gone. There was no traffic on the highway as we got closer to the base; Harbinger sped the car up, then slammed on the brakes making the car spin around. "Motherfucking racist," he yelled. He was trying to show me how mad he was, but I was becoming frightened by the speed and afraid that he would lose control of the car. He spun the car around two more times before we reached the base. I heard that Harbinger once experienced a May West on his fourth jump while he was at the academy. He had to deploy his emergency parachute. It got tangled in with his backpack parachute but slowed his descent so that he only suffered a broken leg. Everybody thought that he would quit, but after his leg healed, he went up for his fifth jump. It was something he didn't like to talk about, I was told. But my whiskey told me that this was a good way to change the subject and slow down his reckless driving.

"I heard you once had a May West," I said.

"What of it?"

"Nothing, I just want you to know that I think you're a brave dude."

"Airborne pays fifty-five dollars extra a month. I have a baby home and I send money to my girl who I'm gonna marry in nine months when I get out."

Even drunk I knew that I was getting into more of his business than was necessary, so I fell silent as we entered the base checkpoint.

<u>2</u>

Each week another mile was added to our morning run and the amount of loud harassment increased. They wanted to gauge how we functioned under pressure. We were called turds and continually reminded to take our heads out of asses. The instructors were all over each of us it seemed. There were twenty-five people in my group at the outset, and six instructors. One instructor to every five students and me with a number that stood out. "333 gimme twenty." By the third week there was twenty-two of us left, which made it more difficult for the instructors to miss any incident. "333 gimme twenty."

We had two more jump towers to conquer. Over the next two weeks we would begin free jumping from the four-foot tower, which replicated the speed we would have reaching the ground from a real jump. This was to perfect our PLF skills and accustom us to the hard landing. The final two weeks, we would work the fifty-foot tower. We would jump from it in full gear hooked to a harness that simulated the parachute. This would be the time to remember to make that quarter twist away from your testicles with the leg harness. In between this time, there were classes to build up our confidence about the people who rigged our parachutes. The riggers and inspectors had to sign a card on each parachute. "So if your chute don't open, we can trace it back to the person who rigged it and the person who approved it," one instructor assured us. "And after we scrape you up from the drop zone, they will be given additional training," he laughed.

We were taught how to get out of the harness if you landed in a tree. How to use the wind to collapse the parachute if you landed in high winds to prevent it from dragging you before you got a chance to get out of the harness. They told us how night jumps were different from day jumps and how jumps from helicopters felt like a sudden drop in an elevator. We were taught how to maneuver the parachute by pulling the correct harness in the direction you wanted to float. And, that the big hole we saw up in the parachute was called the "Apex." It allowed us to come down by regulating the flow of air. They explained to us that the airplanes descent to twelve hundred and fifty feet, the height of the Empire State Building as it approached the drop zone. This gave the enemy less time to shoot at us. All of the training drop zones were named after places that the 82nd landed in the D-Day invasion during World War II—places like Normandy and Sicily.

Every evening I returned back to the barracks so tense that it was difficult to sleep. I found out that reading changed the mood for me, it got my mind away from the pressures of the day and made it possible for me to relax. Over the six weeks of jump school I finished "The Hemingway Reader" and re-read "The Prophet." I was half way through the book on improving my vocabulary. I was up to the word "malingerer" and had even heard it used on that same day by an instructor bellowing at a soldier who had passed out from exhaustion. Some evenings I would read "Fundamentals of Good Writing " by Robert Penn Warren with chapters like "The Motivation of the Writer," and "Your Background for Successful Writing." Two chapters that espoused the idea that the more interesting a life one lived the better writer one could be. And, that notion was supplemented by the assertion that a writer should only write about what he knows. It was these kinds of distractions that took my mind away from the weariness of the day and the thought that the time was nearing. Reading reinvigorated me and got me ready for the next day. During the day, I soaked up what was being taught at jump school. And at night, I read to relieve the stress and to study the craft of writing. I was slowly turning into a person even I would not have recognized a year earlier.

After chow one evening, I found three letters on my bunk. One was from Joan. It was a happy letter. She won a beauty contest and was designated "Miss Subway." For a month, her picture, body statistics and general information were posted in every subway car in the New York City subway system. She was working on becoming a model. She didn't mention Butchie, but she asked if I knew where Ozzie was stationed. The second letter was from my brother Ed Lewis. He wanted to know if I had jumped out of an airplane yet and when I would come home again. The third letter was from Evane. She give birth to a baby girl. Evane would be eighteen on her next birthday. Then in the last paragraph of her letter, she told me that Maggie and Willie Clark's mother died. This was really bad news for me. Mrs. Clark was a lovely lady who always spoke well of me. She'd praised my manners in my presence. "He always says good morning or good evening and when he leaves, he always say goodbye," she told a visitor at the kitchen table. I wrote Maggie a tear stained letter telling her how much I regretted her mother's passing and explained how much I wished I could be there to console her…but.

The fifty-foot tower was a monster. It eliminated more students than any other phase of our training. It got rid of those who were afraid of heights and didn't know it until they got up into the tower and those who couldn't stand a little pain. I had no way of telling for sure, but I imagined that we were nearing the ten- percent drop out margin they told us about on that first day. The climb up the tower in full gear was itself, exhausting. Then you hooked your static-line to a cable that ran down to a mound where you glided down to after the jump. The instructor situated you in the door with the correct bend at the knees, your hands on the outside of the door. Then the instructor slapped your butt to signal you to jump. We practiced keeping our heads down during the jump to keep the harness from slapping the back of our necks when the parachute deployed. They also taught us to keep our elbows in to our sides and our hands grasped around the emergency parachute pack.

We were taught to make a vigorous jump out and away from the body of the plane. Once we made the jump, we were all instructed to make the count, one thousand, two thousand, three thousand, four thousand, then to look up. If you didn't have an open parachute above you, it was time to pull the ripcord on your emergency parachute. We simulated all of this during the tower jumps. Looking up after the jump was emphasized heavily and the instructors on the ground under the tower watched carefully to see if we all looked up after we jumped from the tower. "Do you have an opened parachute 239?" an instructor yelled at a student who did not look up after jumping. "You're dead 239. You hear me, you're dead." Then he took the student to the side, spoke to him with animated gestures, then sent him back up the tower.

During the last three days of training before the big qualifying run in full gear, we worked on a mark up of the C-130. There were long benches on each side of the airplane that are called "sticks." Each stick held twenty men. About seven feet above the sticks were cables that are called static-lines. This is where we, on command, hooked up the static-cords clipped to a strap in the front of the parachute shoulder harness. An instructor stood by the door of the marked up airplane with forty seated men. "Stand up," he shouted as if over the roar of the plane's motor. We all stood up. "Hook up," we all turned facing the front of the plane and hooked our static-cords to the static-lines. "Check static-lines," at which point, we yanked on our static-lines to be certain that the locking clip encircled around the static-line. In a real jump, at this point we would be ten minutes away from the drop zone. At five minutes from the drop zone we'd get the command to "Shuffle to the door," then the first man in each stick shuffled to the door and got into a jumping stance, while the rest of the men in the sticks shuffled up one position.

We practiced this over and over again. While we were seated we looked at the men across from us with smiling eyes. There were no sign of fear on any of our faces and we, unwittingly, thought that this was how it would be during the real thing. We had one more formidable obstacle before jump day and that was the ten-mile run in full gear. Full gear is everything a soldier carries to battle. His rifle, helmet, bayonet, canteen, entrenching tool and backpack containing a blanket and a half tent. All we had to do on the last day of training was to complete the ten-mile run and we would have the afternoon off. The morning after the run, we would make the first of five jumps from a C-130 over drop zone Normandy.

The temperature in North Carolina in September is still fairly hot. Most days are in the high 70's and 80's; not good weather to run ten miles hauling thirty pounds of equipment. That morning when we unloaded from the trucks at the jump academy, it was humid and I could tell that the sun would take its toil that day. While we awaited the start of the run, all of the instructors present were huddled together in what appeared to be an impromptu conference. When they were finished, they had us to stack our arms. Then they put us back into formation and had us put our field packs at our feet with our helmets on top. Then we stepped out from the formation of field packs and helmets to begin the run. We were all puzzled and pleased by this act of mercy. The run began at the jump academy and would end at Pope Air Force base. There we would get a tour of the planes and meet the flight crews who would ferry us to our jump zones. Our convoy of trucks would be there to take us back to retrieve out gear.

We jogged along at a pace of about twelve-minutes a mile. The run was to take two hours, but two hours passed and we had only reached the eight-mile mark. Our pace slowed considerably and people were beginning to stagger behind. The neat formation that we began with stretched out over a half mile. Instructors jogged along-side stragglers shouting at them to continue on. "You've gone this far, don't give up now." And, for the first time, these jump instructors showed genuine compassion. They wanted everybody who had gone through all the blood and tears of the last six weeks to reap the victory. I was jogging next to a short, heavy-set black guy from Memphis, Tennessee, who we dubbed "Memphis Slim," when Cohen, who was ranks in front of us, fell behind. He had a desperate look in his eyes. His face was red, his arms flung like rubber and his legs moved stiffly. He was giving up. As he fell behind us, I caught his eyes. "Catch up to me," I said.

"I," Cohen meant to say "I can't," but only "I" came from his mouth.

"Catch up to us," Memphis Slim called out to Cohen, "hold on to us."

Cohen made a last ditch effort and when he reached us, we each put one of his arms over our shoulder and our arm around his back. All he had to do was to move his legs. We held up most of his body weight. An instructor looked at us with pride and gave us the thumps up sign. We carried Cohen for nearly two miles and when we reached the finish line, we all collapsed in a heap, but we made it. At the air base, they gave us water and salt tablets. The mood was jubilant, even the instructors displayed a temporary glee.

Pope Air Force base is older then Fort Bragg. It is home to the 23rd Fighter Wing, as well as being the strategic transporter of material and personnel. We were taken to the runway where seven C130's were lined up to take us up and to the drop zones the next day. Each plane had four crewmembers. They showed us on and around the airplanes. We saw that the inside were just like the mark-ups that we had trained on. Then we loaded on to our trucks and were taken back for our gear and then back to our barracks for lunch. We had the rest of the day off.

That afternoon I lay on my bunk rereading "The Old Man and the Sea" from The Hemingway Reader. I read how the old Cuban, who always talked about catching the big one, had finally hooked a giant marlin on his line. The old man fought the marlin several days and several nights determined to triumph over the fish. During this time, his skiff was towed far out to sea by the stubborn denizen of the deep. Wearied, sleepless and hungry, his back and hands seared by the line, the old man finally outlasted his fish, pulled it to the boat and killed it. The fish was too heavy for him to haul on board, so he lashed it alongside, raised a sail, and headed for home. But there was a far greater battle to come. He was in shark infested waters and, as the Chinese say, beyond the mountains there are mountains. A shark hit the marlin, taking a bite out of it. Other sharks would, in time, pick up the scent the blood of the marlin left in the water. And then the old man had to fight off the sharks for days and nights, his only weapons a harpoon, a knife and two oars. This is a story of one man's endurance and determination to share his dream with his village and a little boy who believed in him. It is a testimony to what human dexterity; tenacity and courage can achieve. It is also the story of an old man who still believed in himself. This is what I wanted—to believe in myself. I began to dose.

3

Cohen shook me for mail call and five o'clock chow. This was the first day I was at the barracks during mail call in six weeks. The entire company of men gathered outside in an informal way while a sergeant calls out the names of those with mail. It is a time of great expectation and often even greater let downs. This day my name was the fifth one called. I had one letter. After I ate chow, I took my letter up to my bunk and sat down. The envelope was smeared and tattered like it had seen hard times. It was from Ozzie. I tore the top off the envelope and looked in. There was one sheet of paper. I unfolded the sheet of paper and couldn't believe my eyes. I looked around quickly to be sure that no one was looking. Ozzie sent me a picture of himself in a folded sheet of writing paper. There were two other guys in the picture. They all stood by a military looking wooden building. Behind the picture was a joint. On the back of the picture, he wrote, "I'm fucked up here." The sheet of paper was blank. I assumed he wanted me to see how good the marijuana in Korea was, but this was a dangerous act—sending a reefer through the United States Post Office from South Korea to North Carolina. That took both spunk and stupidity. I didn't know what to think of it. I was surprised that the letter came undetected, but how was I to know that for sure. This cat is risking getting us both kicked out of the army, I thought. I stuffed the joint in my pocket. I put the picture in my locker. Then I went to the toilet and flushed the joint down.

Later in the week, when we had finished the five jumps and had graduation day with a big military parade and ceremonial presentations of our certificates as paratroopers, I wished I had saved that joint to celebrate with. To compensate, I found Elroy Jones, the pimp, and celebrated with two of his girls. But the evening the reefer came, I needed to illustrate to myself that I was in control. I hadn't worked so hard to give in to a minor temptation. Something else was happening to me. It was subtle and harder to recognize, but it had to do with the changes taking place in my character. I was no longer just a street hardened kid who would do anything to get over. In certain areas of my behavior, I was developing integrity. After I flushed the joint down the toilet, I went to sleep.

That morning I was surprisingly calm. Cohen was absolutely gleeful as we walked to the trucks. "This is it," he said. "How do you feel?"

"I'm okay—just be glad to get this day over."

"I want you to know that I really appreciate what you and Memphis Slim did for me. I wouldn't be here if it wasn't for you guys."

Cohen had that big broad smile on and I found his confidence reassuring.

"Think nothing of—it's all in the training. Don't they teach us to help each other out?"

"I just wanted you to know how I feel."

The truck ride had a different feel to it this morning. Not only were we bypassing the jump academy and going straight to Pope Air Base, but the mood of the men was also different. There was less talking and clowning around and a feel of more introspection. People were talking to themselves in their heads. The trucks stopped on a strip across from the airplanes and we unloaded. They didn't waste any time. We were issued parachutes and got chuted up with the aid of the instructors. We were each checked to make sure everything was in order. We had our rifles in the weapons pouch and it was strapped to our sides. We had all of our field gear on. The parachute harnesses were pulled so tight that it was impossible to stand erect or to walk in a normal stride. They had a photographer to take our pictures individually with the planes in the background. I managed a slight smile through the discomfort as the photographer took my picture. As we each had our pictures taken, we were assigned to an airplane and we kind of shuffled off to the instructors at our assigned plane.

"When I call your number," an instructor said as the last man joined our group, "move onto the plane and the jump instructor there will get you loaded. 333, you're the first man of the right stick. 323, 335,320,336…"

That jolted me. I never learned how that got to be, but I've always suspected it was because of the number. I didn't let on that I had been jolted by the fact that I would make that long stand in the open doorway and be the first one out of the airplane on my stick. The back ramp of the plane was down. The instructor waved me on and pointed to the first spot on the right stick. The others were right behind me and both sticks on the plane are quickly filled. We were all seated. The C130's powerful engine was switched on. A crewmember came to the back to be certain that the ramp was clear. Then he signaled to raise the ramp. The chief jump instructor was explaining something but all I heard was the roar of the engine. All of our eyes were on him and would remain so until the airplane took to the sky. From here on we would react to a combination of voice command and hand signals.

We sat there with the engine roaring for what seemed like an exceptionally long time, but may have only been minutes. There are no windows in the body of C130, so we couldn't see the other planes but, I think, we could hear them and feel their aura. We knew they were there and we knew our position in relationship to them. We were the fourth airplane on the runway. We began to move forward slowly. Then we made a turn, went a little further, then the plane stopped. We sat there for a minute or two and then we began to move again. The plane paused and the engine began to roar like it hadn't before, then we sped down the runway. Then I felt it leap into the air and climb to the sky. When the airplane leveled off, the chief jump instructor rose from where he was seated during take off and he smiled. He was back in command of what was going on.

The attitude was different than they had been on the mark-ups when we made contacts with smiling eyes. This was the real thing. Most everyone avoided making eye contact with anyone. We were handling our own fear, but we didn't want to see anyone else's fear. People held their heads down or lowered their helmets over their eyes. Some people closed their eyes. I think we were all praying. I know I was "It's not sit-ups this time Lord, it's life itself." The demeanor amongst us was that of subdued panic and no one wanted a stampede towards mass apprehension.

This is how we controlled our fear on the first jump. By the second and third jump, there was far less apprehension. On the fourth jump there was hardly any. By the fifth jump, we made eye contact with smiling eyes.

A red light went on and two crewmembers opened the latch on the side doors, slid the doors back and secured them. The roar of the airplane grew louder and we could feel the wind that seeped into the plane's body. Our eyes scrambled searching for reassurance, then we withdrew back into ourselves. Actually my position as number one on the stick was, in this regard, an advantage. I couldn't see far down the opposite stick, even the men across from me were partly hidden by a bulky crane that was used to haul pallets of heavy equipment onto the plane. The crane was in the center of the plane across from the doors. The chief jump instructor signaled for our attention. He pointed to his watch. He was telling us that the time was nearing. He had a cheery expression on his face. Two other jump instructors with parachutes on took up their positions by the open doors. Although their static line cords were hooked up, they weren't going to jump; their chutes were a safety measure.

The yellow light came on. The chief jump instructor signaled and shouted "Stand up. We stood. "Hook up." We turned to face the front of the aircraft as we hooked our static cords to the static lines. "Check static lines." We pulled the harness to make sure our static cords were locked into the static lines. We were ten minutes away from the drop zone. I was three feet away from the open door. This was agony, I wanted to get to the five-minute mark and stand in the door to confront my past and face my future. I had become aware of the symbolic nature this whole event had for me. Jumping from the door of this airplane meant transformation to me. The symbolic flight from the past to the present and the future. Evangelicals would say I was being born again. The yellow light came on. "Shuffle to the door." I shuffled to the door and turned into it. I lay my hands on the outside of the airplane and got into a crouch that would allow me to spring from the plane when it was time. We were five minutes from the drop zone. I stood in anticipation of the tap on the butt from the jump instructor. At first, I kept my eyes looking forward but I could still see the trees at a distance move by. Then, in a weak moment, I looked down and saw that we flew over the top of a forest. A moment of fear seized me; I looked straight ahead and cleared my mind.

Up to this point in my life this is as near a true Zen experience as I'd ever had. My mind was a complete blank. I was truly in the moment. To this moment, I had done so many things unthinkingly, so little of my time was ever spent thinking and acting in the moment. So little of my life had been lived aware and focused on the present moment. Although this time it was the weightiness of the event that focused my mind, it had the same feel, I later recalled, as a meditative state of inward harmony—a brief glimpse of enlightenment. I was focused on the moment at hand as never before. For this short instant in time though, right then, it seemed an eternity, I found my center. It was if in an instant I was able to sort out the virtuous from the wretched in my life and had instantaneously determine to adopt what was benevolent. I felt the most deviant of my experiences in the projects slip away. The green light went on. I felt the tap on my butt and heard the word "Go." With a vigorous leap, I sprung from the airplane, my head down, my arms to my sides, my hands grasping the sides of my emergency parachute pack as I yelled out "Bozo, Battlemozo, Kazan, Airborne."